© Paige K. Parsons Photography

Arlie Russell Hochschild is the author of *The Time Bind, The Second Shift,* and *The Managed Heart,* all named as *New York Times Book Review* Notable Books of the Year and translated into thirteen languages. With Barbara Ehrenreich, she coedited *Global Woman.* A longtime University of California at Berkeley sociologist, she lectures widely and has written for *The New York Times, Mother Jones, Harper's Magazine,* and *Psychology Today,* among other publications. She and her husband, Adam Hochschild, live in Berkeley.

Also by Arlie Russell Hochschild

The Commercialization of Intimate Life: Notes from Home and Work

Global Woman: Nannies, Maids, and Sex Workers in the New Economy (coeditor)

The Time Bind: When Work Becomes Home and Home Becomes Work

The Second Shift: Working Parents and the Revolution at Home

The Managed Heart: Commercialization of Human Feeling

The Unexpected Community: Portrait of an Old Age Subculture

Coleen the Question Girl (a children's story)

The Outsourced Self

Arlie Russell Hochschild

THE OUTSOURCED SELF

What Happens When We Pay Others to Live Our Lives for Us

PICADOR

A Metropolitan Book
Henry Holt and Company
New York

The names and identifying characteristics of some persons in this book have been changed, as have dates, places, and other details of events in the book.

 For information, address Picador, 175 Fifth Avenue, New York, N.Y. 10010.

www.picadorusa.com
www.twitter.com/picadorusa • www.facebook.com/picadorusa
picadorbookroom.tumblr.com

For book club information, please visit www.facebook.com/picadorbookclub or e-mail marketing@picadorusa.com.

Designed by Kelly Too

The Library of Congress has cataloged the Henry Holt edition as follows:

Hochschild, Arlie Russell, 1940–
The outsourced self: intimate life in market times / Arlie Russell Hochschild.—1st ed.
p. cm.
Includes bibliographical references and index.
ISBN 978-0-8050-8889-2
1. Families—Economic aspects—United States—History. 2. Interpersonal relations and culture—United States—History. I. Title.
HQ536.H628 2012
306.850973—dc23

2011044135

Picador ISBN 978-1-250-02419-0

Picador books may be purchased for educational, business, or promotional use. For information on bulk purchases, please contact Macmillan Corporate and Premium Sales Department at 1-800-221-7945, extension 5442, or write specialmarkets@macmillan.com.

First published in the United States by Metropolitan Books, an imprint of Henry Holt and Company, LLC

10 9 8 7 6 5 4 3 2

For Neil Smelser

Contents

Introduction

Villager and Outsourcer

You might say this book began on those August mornings when I was a child picking pigweed from the corn rows in my grandmother's vegetable garden on a gently sloping hill in Turner, Maine. My widowed grandmother would point her crutch at the tall corn, "Aa-lee"—she always dropped the *r* from my name—that 'corn looks just fine. But now, look how the weeds have gotten ahead of the broccoli over there. . . ." Afternoons, my brother and I and a gaggle of cousins husked corn, shelled peas, peeled apples, knocking off around four to swim in a nearby pond. As a plate of steaming corn was later passed hand to hand among a dozen family members seated at a large kitchen table for supper, I would hear my name praised as a "good weeder and husker."

I didn't love farmwork. But I remember it vividly, partly because it conveyed a lesson that I came to understand only much later. My ancestors, thread lipped and grim in sepia photographs hung on the farmhouse parlor walls, had tilled the soil of this farm since the first one chopped and plowed it out of the stony wilderness in the 1790s. By the late nineteenth century, when my grandmother was a child, it had grown to medium size: sixteen milking cows, a dozen chickens, some pigs, sheep, and a retired milk truck horse named Frank, credited with great empathy for small children. My grandmother married in 1904 and moved with her husband to Boston. When her parents died, the farm passed to her. Now based in Boston, my grandparents sold off the sheep, hogs, and most of the cows, but otherwise maintained the Maine farm year-round. In the winter, two hired hands, and in the summer, my father, his brother, and two sisters tilled, planted, and hayed the fields, milked the cows, and fed the chickens. My grandparents had left for the city but kept the idea of a farm alive.

One photograph from 1933 shows my father beaming in a white hat and glasses, atop an enormous haystack, pitchfork paused in the hay. My mother, his new bride, leans over the hay, face to the camera. The pitchforks of two hired men in overalls on the ground below create a photographic swirl of motion. Shown this photo a few years ago, my then ninety-four-year-old aunt Elizabeth, born in Boston but returning in her twenties to settle in Turner year-round, quipped subversively, "City folk. A *real* farmer could do the job single-handed in half the time." She was onto something.

To some extent, we were playing at farming. By the time I was weeding the pigweed out of the corn—three weeks every summer in the 1950s—there was no hay to reap, cows to milk, pigs to slop, or eggs to gather. But that didn't mean there wasn't a barn to paint, path to clip, or peas to shell. "Aa-lee," my grandmother would call, "now be a good girl and dust the paa-laah." I would aimlessly whirl a feather duster over a seashell collection and small tintype photos set on lace doilies atop spindly legged wooden tables in a formal and seldom-visited front room. "This is silly work," I'd whisper to my older brother. "You have it lucky," he'd whisper back. "Grandma has me stacking shingles in the barn with the edges *even*." Such tedious tasks seemed like empty rituals. They weren't necessary or fun or educational in any way we could see. So what was the point? we wondered. Still, my grandmother—with nodding approval from parents and aunts and uncles—gave us task after task with such serious, kindly intent that we sensed the presence of some larger purpose.

No one outright said what it was, but we sensed it nonetheless. Our farm was indeed different from the real farms up and down the road, but it was not a gentleman's farm that simply consumed the freshly picked results of someone else's labor. We were a gentleman's farm without gentlemen. For us, the point of pride was the labor itself. That was the lesson: the near-sacred value of working together to grow our own food and put it on the table.

When I was twelve, my father was posted as chargé d'affaires to the American Embassy in Tel Aviv, and I was transported to an utterly different world. We moved into an enormous white stucco mansion protected by a uniformed guard with a military-type hat who stood to salute my father each time he walked from house to car or car to house. If I tiptoed into the kitchen looking for some melon in the refrigerator, the white-coated cook, Josef, politely shooed me out. I snuck back during his off-hours, though, leaving serial, anonymous scallops in open-cut melons. Maisel, in black uniform with a white lace collar, daily mopped the stairs, laundered our clothes, and answered the door.

To my great embarrassment, a liveried chauffeur named Shalom drove me to school in a long, black limousine, letting me off at the entrance in front of a sidewalk cluster of whispering schoolmates, pointing, some hesitantly touching the metal rod on each side of the hood where small American flags fluttered whenever my father rode in the car. I made a deal with Shalom to drop me off a block early, but there, too, a few children would bend forward to peer through the darkened glass, hands cupped around wide, curious eyes.

My life was unbelievable to them, as it was to me as well. At the embassy residence everything we normally did for ourselves was now done for us by someone else, conspicuously so. On the farm in the summers, we children sensed ourselves on a stage subtly designed to teach the value of self-reliance and communal work. Now I discovered myself on another stage created to display American wealth to our poorer hosts and to diplomats from around the world. On the farm, I had wondered why we had to do everything from scratch. Now I wondered why we couldn't do the slightest thing for ourselves.

I did nothing. I didn't set the table. I didn't clear the dishes. I didn't fold laundry or tend our beautiful flower garden. What made an impression on me was not simply the contrast between hoeing the pigweed in Turner and being waited on at our embassy dining table. It was the feeling I had about myself in each place. In Turner, through doing my jobs, I felt a part of a larger whole. To my ten-year-old self, the farm tasks were not just tasks; they joined me to my playful cousins, to stories of family pranks, to rippling laughter around the dinner table. Those three weeks in August, which stretched in my imagination to half a year, offered a taste of a village style of life. As a minor contributor to this village, I was less free in one way (the chores were a bore), but more free in another (it gave me a reassuring sense of belonging to something larger than myself). This childhood experience became a prototype for later experiences—of being part of a circle of friends, a neighborhood, an academic department, a social movement.

Our embassy life offered a different way of relating to the world. Household tasks were outsourced to Maisel, Josef, Shalom, and others with whom I was not expected to have meaningful or lasting bonds. And while I lost the feeling of belonging to a community, freshly ironed clothes and favorite meals appeared as if by magic, the final product of someone else's work. As in the best market arrangements, the pay was fair, the household atmosphere pleasant. But after five months, Maisel and Josef left for England to be replaced by a jolly Greek Cypriot couple, Sharley and Jorge. A new cook, Victor, presided in the kitchen. Sharley, Jorge, Victor, and Shalom came, as it were, with the house. If household relations in Turner were as in a village, relations in our embassy home were as those in the marketplace.

Embassy life—ours and that of all the top officers in other embassies—was a project in status display, as I came to understand later. The farther away my father, and by association, his family, seemed from hoeing corn or doing any necessary work, the greater the respect and honor accorded him—a dynamic that Thorstein Veblen observed in his *Theory of the Leisure Class*. Our "help" embodied our detachment from the essential tasks of life and, since it was my father's job to represent the United States, such display bestowed honor on it as well.[1] As a young sidekick to this status display, I felt pampered and oddly important myself, but vaguely wondered why.

Since those days of weeding corn and riding in the limousine, a great deal has changed. After my grandmother died, the warm summer gatherings around the Turner dinner table came to an end. The farm burned down in an accidental fire in the 1960s and the family built two clapboard houses on the land, one for my aunt and one for us to visit in the summers. Meanwhile, my parents moved from post to post, replaced, in each residence, by new come-and-go diplomats. By the time I was twenty, my parents were living in New Zealand, and my brother and I in different cities in America. We corresponded by loving weekly letters and each of us had long-distance friends. But we didn't share, in my grandmother's sense, a community. And we missed it. Long after my father died, my aunt told me that he had mailed from New Zealand, Ghana, Tunisia, year after faithful year, annual dues to the Turner Grange, an organization of local farmers who met over paper plates of baked beans and hot dogs to talk over seed prices, soil depletion, and rain. Today, my grandmother pointing her crutch, my father beaming atop a hay pile, my brother straightening shingles—all of them have gone. Pigweed and chauffeur—each life highly privileged in its own way—have passed into private memory.

In my child's mind, these two ways of life seemed like irreconcilable opposites. But of course in reality they were never absolutes. The farm—our farm but also the real farms—had hired help, and there was plenty of teamwork and generosity at the embassy.

Nonetheless, the two do correspond to very different sets of social arrangements, and in the intervening years, one has fared significantly better than the other. So much of what we used to do for one another as neighbors, friends, and family—what I experienced as village life—we now secure by turning to the market.

My aunt Elizabeth had a phrase for the relations of the village: "Just do" she called it. "When a need arises," she explained, "neighbors and friends don't ask themselves, 'Do I want to help?' They don't think about it. It's in their bones. They *just do.*" "Just do" meant neighbors in town keeping a casual eye out, carrying on—through exchanges of baked goods, borrowed tools, know-how, babysitting, and spur-of-the-moment drop-ins—"the spirit of the gift," in the words of French anthropologist Marcel Mauss.[2] Neighbors who had bumper crops of tomatoes or more venison than they could freeze for the winter would expect to share and it would be a measure of a neighbor's character if he or she did not. Less money changed hands than in the city but more gifts were exchanged. When money did change hands, it did so differently. Along the edge of lawns, signs would appear—FRESH CORN, GLADIOLAS, CHRISTMAS WREATHS—with the promised goods set on small stands by a change jar. By exchanging goods and services in this way, people were affirming a basic tenet of small-town life—"around here we trust one another."

In this modern expression of a pre-market way of life, gift and repayment came in the form of promise and gratitude, and underlying these was a faith in memory. If a friend did you a favor, you weren't obliged to repay it right away, as when we pay for a service. In fact, that might have seemed rude. It would have defeated the purpose of the gift exchange, which ensured long-term bonds. People didn't give practical help just to get things done; they got things done, in part, to affirm their bonds. Part of such bonds expressed love of one another's company, but they also represented an unspoken pact: "I'm on call for you in your hour of need and you are for me." Villagers might quarrel, gossip, get bored, and leave. But living there, they paid a moral tax to the community in this readiness to "just do."

As time went by, many supports for village life disappeared. For one thing, Americans left farming—38 percent of all workers were farmers in 1900, and less than 2 percent were in 2000.[3] In Turner, local apple and dairy farmers were hard hit by national and global competition. FOR SALE signs went up at the small farms first, then the midsized ones, then a few of the biggest. Developers bought the land. The hills filled with modest, well-tended homes, red tricycles in the driveway, chalk drawings on the sidewalk, freshly mown front lawns. Here and there an apple tree remained where an orchard once stood. Young working couples and single parents moved in, commuting to jobs in the schools, colleges, hospitals, grocery stores, lumber yards, nurseries, and call centers in nearby towns or to a miscellany of older, dilapidated malls and roadside diners. The shoe mills that had once flourished in the nearby towns of Auburn and Lewiston, a dozen or so miles from the family farm, closed or relocated, in search of cheaper labor, to southern states in the 1970s and then to central America, Mexico, and China.[4] A Walmart regional supercenter moved into a thirty-seven-acre lot next to a row of other big box stores, with dreary stretches of used car lots lining the highways leading to it.

Over time, many people moved to cities in search of better jobs and more services. In 1910, a quarter of Americans lived in metropolitan areas and, by 2000, 80 percent did.[5] Now more urban, Americans continued to express some village ethic of "just do" with neighbors, friends, and coworkers. But for an increasing number, family became their village.[6] At the same time, that family was not immune to the broader transformations taking place. The two most significant—the rise of the working woman, and the increase in divorce—greatly undermined the family's ability to care for itself. Steadily from 1900 on—and dramatically after the 1970s—the homemakers of yesteryear became the working women of today. Women made up 18 percent of the American workforce in 1900, 28 percent in 1970, and a stunning near-50 percent by 2010. Today, 70 percent of all American children live in households where all the adults work.[7] So who now would care for the children, the sick, the elderly? And who would provide, as nineteenth-century middle-class homemakers were said to do, "the sunshine of the home?" Mothers were trying hard but they were also out billing customers, stocking shelves, teaching classes, and treating patients. And so were the once-available maiden aunts, grandmothers, friends, and "give-you-a-hand" neighbors.

Meanwhile, marriage in America became less secure. In 1900, about 10 percent of marriages ultimately ended in divorce, while today, for first marriages, chances stand at 40 to 50 percent. Those who marry a second or third time are yet more likely to divorce and do so more quickly. Moreover, the percentage of babies born to single mothers reached 40 percent by 2011, and studies revealed that half of American children spent at least part of their lives in single-parent households.[8] There were simply fewer people to shoulder the tasks at home.

During the same period, for both men and women, the workplace became more demanding and insecure. As Robert Kuttner noted in *Everything for Sale*, from the 1970s on, many people lost confidence that they could hold on to their jobs.[9] "Relentless layoffs are not merely a temporary response to business cycles," he wrote, "but a way of life."[10] The long-term contracts once enjoyed by white-collar and union-backed blue-collar workers all but disappeared as companies downsized, merged, and restructured. Stable careers, along with pensions and benefits, were increasingly limited to the privileged, with other workers treated as casual labor. Manpower Temporary Services—a Milwaukee-based company with 4,400 offices employing over 30,000—became one of the biggest employers in the United States.[11]

With women in the job force and all Americans working longer hours and having less secure jobs, modern families became ever more hard pressed. Where were they to turn for help? The government? Europeans have long been shocked at the basic public services we lack: paid parental leave, high-quality paid child care and paid family and medical leave that would permit a worker to tend to an ill child or elderly parent. At least on paper, 186 countries offer government-supported maternity leave, and the United States has never been among them.[12] If anything, over the last five decades, public services have dwindled. As child-care expert Edward Zigler noted, during the 1980s "the government's role in child care did not expand in proportion to the growing need but in fact declined."[13] In the wake of recent events—the great recession of 2008, expensive foreign wars, and a looming budget deficit—the prospect of government help has grown dimmer still.

Nor could nonprofit organizations fill the gap. Parent-initiated cooperative nurseries, the YMCA, the Jewish Homes for the Aged, nursing homes, community recreation centers based in schools and privately funded—all these have been a worthy but minor sideshow.

With no community of yesteryear to lean back on, and no European-style government supports ahead, people looked increasingly to the one remaining option—the market. Families who could afford it have always made use of paid services, of course; at the turn of the century, they hired servants, matchmakers, governesses, chauffeurs, wet nurses, and more. But over time, Americans in ever greater numbers have turned to more market solutions. To give just a few examples: In 1900, over 95 percent of American food dollars went to food prepared and consumed at home. Today, nearly half such dollars go to food prepared behind take-out counters or eaten in diners and restaurants. Dressmaking has moved from home to factory, hair care from home to beauty salon.[14]

The trend has accelerated particularly in the last forty years, a period when the market came to dominate American life as never before. Voices calling for larger market control—for deregulation, privatization, cuts to government services—grew louder.[15] Accordingly, many aspects of post-1970s American life slipped from the realms of community, commons, and government into the market. Prisons, parks, libraries, sectors of the armed forces, security services, schools, universities—these have moved, in full or part, into for-profit hands. The market, it is said, can do things better—even in the home.

Today, the market offers families an extraordinary array of possibilities. Americans now live within a cycle of market take-away and give-back. While market forces have eroded stability and fostered anxiety at work and at home, it is, ironically, mainly the market that now provides support and relief. Along with the more familiar resources of child care and home help, Americans can now readily employ personal trainers, event planners, life coaches, and dog walkers, to name a few. Once reserved for the elite, personal services have been increasingly extended to the middle class, with more Americans living or being hired to provide them than ever before.

Outsourcing of work once done at home is most highly developed in big cities, of course. But even in small towns like Auburn and Lewiston, Maine, shop bulletin boards and local papers might display a notice for Rent-a-Husband, a handyman service, that cleans out your garage and hangs your pictures. If in 2011 you called 1.877.99.HUBBY, you would be contacting a nationwide chain with five offices in Maine, one half hour's drive from my aunt Elizabeth's home. A local event planner will organize your daughter's Sweet Sixteen party. One June morning I heard a radio announcer advertise a Fourth of July service that pats together your hamburger patties for the grill "so you can sit back and enjoy the holiday."

But we have not just democratized the old services. We've made them more specialized, as the hamburger patties suggest, more professional, and more technology-based than in the past. A household with small children might employ a van driver from Kids in Motion to escort children to and from soccer games and music lessons, a potty trainer who graduates a child from diapers to pull-ups, and a doula for a sleepless child if the sound track of "Sleeping Baby," available for download from eMusic, doesn't work.

There are specially tailored options for every category. For those on their own, a pluckily titled Rent-a-Friend service provides a paid "pal" with whom to eat dinner, see movies, work out at the gym, sort photos, or go on trips—no sex included. For those who yearn for the feel of a "traditional" family dinner, Rent-a-Grandma will let you shop, cook, talk, and share a family dinner with an older woman of your ethnicity—choices include Italian, African American, Mexican—who can, in the course of this, teach you about your "traditional" cuisine.

Personal services are increasingly using new technologies. eHarmony and Match.com, for example, attract millions of fee-paying clients to a keyboard search for love. Through new reproductive technology, artificially inseminated commercial surrogates carry the babies of infertile couples, gay men, or even women who fear pregnancy. The revolution in technology has also allowed the market to go global. A young man late for an interview with me in San Francisco couldn't locate his car so he e-mailed Misha from "Your Man in India," a Bangalore-based concierge service, to check all the municipal tow lots in the Bay Area. Students in America can turn to the India-based TutorVista, which at twenty dollars an hour offers help for less money than many tutors closer at hand.

But the greatest innovation of the contemporary scene are those services that reach into the heart of our emotional lives, a realm previously more shielded from the market. A love coach guides his shy client on what to do and how to feel at each step of online dating. A wedding planner helps select a suitable "memory" to set the theme of the ceremony, the inscription on place cards, and the subject of a heartfelt speech. A marriage counselor helps couples learn to shut their BlackBerries in a drawer to enjoy a romantic evening together. A paid carer offers to visit and love an elderly parent. A wantologist helps a woman figure out if she really wants a bigger home. A dog walker offers to "relate" to a dog. Attached to each practical step of dating, wedding, and divorcing are the subtle issues of what, how much, and when to feel.

The proliferation of such intimate services suggests that the market has made inroads into our very understanding of the self. In the marketization of personal life, acts that were once intuitive or ordinary—deciding whom to marry, choosing a name for your newborn, even figuring out what to want—now require the help of paid experts. In some ways, market services are very welcome news. But they raise, at every turn, the specter of a profound shift in American culture: the commodification of intimate life, which may be the great unnoticed trend of our time.

To explore this shift, I immersed myself in the world of the outsourced self, discovering in the process that every stage of life has its corresponding market service. I interviewed love coaches and wedding planners, birth surrogates and parenting counselors, paid friends and mourners-for-hire. I spoke to the people who engage them and saw how they struggled with the desire to rely on family, friends, neighbors, on the one hand, and the need for professional assurances, on the other. I wanted to understand the meaning of what it is that we're doing when we outsource a personal act to someone who will know part of our knowledge, do part of our work, feel some of our feelings for us.

One thing, I discovered, was that people drew lines between what seemed to them "too village" and "too market." Some things were obvious. A sidewalk vendor wearing an apron with dot eyes stands before a customer, in a *New Yorker* cartoon, a printed sign above his stand: "EYE CONTACT, $1.00." Everyone I showed this cartoon to laughed. That's "going too far," they said. But other cases were not so clear-cut. One man was happy to pay someone to walk his dog Monday through Friday, for example, "but not on Saturday. Why *have* a dog if you don't walk him on Saturdays?" It was fine, one woman told me, to hire a friendly visitor to drop in on her elderly mother because she lived three hundred miles away. But the woman's sister lived only ten miles from her mother. Why hire a visitor, she asked, when my sister lives ten miles away? Another man drew a line regarding commercial surrogate mothers: "One or two babies, that's fine. But if the surrogate has three or more, then she's turning into a baby factory. Then it's just about money." On issue after issue, people sought to protect the personal from the purchased, the village from the market, the self from a strange new emotional capitalism.[16]

The challenge is immense. We are bombarded with language that urges us to think in market terms. "You're the CEO of your love life," one coach advised a lovelorn client. "You need to brand yourself better," another advised. "You're a 4 on a 10-point scale in the partner search market," another client was told. "Isn't it time to outsource your dating life?" read an ad for a dating service in United Airline's *Hemispheres* magazine: "My clients look to me as their personal dating headhunter." People scrambled to decipher such market metaphors, to try them on, to take them off, to figure out what stance to take in relation to their own selves.[17] Service providers also came bearing the opposite message. "Remember, you're not a number, you're unique," one coach reassured his client. But of course "unique" is one of the most valuable marketable traits of all.

We have shifted, the philosopher Jerald Wallulis has noted, from being a society based on marriage and employment to one based on "marriageability" and "employability." And in light of our new insecurities, the more the market becomes our main source of help, the more powerful its aura of inevitability. This in turn makes it more acceptable to hire someone to do such things as pat hamburgers for the Fourth of July grill, if not yet pass a plate of them to a Rent-a-Friend.[18]

Those who are most insecure are America's poor, who also, of course, can least afford the tempting offerings of the market. In their ever-increasing insecurity and isolation, the poor need and yearn for personal services. But one message of this book is that the answer to the dilemma posed by the market may not be found in universal access to private outsourcing. The real answer may lie in a greater commitment to public life and community. In this case, the proverbial canary in the coal mine may actually live in a gilded cage.

Americans are used to faulting themselves for being too materialistic.[19] In a 1995 survey commissioned by the Merck Family Fund, 82 percent of Americans agreed that "most of us buy and consume far more than we need."[20] We often contrast a materialistic focus on the external aspect of life—the stuff we buy—with a noncommercial internal self that we protect. We either overstock at the mall or sit straight-backed in a yoga position, thumb to forefinger, focusing on nature, God, or our inner essence. But the deeper truth is that the two are no longer so distinct. Despite everyone's best intentions, personal experience can become a thing we purchase—the "perfect" date, birthday, wedding—detached from our part in creating it. This book, then, is about the market's pressure to commercialize the self, and the ways in which we accept, resist, and grapple with that challenge.

It was through my aunt Elizabeth, my last living connection to those summers at the farm, that I came face-to-face with the dilemma that drives this book. At ninety-four, she became too sick to care for herself. She had spent most of her life in Turner. In her younger years, she had taught grade school. Generations of townspeople learned from her how to hold a pencil, sing in unison, and line up at the door of a small, wooden, one-room schoolhouse that her mother before her had once attended and where she, too, had taught. Late in life, Elizabeth married a man who lived "down the ro'd a piece," as they used to say in rural Maine, and was widowed after five years. Later in life, she inherited the family farm and moved into the white house she had built after the farm burned down.

This she let go to pot. Shingles dropped from the roof. Chipmunks hopped through a tear in the screen of the open front door, scampering toward a large, open bag of seed by her chair. Fleas multiplied. Mice rustled in the corners of back rooms. Peanut butter jars held up the living-room windows. Retired, alone, lame, and half deaf, she sat for years looking out the window onto the gently sloping pastures her ancestors had plowed over two hundred years ago.

When my parents were still alive, they would look in on her, and tried to help as much as she would allow. That wasn't much. My father would walk down the hill from our house, a windowpane under his arm, tool kit in hand, prepared to replace a broken garage window he'd noticed. *"I don't need help!"* She'd crack her schoolteacherly voice like a whip. My father would patiently return, set aside pane and tools and wait for the next chance. But the frailer my aunt became, the more fiercely independent she wished to be. Then, one after the other, my parents died, and it fell to me to keep an eye out for Elizabeth.

And that's all I did at the beginning—keep an eye out. From the safe distance of San Francisco, I followed my aunt's quirky life with affectionate interest and listened with great admiration to lively accounts of the help her neighbors gave her. During summer vacations, we flew to Turner, Maine, to stay in my parents' old house up the hill.

A day or so after we arrived, I would walk down to Elizabeth's house, knock on the front door, and wait.

Silence.

I would knock on a window and call, "Elizabeth?"

Silence.

I would call out again. "Elizabeth? It's Arlie."

Silence.

Then a slight stir. A shuffle.

After five minutes she would press open a stuck door, limp out in frayed slippers, holding two worn lawn chairs. These we ceremoniously set up in the knee-high grass outside her front door. In those years she almost never invited anyone into her house and always refused my offers to mow her lawn or plant flowers, the first step in a ritual of slowly conceded consent. "No, no, thank you," she'd say, then ask with genuine interest how my year had gone. After a certain number of offers to help and refusals, she could be coaxed to dinners with my family up the hill. During winters when we were gone, kindly elderly relatives and neighbors visited, recycled her bottles, and eventually took on feeding her Lean Cuisine dinners, paying her bills, and washing her hair.

Despite the plethora of services that had begun to appear in rural Maine, the spirit of "just do" had not vanished. In February 1998, a fierce ice storm hit Turner. It buried cars, felled trees, froze water pipes, knocked out the power, and so chilled the air in my aunt's small living room that, sitting in her wingback chair, Elizabeth could see her own breath. As the temperature dropped, my aunt donned a sweater, a coat, three pairs of socks, two caps, and in a paradoxical expression of independence and helplessness, went to her bed in the living room, pulled up two blankets, and waited.

Help came. A parade of kindly neighbors in touching acts of small-town kindness stocked her refrigerator, brought extra blankets, set up an electric generator, and placed flowers by her chair. Other elderly or disabled residents more mobile or less stubborn than she were moved, with pets, to cots set up in the town fire station. Volunteers served three hot meals a day until the crisis passed. It didn't occur to my aunt to calculate her neighbors' time, add in gas, and write out checks to her rescuers any more than it would have occurred to them. In truth, Elizabeth was loath to pay anyone for anything. But even so, it sat right with both her and them that her rescuers were kindly, civic-minded townspeople and not professionals delivering skillful, friendly service.

Then one summer morning, when fortunately we were still close by, Elizabeth awoke to discover she could not swallow. After a day of no food or drink, she could not rise from bed. A neighbor called Turner Rescue, the town ambulance service. A soft-spoken EMT named Ross emerged from the van, sat on a stool beside my aunt's bed in her living room, as he had from time to time for years, and asked: "So how d'ya feel?"

"Fine," came her reply.

"Fine really?"

"Fine enough."

"Fine enough how?"

"Fine enough so that I don't have to leave here."

After a half an hour of gentle, steady banter, Ross coaxed my aunt into the ambulance and drove her to a local hospital where a doctor discovered a hernia blocking her colon. If he didn't operate, he explained, she would die. He operated and from this—she was now ninety-four—she miraculously recovered. She was transferred to a convalescent home where she was helped to stand lean on her walker, and haltingly walk.

A month later, the doctor declared her well. She could not stay in the convalescent home indefinitely, but, given the doctor's assessment of her condition, she could not legally be released without around-the-clock care in place. As Elizabeth's nearest of kin, it fell to me to figure out what came next.

My Berkeley classes started in a week. The two couples who had previously pitched in with shopping, paying bills, and washing hair, could do no more. But Elizabeth—childless, lame, nearly blind, unable to drive—only wanted to sit in her wingback chair on her beloved hill and be, as she imagined, "independent."

Would she move to San Francisco? I asked. "I could find you a place. We could visit." "No," she said, "just take me *home*." But at home, she had no thought of bringing in a person to care for her. "Strangers in my house? No need for that." And as for paying such a person? "No need for that either." My aunt Elizabeth had in mind an older world of "just do." But I couldn't quit my family and job in California to care for her in Maine myself. I couldn't "just do."

I now faced a care crisis of my own, so I ventured, alongside the people in this book, out onto the market frontier.

Chapter 1

You Have Three Seconds

A century ago in America, courtship was mostly a community affair. We can imagine my grandfather James Porter Russell, age twenty-three in the summer of 1900. He is riding his penny-farthing bicycle, with its large thin front wheel and smaller back one, over twenty-nine miles of dusty, washboard road from his home in Farmington to the farm in Turner. Five hours coming, five hours back, all in one day. Once there, he courts Edith, and her younger sister, Alice, local schoolteachers. One of the two will become my grandmother, the other the wife of a ne'er-do-well farmer. While paid matchmakers plied their trade in the ethnic enclaves of the great cities, they seldom entered the parlors of small-town New England[1] where courtship tended to be a do-it-yourself thing.

The sisters and their visitor might well have been seated on the front porch of the farmhouse facing the dirt road. A neighbor's son, passing by, might have raised a palm to wave. The girls' father, a shy man who fought with the 16th Maine Regiment in the Civil War, would likely have been milking cows in the barn with his two hired hands. Their mother, chronically ill, was probably resting but would have come out if one of the girls called for her. This was the sort of situation an honorable suitor in 1900 might have found himself in: expected to court under the watchful eye of family, neighbor, and village. J. Porter, as he called himself, had met Alice at a teacher's training college in Farmington and took a liking to her. But once he met Edith, the spunkier of the two, and saw her combing her resplendent brown hair in the sun—so the story goes—he made up his mind to choose her as his wife.

J. Porter was looking for a traditional girl, a homemaker and future mother, in a traditional way: a face-to-face meeting arranged through friends who also knew each other face-to-face. A typical turn-of-the-century advice book would have recommended he search for a modest, frugal, clean, courteous, industrious woman who reflected in her comportment "sobriety of conduct" and "chastity of intention." One such advice book cautioned a suitor to "marry no woman who sleeps till breakfast" because early risers "exhilarate the mind and induce prosperity." Another warned a man not to propose "before you have had time to notice whether her front hair and back hair match."[2]

One hundred and nine years after J. Porter pedaled his bike to Turner in search of a wife, Marcel Singer began his twenty-first-century courtship of Grace Weaver.* While J. Porter courted Edith in the presence of family and neighbors, Marcel and Grace first met through Match.com, a commercial Internet dating site, and Grace, who lives in Boston, received advice by phone from her love coach in Los Angeles.

"I Need a Consultant"

Grace's Internet profile photo on Match.com showed a green-eyed woman with loosely curled short blond hair and a radiant smile. At

* I have changed the names of all interviewees—except those who didn't mind being identified—as well as many defining characteristics. But I have tried to faithfully describe their experiences and accurately report what they have said.

age forty-nine, she was a full-time engineer and the divorced mother of a twelve-year-old daughter. She was looking not so much for a husband, as for what she called a "partner for the long term," an "emotionally engaged" new-fashioned guy, in a new-fashioned—screen-to-screen—way. Grace's ideal had far less to do with frugality, modesty, or industry than with emotional warmth, openness to mutual self-disclosure, and sexual fulfillment. Compared to J. Porter, she was seeking a far more intimate bond in a far less intimate way.

Her voice was spritely and warm when I called for the first of a series of telephone interviews. I began by asking her how she came to hire a love coach.

> I remember waking up the morning after going out to a New Year's Eve party. I felt disappointed I hadn't met any interesting men. I flipped on the television and watched a *Wall Street Journal* show on Internet dating. I'd always thought Internet dating would be tacky, and leave me feeling icky, overexposed, and naked. But then I heard this coach Evan Katz say, "Come on, guys. There's nothing embarrassing about Internet dating." I jotted down his name and wondered if this shouldn't be my New Year's resolution: hire a coach, take control of my life.

To do that Grace would need to leave behind the last remnants of J. Porter's face-to-face village and outsource to a paid professional what has, for the last century, been imagined to be a personal matter. When friends still inhabiting that older world asked her, "*A coach?* Are you out of your mind? Get us to set you up. Pass the word. Join clubs. Meet a guy *naturally*," she told them, "I've tried that, and I don't want to waste more time."

> I work 8:30 a.m. to 5:00 p.m. With cooking, shopping, driving my daughter around, beekeeping, and gardening, I don't have time to look for a long-term permanent relationship—the basic thing I feel is missing from my life. My sister-in-law set

me up with perfectly nice friends of friends, but no one special. Once you exhaust those possibilities, what do you do?

Then one morning as she rode her bedroom exercise bicycle, the thought came to her: Finding love is like an engineering project. I need a consultant.

So Grace Googled Evan Katz, whose online name was e-Cyrano—named after the secret wooer who fed lines to his handsome, lovelorn but clueless friend—and whose Web site read: "I am a PERSONAL TRAINER for women who want to FALL IN LOVE." (Evan actually had male clients, too.) She signed up for his medium-level $1,500 Premium Package and simultaneously enrolled at Match.com for $17.99 per month. (In 2009 Match.com was charging its 1,438,000 paid subscribers $34.99 for one month or $17.99 a month for a six-month contract.) Grace declined Match.com's further offer (and fee) to advise on the next step—getting a prospective date to exchange phone numbers. She also declined "First Impressions," a service that, for yet another fee, moved messages to the top of the inbox of all new Match.com subscribers.

Wondering how a love coach went about his work, I flew to Burbank, California, to interview Evan Katz. He answered the doorbell and, with a friendly nod, welcomed me in, head tilted into his cell phone, alternating silence with soothing words to a client. Thirty-five years old, Evan was a tall, lean, wide-stepping man with a halo of curly brown hair and alert, curious, slightly worried blue eyes. Over tea, he described with disarming modesty his initial venture into coaching, "I had a BA from Duke in English literature, and I wanted to write romantic comedy screenplays for television. That didn't work out but I thought I'd hold on to the romance part and try this."

With the help of a business coach, Evan launched what became a highly successful company. He was featured at the International Internet Dating Convention in San Francisco, and has been a panelist on the Flirt-A-Thon Expert Panel in Los Angeles. He appeared on NBC, ABC, and CBS. He was the author of *Why*

You're Still Single: Things Your Friends Would Tell You If You Promised Not to Get Mad.[3] He maintains a monthly newsletter, and has produced audio CDs based on a tele-class (an interactive workshop via telephone) on "How to Write a Profile that Attracts People You Want to Meet." When I met him, in May of 2009, he had written more than five hundred personal profiles for his clients, most of them heterosexual women.

Recalling Grace's hesitation, I asked Evan if his clients felt ashamed to hire him. "Oh, I'm their dirty little secret! They think they're supposed to be able to do this on their own," he answered. A lot of them believe that "when you're ready, love finds you." But actually, he said, "finding love takes skill and work." And to learn that skill, you need to pay an expert.

Evan offers three coaching packages for online daters—Basic, Premium, and VIP. For the Basic package, he helps clients write a profile for the online dating Web site of their choice; pick a headshot from LookBetterOnline, a photo service for online daters; create an alluring username; and write a catchy subject line. He also gives tips on how to correspond with an interested party—that is, date online, and how to date IRL, that is, In Real Life, afterward. The Premium package included a month of private coaching sessions. The VIP package adds sixteen hour-long coaching sessions over four months.

Like other love coaches, Evan also offered to read all the responses sent to Grace's online profile and help pick out the most promising. But that felt "over the line" to Grace. "I'm the only one who can tell who is and isn't promising. Plus, I want to be able to tell my partner, once we're together, I chose you *myself*." Unlike Evan Katz's service, eHarmony, another Internet dating service, sets out guidelines for what to talk about after a couple has decided they are seriously interested in each other. But Grace found that unacceptable, too: "If one coach is feeding lines to the guy and another is feeding lines to the woman, isn't that one coach courting the other?" A Double-Cyrano, for Grace, was just "too much."

In all of these decisions, Grace had to consider the extent to which she should adopt Evan's businesslike approach to finding love. To begin with, he told her that looking for love was like finding a job. That made a certain sense to her:

> I'm an engineer. So it was easy for me to think of dating as a work project. Just get it done. I know that sounds unromantic, but that's okay, so long as I get to my goal. Evan kept my nose to the grindstone.

Other online daters writing on Evan's blog also seemed determined to stoically embrace courtship as work. One woman said she was "working at" meeting men online and even on "putting in face time." Another who identified herself as *offthemarket4now* described her schedule: "I kept plugging away, TableForSix [a service that sets up dinners with other singles], poetry readings, volunteering, and it's hard work." One playful poster remarked, "If dating is work, you may want to avoid people who have too many dates, like employers avoid job-hoppers." Another wrote defiantly, "Looking for love is *not* like work."

According to Evan, however, looking *was* work:

> When you're unemployed, what do you do to find work? When you are single, what do you do to find love? I'm not telling clients to spend forty hours a week looking for love, but I tell them, "You can give it three. Do the numbers—and don't resent it."

More than not resenting this work, Evan believed a person should enjoy it. In fact, trying to enjoy the work was part of the work.

Evan advised Grace to relax and to "put her real self out there." As Grace recalled:

> Evan told me: "Okay, Gracey, you can't hide behind generalities—fun-loving, athletic, musical. You have to show the real you through real stories."

So Grace proposed a real story:

> I once paid good money to go to a Zen monastery where I was guided to get on my hands and knees and scrub the men's bathroom, to teach humility. And I didn't mind. I'd cleaned Trudy's [her daughter's] bottom many times.

"That might be a little too out there," Evan cautioned. "Why don't you save that for when you're actually on a date?" In other words, he urged her to be "real" but not "too real," distinguishing between off-putting and enticing real stories.

The best real self, Evan assured Grace, was an "average" one. The Internet was not, as he saw it, a brilliant new medium for like-minded oddballs to find each other. It was a place for one wide-appeal average to meet another. "Everyone needs to aim for the middle so they can widen their market," he counseled. "Don't appeal to a small niche." It was a common mistake clients made, Evan said:

> I had this MIT brainy double-helix guy who worked for a suicide hotline, but I told him, "You can't lay that out on the first date. It's too much. You have to learn to talk about the weather."

So part of getting the "real you" out there required the suppression of the too-real you. In your local community, Evan reasoned, a simple "this-is-me" approach would work, since people have had years to inquire of others and observe who you are. But the Internet, Evan said with awe, has revolutionized courtship:

> The Internet is the world's biggest love mall. And to go there, you have to brand yourself well because you only have three seconds. When I help a client brand herself, I'm helping her put herself forward to catch that all-important glimpse. A profile could say, "I talk about myself a lot. I go through bouts of depression and Zoloft usually works." That might be the truth, but it's not going into her brand.

Nor would excessive reticence do the trick:

> One client told me, "I'm really good with my nieces and nephews." But I told him, "Look, man, this is your job interview. Bring on the A-game. You don't want a woman to ditch you because you bored her. The burden's on you to reach out, not for her to see through your shy mask." It's a bitter pill to swallow.

Evan urged clients to use humor to persuade others that the edited sliver of their "real" self was them. He told me proudly of a success story.

> Tony was bald and short, five foot two. I didn't deny he was short, but I also didn't focus on the height he didn't have. I focused on the sense of humor he did have. We put "Are you afraid of spilling things on me? Don't answer my e-mail. Worried about falling objects? Look for a taller person. A man you can look up to." Before the new profile, he was hardly getting any e-mail response. Now he gets fifty or sixty page views and ten to twelve e-mails a week. I made the guy larger than life.

Applying Evan's approach, one inspired online dater wrote: "Putting the 'rarin' back into 'librarian.'"

Pressing the Button

Grace was ready. She had paid her fees and, with Evan's help, had written her profile, posed for her photograph, collected additional shots of herself gardening, skiing, and hiking. She had prepared an e-mail subject line: "Nature Girl Looking for Serious Relationship." Now all she had to do was click "submit." Her voice trembled slightly as she recalled the moment:

> I froze. It was hard to push the button. That was *my* photo, and there are twenty million viewers who are going to see it. What if some creep downloads my photo? I work in a state office building. What if someone walks in and recognizes me? It made me squirm. But Evan kept telling me, "You can do it." So I pushed the button.

The next day, Grace's profile went online, and, given her beautiful smile and artful description, e-mail responses flooded in.

> Wow! People deluged me. Look at all these men interested in me. I felt so good about myself. A few hundred page views every few days—e-mails and winks [a Match.com option by which a viewer can express interest in a post]. I was like a kid in a candy store.

Grace felt she had to cull these responses on her own, without Evan's help. Going through the messages gave her a sense of who was genuinely looking for love, and who was out for sport.

> I discarded men who seemed to want a fling, or serial monogamy or pretend-monogamy. I wanted someone to grow old with, someone as morally upstanding as my dad, a sex god, and crazy about me, physically active and emotionally and spiritually mature. With this much choice I felt I didn't have to settle for someone who wasn't really exceptional.

"You're getting good ROI," Evan told Grace—Return on Investment, a term widely used on Internet dating blogs. Having now invested money and time, Grace focused on results; if dating was a job, you measured success by the quantity of high-quality responses.

Grace corresponded with many men. Some were sweet but implausible—like an Alaskan musher with forty dogs who'd noted that she owned a Labrador retriever and thought they might share a love of dogs. Others were unnerving, like the man who, when she met him in person at a bar, turned out to be twenty-five years older than he'd claimed to be online—a fact he tried to remedy by applying a great deal of face cream and powder. As a friend put it to Grace, "You have to kiss a lot of frogs."

But Evan didn't talk about frogs and princes; he talked about numbers. As he explained, "Even if daters don't think in numbers, numbers apply to them and they should know it." His rating system went from 1 to 10. "I see a lot of 5 men looking for 10 women, and that leaves the 4 and 5 women in the dust," Evan observed. A "10" woman, as he explained it, was twenty-four, never married, had a sexy 36–24–36 figure, a face like Nicole Kidman's, a warm personality, a successful but flexible career, and a love of gourmet cooking. Grace was very pretty and sexy but older, divorced, and low on time for gourmet cooking. So maybe she was a "6." How volatile such numbers were, Grace realized when she updated her profile the day after turning fifty. "Like stock prices, overnight, my ratings fell by half. I asked myself, 'What happened? I'm the same *person* I was a day ago—but not the same number. Now I'm a 3 and a half.' "

Complaints sprinkled through Evan's Internet blog were often couched in numerical terms. A woman who described herself as "nice, average looking, intellectually fun and creative" wrote, "I am SO SICK of these men who are fives (or lower) who think they're going to wind up with supermodels."

Before she met Marcel, Grace had had two half-year-long relationships. In each case the relationship ended because the man couldn't get along with her preteen daughter. But what shocked Grace was how casually these men treated the breakups and how confident they were about their future prospects. "It was eerie," she told me.

> The first guy said, "I'm getting back on Match.com. It was so easy to find you; there must be others out there like you."
>
> I said, "Are you kidding me?"
>
> He came back months later, "Oh, my God! What did I do? There are no other you's out there."

> I said, "It's too late." I'm not dealing with someone who thinks people come in facsimiles. It's very weird, but the second guy said exactly the same thing. "It was so easy to find you." Ten months later, he tells me, "There's nobody out here like you." In his mind, I was a box of cereal on the shelf with dozens of others. I was replaceable.

Both suitors had taken the idea of a "6" to heart. One 6 seemed equal to another. So if you lose one, you can get another just like it. In Grace's eyes, they had taken market logic "too far." Grace might be using the market to find a man but she didn't want to end up with a man who saw her in a marketlike way.

One day, in a moment of great loneliness, Grace's second boyfriend paid her a late-evening visit. Despite her strong reservations, she was tempted by his profuse apologies and entreaties. But Evan counseled her, "Gracey, has anything changed? Does he get along with Trudy any better? Has he grown more flexible? No? So don't take him back. Mr. Right is out there. Keep going." Here Evan was more than her guide to self-marketing. He was a friend, or at least friendlike. Maybe the suitor didn't see who she really was, but her coach evidently did.

A few months later, Grace met Marcel, a twice-married musician and teacher. "The first thing that impressed me was that he put himself out for me. We live an hour and a half's drive apart. But he told me, 'I'm happy to drive to you.' From the start, he was generous-hearted." Something else also struck her. Many of Marcel's attributes did not match the list of desirable traits she had given Evan earlier in the process: tall, good looking, possibly an accountant or engineer. Evan hadn't put much stock in her list, and now she saw he was right.

> The first time Marcel came to my house, he serenaded my Labrador retriever and me with his tenor saxophone. As I was watching him, I realized Marcel didn't have many checks on my list. I wasn't looking for a musician. I wasn't looking for a

> bald man. And he's tattooed! But he's gone out of his way to introduce me to his friends and family, and they all smile knowingly and say they've heard all about me and they're thrilled for him. After he'd known me for less than a month, he invited me to his high school reunion that was to take place four months later. We've been dating for just five months now, but already it feels deep.

Part of Marcel's appeal, never considered on Grace's list, may have been his own readiness to weave her into his life in nonmarket ways.

When I talked to Marcel by phone, he explained that his decision to put his money down for Match.com evoked little of the anxiety Grace had felt, even though he was, as he put it, "an Internet dating virgin":

> I just sat at my computer one summer day, punched in my Visa number, attached my photo and—zip—I was online. I didn't hire a coach and didn't have a shopping list. But I was excited to try it out. I'd gone on a bunch of ordinary dates but it was the sweetness in Grace's eyes and smile in that photo that caught my attention.

After Marcel and Grace had exchanged messages, he visited her. "On the second date," he recalled, "Grace packed a sushi lunch and a bottle of wine, and she asked to kidnap me to drive to a place very special to her—an organic herb farm. She was as sweet inside as out. She's a giving person."

Marcel had never heard of 1 to 10 ratings, brands, or ROIs. After meeting him, Grace, too, began brushing them aside. "I never would have gone out with him if I'd stuck to my checklist!" The old language of romance crept back into her dating life. "It seemed to happen organically," she said. "We feel natural with each other." At one point, she even mused, "The way I think about it now, I wonder if meeting Marcel wasn't fated. It's like he was sent to me." In the realm of love, Grace had entered the market, exposed herself to its ratings of investment and gain, encountered men who saw her strictly as a commodity, and recoiled. The market could take you only so far. It might make the introduction but for the rest what was required was the spirit of the gift.

Others Not So Lucky

Grace was one of Evan's success stories. She had achieved her goal and felt happy to have hired Evan and gone on Match.com. Other Internet love-seekers, though, were not so lucky and ultimately felt hurt by their experiences online. As a woman who posted on Evan's blog remarked:

> There probably isn't a single guy I wouldn't have given a second chance to, but out of the many, many men I met, only two ever gave me a second date. You may read this and think I'm a terrible date. But I'm not. And I'm not looking for a movie star. I don't care if he has money, career, or a car. I'm just looking for a guy who's nice to me, makes me laugh, and uses his brain. Personally I don't feel the need to subject myself to this kind of rejection anymore. You know what I'm doing? I'm having a rich and active LIFE. . . .

A chorus of sympathetic online nods followed: "I know what you mean. . . . I'm in the same boat." Men overrate themselves, women complained, leaving more women—especially older women—forced to lower their standards and demean themselves to elicit interest. One woman sadly admitted that in order to attract a man, she had falsely claimed she wasn't interested in marriage. Another proposed mobilizing a voluntary nationwide women's cartel against callous men in order to raise the general standard of respect for women. "We should all refuse to go out with men who treat other women poorly," she suggested. But this idea fell by the wayside in the unregulated, nonunionized market of love. Evan countered with a simple "Sorry, darlin'."

Internet dating could be hard on men, too, Marcel explained:

> I didn't anticipate some of the anger you can run into out there on the Internet and in person. I remember I asked a woman out. And when she got out of her car, I saw she was thirty pounds heavier than her photo showed. We had drinks. Then when I was walking her to her car, she excoriated men who cared about a woman's weight. When I later e-mailed her to say that I didn't think we were a match, she wrote a venomous reply. It was hands down the worst date I ever had.

Thinking of Marcel's experience, I asked Evan Katz why he thought Internet dating was so unrewarding for so many. For one thing, he felt, some people were simply too old, too fat, too unattractive in person or personality; their "numbers" were low. What about the fact that so many divorced men remarried much younger women, leaving attractive older women with fewer options? Nothing to be done about that. Work hard. Tough it out, he advised.

More to the point, he felt, was a general lack of clarity about just how close a bond really was:

> People get very confused. They want to know when a relationship is serious. Here's how it is: A relationship isn't real until you've committed to being boyfriend/girlfriend. Everything prior to that—phoning, e-mailing, dating, preliminary sex—all that isn't real until you have each committed. I've had clients devastated to realize that they've fallen in love with someone who is still looking online.

Another reason Evan gave for failure was—paradoxically—that his clients acted too much like shoppers:

> People think they are shopping, and they are. But they want to quickly comb through the racks and snap their fingers, next . . . next . . . next. . . . They make low-investment dates, so they can quickly move on to the next appointment, and they set up a short meeting at Starbucks where all they have time to say is, "Oh, is that a soy latte?"
>
> You need to slow down. Hold out for high-investment dates—a nice dinner, a play afterward. You can be too efficient, too focused on your list of desired characteristics, so intent on getting the best deal that you pass over the right one.

Many clients clicked through dates—next, next, next—out of anxiety, Evan surmised. Part of his job, he said, was to tell them, "Relax. You have time."

And even as shoppers, he pointed out, his clients often misunderstood the market. Many held the illusion, for example, that highly desirable partners were there for the picking.

> Imagine you talk one-to-one to a beautiful woman at a party. She seems available. You feel lucky. Maybe a guy comes up; you see your competition. But what if, after you talk with her, you notice a line of five hundred men behind you. It's like that on the Internet. If the supply of competitors goes up, your rating goes down. You just can't see it.

On the farmhouse front porch in 1900, my grandmother was, lore has it, sitting next to her competition, her sister. It was a village courtship, and surely for her sister, all the more painful for that. To Grace, Marcel, and millions of other American online daters, however, the competition was anonymous; so for disappointments, there seemed no one to blame but oneself.

Evan also cautioned against looking for just what many love coaches professed to sell—a soul mate. Clients, he was convinced, were often scanning the listings for the wrong thing. As he observed ironically:

> Online daters listen to coaching ads. "Find your soul mate. Find perfect chemistry. Fall in love." And so they come into my office with long lists of characteristics they want: The man should be successful, tall, handsome, funny, kind, and family oriented. The checklist goes on. Does he like to dance? Is he a film aficionado? A real reader? They want a charismatic guy who doesn't flirt, a CEO who's home by 5:00 p.m. Some women are so touchy about not wanting to settle for less than their complete list that they price themselves out of the market. Then they get discouraged and conclude it's impossible to find real love.

"Soul mate," as Evan saw it, was a retrospective category. "It's only when you look back after twenty years together that you can say, 'We've been soul mates,'" he observed. The term implied, even created, a certain chemistry. So Evan didn't use it. Still, many people do. Eighty-five percent of online daters in a 2004 study by Dr. Courtney Johnson said they believed "everyone has a soul mate." Over three-quarters believed in "love at first sight."[4]

How might all this have looked to J. Porter? I wondered. For one thing, the search for a soul mate with great sexual chemistry would probably have startled him, given his era's greater focus on a woman's steadiness of character and motherliness. He would have been astonished, too, at the modern celebration of—and expansion of—choice in the world's "biggest candy store." After all, as far as we know, his choice was between Edith and Alice seated together on the same farmhouse porch. Grace Weaver's Match.com profile, on the other hand, went out to many millions of viewers, 1.3 million of whom paid for the right to reply to her or other paying clients. In 2009, Match.com reported 56 million introductory e-mails sent, and 132 million "winks."[5]

J. Porter might also have been nonplussed by the very idea of a hired e-Cyrano, self-branding, 1–10 ratings, and ROI. He would have been baffled by the paradox of the love mall: if everyone is invited to shop for ready-made, off-the-shelf love, the opportunity gained in numbers may be lost in the brusque efficiency with which seekers treat prospective partners. "Isn't it strange," Evan later mused, "how we forget the biggest thing—kindness?"

There were other problems in Internet dating that Evan did not mention. Some daters lied about their age, drug habits, and marital status. In the absence of a watchful community, some felt free to brand themselves in deceptive ways. Some were rude, mean, or worse. One Internet dater I interviewed contracted a venereal disease from a man who lied about having it. This woman confided her revenge fantasy: "I wanted my brother to go over to that guy's house and spray-paint 'clap' on the front of his garage. I wanted people to know." Another woman had a similar revenge fantasy about a man who, she later discovered, was married. "When he told me not to call him at home because he was visiting his sister, I got suspicious. And he wouldn't give me his cell phone number. The clues added up. That was the one thing I specified in my post: no married men. I felt like calling his wife to warn her—but I didn't have her number."

And that was not the worst.[6] Marcel related a disturbing story he heard through a close friend. A woman, a divorcée with two children, met a man on Match.com and agreed to go to his apartment for a drink. He drugged her, raped her, and stole all her money. Stunned and drowsy, she managed to dress herself and begged for money to get a taxi home. The rapist threw her twenty dollars and she staggered out the door. Wanting to shield her children, she didn't prosecute the man. Nor did she report it to Match.com. As far as Marcel knew, that man was still on the dating Web site.[7]

A Booming Love Business

In one out of six new marriages, the couple met through an Internet dating site.[8] Of those I spoke to who were looking for love, all were intrigued by Internet dating but kept it as a backup in case friends' parties and office meet-ups—more "natural" ways of meeting—didn't work out. But within the Internet dating industry, Gian Gonzaga, senior director of research and development at eHarmony explained, such person-to-person meetings are called "off-line dates." Others in the industry call them "dating in the wild." Match.com is only one of many Internet sites, and estimates vary on how many people click in. A 2005 Pew Center survey of online dating found that 16 million people—"11 percent of all American Internet-using adults"—had visited an online dating Web site at some point. During the September to December period of the survey, 10 million single Internet users said they were currently searching for romantic partners, and over a third—3.7 million—were doing so through dating Web sites. A third of all Americans at that time said they knew of someone who'd visited a dating Web site. A quarter said they knew someone who had gone on a date with someone they met through such a site, and 15 percent—or 30 million people—said they knew someone who had been in a long-term relationship or married someone he or she had met online. Estimates of online daters vary wildly—from 20 million unique users now visiting online dating sites in the United States to 40 million—or about half of all single adults in the United States.[9]

A 2007 survey of a random sample of nearly one thousand Californians of every age tends to confirm the estimate of 20 million. I asked people to "Imagine that you're looking for a serious romantic partner, haven't been able to find one, and you had enough money to pay for what you needed. Where would you go for help first? Family and friends? Religious leaders? TV or radio figures? Free Internet dating service? A for-pay dating service that finds you a partner and leaves it at that? A for-pay dating service that finds you a partner and sets up a meeting with him or her? Or a for-pay service that finds you a partner and provides monthly checkups to keep the relationship in good order?" Extrapolating from the survey, of all Californians, more than two million of the state's twenty-eight million residents would opt for one of the for-pay services. Extrapolating to the United States, that would add up to some twenty-three million for-pay potential daters.[10]

The second largest online dating company, eHarmony, administers a 458-item questionnaire. It matches new members' answers with those of other paid clients, thereby preselecting a few theoretically suitable applicants. eHarmony's goal, according to its publicist, is to "capture the M market"—marriage market—by applying science to love. In 2011 the dating site claimed nearly one hundred thousand marriages a year.[11] Perhaps to improve its marriage numbers, eHarmony does not admit physically ill, thrice-married, or—until a 2009 policy change—gay clients. eHarmony also for a while offered a marital tune-up service to help its marriages last.

The company is searching for other ways to improve its numbers, too. Gian Gonzaga, the psychologist who directs eHarmony's research and development lab, told me in a telephone interview:

> We'd love to move into "sparking" or what I call interpersonal attraction. Evidence shows that people are attracted to those with different DNA-based immunity profiles. Those are probably communicated through smell at close contact and are related to sexual responsivity. But we'd need to collect cheek swabs and that would be hard to do.

eHarmony's technique for predicting long term compatibility involves proprietary information, which Gonzaga calls a "product." If the company ever happened to perfect a method to test for sparking, presumably that would become a product, too.

In a recent expression of the spirit of capitalism, eHarmony, Match.com, and other for-profit dating services now post competitive research bulletins on company blogs, each claiming to lead to more, happier, and longer-lasting marriages. At one point Match.com claimed that twice as many recently married U.S. couples met on its site than on its closest competitor's site. eHarmony countered that its clients enjoyed longer and happier marriages than those of all other companies.[12] The eHarmony survey used pie charts and graphs, rates of statistical significance, and a Couples Satisfaction Index (CSI), and claims to duplicate the sample size and selection criteria of a recent study by Match.com. It also boasts clients who suffer less "loss of spark"—a state they refer to as LOS.

eHarmony also claims that its clients are less likely to suffer LOS or divorce than do married couples who meet at bars and clubs, work or school—and even through family and friends.[13] Company-sponsored research on both sides is often based on Internet-recruited samples[14] and doesn't say whether the service attracts people who for well-documented reasons (such as higher education, higher income, and professional status) tend to stay together, regardless of how they met.

Behind the spirited contest between different company-funded researchers is, of course, the great profit to be made. In 2011 American fee-based dating sites grossed over a billion dollars.[15] In 2008, Match.com was grossing $365,500,000—a million dollars a day. That amounted to $83,000 in subscription revenue for every marriage it claimed. When the stock market dipped that year, traffic on Match.com rose. The more insecure jobs become, some speculate, the more people seek security elsewhere. (The sale of pets went up, too.) And now such Web sites are looking abroad. As Jeff Titterton, the president of PlanetOut—a for-profit Web site featuring personals for gay clients—observed, "The money is in the international markets. . . . The next big wave is to go overseas. Let's see what happens there."[16]

eHarmony's Gian Gonzaga spoke excitedly about the company's future:

> Our compatibility matching systems is a good product; we're already in fifteen countries, including Brazil, Japan, the UK, Australia, and Canada. And we have a partnership with eDarling which services Eastern and Western Europe. I'd love to set up labs in São Paulo and Tokyo.

The company is also expanding its business into other kinds of relationships—the selection of college roommates and company work teams, for example. And it is following married couples into later stages of life, such as parenthood.

Given the profits to be made, it comes as no surprise to see the current explosion of online dating sites: Kiss.com, craigslist, Yahoo! Personals, Chemistry.com, Matchmaker, LoveHappens, GreatExpectations, OKCupid, TheRightOne, PerfectMatch, and more. Sites devoted to matching daters by religion—including Catholic Mingle, AdventistSingles, LDS Mingle—are now commonplace. As are sites focused on particular ethnicity or race, such as AsianSinglesConnection, Filipina Heart, LatinSinglesConnection, JDate, or InterracialMatch. Others address elderly daters: Silver Singles, Prime Singles, and Senior Friendfinder. Still others specify levels of intelligence (GoodGenes), education (TheRightStuff), occupation (FarmsOnly, MilitaryCupid), sexual orientation (GayCupid, PinkCupid, Adam4Adam), or disabilities (DeafSingles Connection).

One company has carried paid dating services one step further—men pay outright for actual dates, the company getting a cut. In the first month after WhatsYourPrice.com went online March 29, 2011, it attracted 50,000 sign-ups and brokered over 5000 dates. As Singapore-born MIT grad, Brandon Wade, its founder, argues, "It's a matter of free market principles really."[17] After all, he points out, a man usually pays for dinner, drinks, maybe a show on a date in America. His middle-man cut only adds a bit more. As for first-date etiquette, he recommends that women accept no personal checks or cashier's checks, and that men pay the women half the price at the start of the date and half at the end. The Web site features images of women, often each body part separately, with captions reading "Wants $80" or "Wants $60." Through other dating sites, too—SeekingArrangement.com, which connects Sugar Daddies (rich old men) with Sugar Babies (pretty young women), and SeekingMillionaire.com, for example—Wade creates many stopping points along a continuum between conventional dating and the clear commercial encounter.

Terms of Engagement

If in the search for love some of us have left the village, people like Grace are developing the ability, it seems, to keep personal life feeling personal in strange new market times. Grace hired an expert to help her. She countered her anxiety about entering the "love mall" by insisting on making her own decisions at various key points—drafting her own self-description and scanning all responses to it. To some degree, Grace was doing as Evan directed, but she carefully reserved a space where she felt in charge: "I'll pay you to do this; I want to do *that* myself."

Grace was lucky to have encountered a coach who taught her both how to "shop" in the online dating mall and how to stop thinking in shopping terms. Evan helped her think of herself as a brand with a market rating but also intimated the need to go beyond a brand mentality in her personal dealings with people. He guided her around an obvious but hidden paradox: if we shop for love in too commercial a way, we may never find it.

And how had things worked out for the master of the modern mall, the thirty-five-year-old Evan himself? I imagined that, as a national expert in online dating, Evan would certainly find his true love online if he hadn't already. Maybe she would be a 9 or 10; he would get extraordinary ROI. And once he found her he might call on Sarah Pease of Brilliant Event Planning, "the go-to expert for designing your marriage proposal idea," to "coordinate every moment until she says yes." So I was surprised to hear Evan confess that, although he had been on two hundred online-initiated dates, he'd met his fiancée-to-be at a friend's party and proposed in the ordinary way. Maybe it wasn't J. Porter and Edith's front-porch courtship, but then again, it was closer to that than to the "love mall" that provided his living. As we spoke, his mother was en route from Florida with his grandmother's wedding ring. Bemused by the irony, Evan reflected:

> I was looking for a never-married, Jewish, Ivy League woman, a little younger than me. Brigitte is Catholic, divorced, older, and a community college graduate. I never would have dated her on Match.com. But I am *so* lucky to find a kind, considerate person who loves me for who I am. You can't put that kind of kindness in a profile. It takes time to reveal itself.

Soul mate and chemistry—these were the core ideals of the industry's love-seekers. Yet Evan did not believe these were something one could instantly find, much less buy. Perhaps it was the abundance of apparent choice that made the ideals seem tantalizingly within reach. Or maybe the intent focus on finding the "right mate" right away reflected an impoverishment in other relationships—with friends, family, coworkers, neighbors. Whatever the reason, Evan was convinced that the imperative to find your instant soul mate was actually preventing his clients from recognizing the soul in the potential mate. That was because they were told to train their attention on finding—not making—connection. They were preparing to become consumers, not creators, of love.

His own case to the contrary, Evan was sure that love coaching and Internet dating were the wave of the future, and Grace agreed. "My twelve-year-old daughter, Trudy, is on Facebook a quarter of an hour in the morning and two hours at night talking to her 'three hundred friends.' She has a whole different sense of what's public."

When I talked to Trudy by phone, she, too, said her three hundred Facebook "friends" were a big part of her life. Yet when I asked her whether someday she thought she would like to go online to find a mate and maybe hire a coach, too, she replied, "No, I'd like to meet him at a friend's party." But when I told my aunt Elizabeth that the people I was interviewing were seeking soul mates on Match.com, she tilted her head back and chuckled in disbelief. Then, to my surprise, she added, "If other ways of meeting someone don't work, maybe a person should try it."

Chapter 2

The Legend of the Lemon Tree

For a rough idea of a wedding in small-town New England at the dawn of the twentieth century, we might consider that of my grandparents J. Porter Russell and Edith Pratt on September 10, 1902. As the bride walked into the small wooden Universalist church in Turner, a few dozen proud relatives seated in narrow wooden pews turned their heads to the aisle to watch for her arrival. Or so Aunt Elizabeth was told. Women in upswept hair, broad feathered hats, long-sleeved puffy blouses, and below-ankle skirts; girls in ribboned braids and lace-trimmed floral dresses; men in high-collared shirts and vests fastened high on the chest: this was the wedding scene. Edith's father might have slipped an envelope of thanks into the minister's pocket before everyone headed back to the farm for cider (soft and hard), sandwiches, ice cream, and cake and an evening of dancing to the tune of hired fiddlers.

Even marriages of the rich and famous in turn-of-the-century America were, by modern standards, often simple affairs. Teddy Roosevelt's marriage to his first wife, Alice Hathaway Lee, in

1880, for instance, took place in a Boston church followed by a reception at the bride's home. His second marriage in 1886 to Edith Carow was a quiet event attended by a few close friends and family.

No longer. Take Laura Wilson, a tall, ebullient redhead with an earnest, cherubic face, who hurried breathless to the table at the noisy San Francisco restaurant where we'd agreed to meet and quickly seated herself, savory details of her event ready, it seemed, to be set free. At thirty-three, she was a successful specialist in what she called "message platform development and rebranding" (though she also confided a wish to work in the future with special-needs children in a nearby poor community). Her wedding—150 guests at a stately rented mansion—had taken place a year earlier and neither Laura, her husband, Trevor, nor Laura's mother had been its central planner. I was lunching with her, in part, because I was curious to know why, like so many young professionals, she and Trevor had decided to hire a wedding planner, in this case, Chloe DeCosta at Happiest Day. I also wanted to learn just what lay behind her giggling telephone account of the planner's purchase of five hundred lemons.

While love coaches like Evan Katz are still somewhat new to the American scene, wedding planners have over the last decades become heroic figures in popular romantic comedies, the human face behind a fussy status display. Today, according to David Wood, president of the Association of Bridal Consultants, about one out of every ten couples hires a wedding planner.[1] So, I wondered, how much could a person give over to experts and helpers and still feel like the author of such an event? At one extreme stood Laura's parents, who had married in a small town in Missouri a half century back and never heard of a wedding planner. "After the wedding, we had punch and homemade cake in the church basement," Laura's mother told me, "and spent a one-night honeymoon in an Indiana motel." At the other extreme were Laura and Trevor, who, living in Los Angeles and with demanding careers, had whittled down their participation to almost nothing. Just where, I wondered, had Trevor and Laura—and for that matter, Chloe—drawn the line?

When I asked Laura how she came to hire Chloe, she began by describing the couple's schedules:

> Trevor was getting up at 3:30 a.m. every morning, heading for the office (a law firm) by 5:00 a.m., and not getting home till around 7:00 p.m. I was working full time, too. We'd only left ourselves six months to plan the wedding. My mother lives in Missouri. My maid of honor works in New York. We were all scattered and low on time.

A divorced father of two, Trevor was twelve years Laura's senior. Within two weeks of meeting, the two were inseparable and, after a year, began talking of marriage, the best time to marry, and then, with little fanfare, of a wedding planner. Laura's mother was all for it, she remembers:

> I began looking for ideas in a Martha Stewart magazine. But we live so far away and my husband and I work full time. When Laura told me about a lady who plans weddings, I immediately said, "Why don't we do that? You hire her and Dad and I will pay for it. That will take the place of me being in Los Angeles to plan it with you."

So Laura and Trevor became clients of the $161-billion-a-year wedding-planning industry. Although neither Laura nor her parents talked about how much the wedding had cost, if it was average for American weddings in 2010—planner or no—the price would have been somewhere around $28,000.[2] "I'm going to spend the rest of my life with this man," Laura said, "so I wanted the wedding to be lovely. If you're going to splurge, do it on your wedding." At the same time, she added, "I didn't want it to be ridiculously over the top."

It sounded as if Laura knew what she was up against. Journalist Rebecca Mead, author of *One Perfect Day: The Selling of the American Wedding*, visited the Great Bridal Expotrade convention in 2008 and discovered stands peddling laser hair removal and teeth whitening (presumably services to be administered before the wedding) as well as wings for pet dogs trained to trot ceremonially down the aisle. One could also purchase "heirloom ornaments"—such as a pewter disk with the image of a blossom on it for the flower girl to keep and pass on. And for Americans who opted to elope, there was an "elopement package," including a ride in a hot-air balloon that lifts off from the parking lot of a wine vineyard in Sonoma, California.

Compared to my grandparents' day, the typical bride and groom today are older, richer, and more likely to juggle two careers. They also spend more. But the fantasy of a big wedding has also caught on among the less well off. Poor unmarried couples who are already raising children together, report sociologists Kathryn Edin and Maria Kefalas in their book, *Promises I Can Keep*, often dream of a grand wedding "some day"—after their partner is released from prison, gets off drugs, or gets a job.[3] Poverty doesn't suppress the dream but rather delays it—sometimes indefinitely. Ironically, the power of the big wedding fantasy, together with the high cost of realizing it, may be one—although not the only—reason why a declining proportion of couples actually marry these days. In 1900, perhaps 4 or 5 percent of births were to unmarried mothers in America—today nearly 40 percent are.[4]

For their own special day, Laura and Trevor had a vast range of wedding services to choose from, suggested by such names as Integral Interfaith Weddings, Twice Is Nice, and Encore Bridal Creations (which catered to second, third, and fourth marriages). They could also opt to wed in an exotic destination—by a secluded lake on a mountaintop in the Sierras, on a stately ship off the Florida Keys, or on a white sand beach in Baja, California. There were equally varied options for the less affluent; Graceland's Chapel in Tennessee offered an Elvis Presley impersonator who would lip-synch an Elvis song before giving away the bride; at Walt Disney World's Wedding Pavilion in Florida, a couple could rent a Cinderella Coach for a post-ceremony dream ride through the Magic Kingdom. And for the thrifty, an open-air chapel with seating was available for twelve dollars an hour outside Austin, Texas.

Laura and Trevor decided against a "destination" wedding and picked Chloe DeCosta to help them plan something closer to home. When Laura told friends, they were unfazed. "If it's a big wedding and you don't have time," one friend said, "hire a planner." A love coach in 2009—that might still raise a few eyebrows. But a wedding planner? Well, sure.

Happiest Day

Chloe DeCosta was in her office in downtown Los Angeles explaining how she determined which tasks were "too personal" for her to take over, when the phone rang. A warm, spirited Italian American with curly black hair, swinging loop earrings, and a wide smile, she picked up the phone in the middle of the second ring and answered:

> Happiest Day. May I help you? . . . Oh! I knew it would be! I *said* it would be! . . . And her name is? Oh . . . and what's her middle name? Oh . . . seven pounds, seven ounces? What a big girl. It was today? . . . How's the mommy? I'm so thrilled for her. . . . Oh I'm sure it is *fine* you told me. . . . I'll act surprised when they tell me. . . . Bye-bye.

Turning back to me, she explained: "One of my brides just had a baby. Her assistant just called but wasn't supposed to tell me. I'm supposed to hear the news from the family. I have three pregnant brides right now. Wedding planning is very personal, at least how I do it."

On the large oak desk between us lay half a dozen thick, leather-bound albums of wedding photos; a cat calendar sat beside a large philodendron—a gift from a mentor in wedding planning. The office walls were hung with large, color photos—of a couple holding hands on a mountaintop at sunset; of a petite, daisy-crowned bride embracing her enormous groom in an English garden; of two tall, joyous lesbians holding up a startled baby in a white blanket, at what might have been a christening. In one photo, a beaming Chloe, playfully waving to the camera, stood wedged between a side-glancing bride and her bespectacled groom.

Laura and Trevor had chosen Chloe, but to do what? Just as Grace Weaver had left some tasks of finding a soul mate to her love coach (devising a brand) while hanging on to others (scanning e-mail messages for nice-sounding men), so it was for Laura and Trevor in planning their wedding. "Some things I just wanted to check off my list," Laura explained, "I didn't care who did them." Chloe boiled down the choices.

Music: Do you like salsa or 1950s rock and roll?

Salsa.

Done.

Flowers: Do you prefer cheery spring, say, red tulips or formal occasion, like white roses?

Tulips.

Done.

But when it came to choosing a wedding dress, Laura felt differently. "For that, I wanted time with my mother and best friend, who came all the way from New York."

Laura's mother and best friend couldn't help with the whole wedding, but they could go with her to the bridal shop, the mother sitting on the dressing-room chair, checking sizes, pulling gowns off hangers appraisingly, her friend zipping Laura into one majestic white gown after another. They asked her to stand, to walk, to turn, to stand again. Much of wedding planning consisted of practical details she could easily hand off to Chloe. Here, chosen from among them, was an act so much more personal, Laura had to reserve it for her mother and best friend.

But some couples outsource even very personal acts. As Chloe reflected:

> If they're too busy, some grooms pay me an extra fee to be their fiancée's temporary best friend. So I go around with the bride, shopping for clothes, flowers, music, caterer, cake-maker. I've had grooms say to me, "I want you to go to every single store with my fiancée and really keep her company." Either the groom doesn't have time to go with her or he's traveling. So he hires me, that way his fiancée doesn't feel like she's doing all this alone. A lot of times I suddenly jump from being this nice person they've talked to on the phone to a trusted confidante privy to *very* intimate details.

I asked Chloe, "Do you ever feel that you're really playing a family role?" She seemed startled by my naïveté:

> *God* yes! I mean, always. I handle twelve to eighteen weddings a year, and I keep up with my couples long after they marry. I know their tastes. I know what gets on their nerves, what relaxes them. I become their grand confessor, their paid best friend. To some clients, I'm a younger version of the mother they wished they'd had.

"Were you that for Laura and Trevor?" I asked. Chloe paused and then responded, "No, more like a knowledgeable friend." Then she explained just how she went about her job.[5]

> When I met Laura and Trevor at their apartment, I noticed how they dressed, the photos on the mantel, the furnishings. As I showed them my wedding portfolio, I watched their reactions to different scenarios—formal church, lavish hotel, English garden. Bit by bit, I get a picture. Then I identify how *involved* they want to be.

How involved, I wondered, did Chloe herself want to be?

> Well, first of all, *I* like to be very involved. My favorite clients are the blank slates who don't know what to ask because they don't know what there is to want and are so overwhelmed they're ready to scream *ARGGG!* Then I can help. Do they want ritual without the church? We'll do an art gallery with a woman minister and self-written vows. Do they want nature and simplicity in the city? We'll do the botanical garden with flute players and a daisy ring in the bride's hair.

Some of Chloe's clients' slates were blank indeed:

> I had a couple in their midthirties who had lived together for three years before one of them said, "Let's marry." But both were too busy to plan a wedding. So the woman called me and commented, "At least now I know we're going to get married, because we hired you."

Laura and Trevor knew they wanted the ring, the marriage, the honeymoon. The works. Laura had also visualized a great many possible kinds of weddings down to the smallest detail. But the last thing Trevor wanted was to get deeply involved in planning the wedding. In a calm, methodical tone, he told me: "We realized that Laura could do eighty percent of the planning, but that left us twenty percent short." In this elusive formulation, I realized Trevor assigned himself no percentage at all.

Grooms on second marriages were typically more cautious and guarded, Chloe observed, than their younger, starry-eyed, first-time brides. But to Chloe, it seemed as if Trevor was outsourcing even *caring* about the plans for the wedding. He didn't participate in any of the small personal moments within the process—a troubling way, she felt, to start off a life together. When Trevor sat through a meeting in Chloe's office, quietly slumped in his chair, Chloe remembers saying to Laura teasingly: "Look at him—he's trying to short-circuit this grand day of yours." Trevor gave her a smirk. She countered with a playful poke, "I'm not talking to you; I'm talking to her." Then Chloe reflected, "I work with the smirk."

Working with the smirk—figuring out how to coax the groom to get more involved—turned out to be a surprisingly important part of the job for Chloe and other planners I talked to. Amelia Montgomery, a veteran New York–based African American wedding planner, recalled a groom who swore he wouldn't marry his prospective bride if she "made a big fuss" by hiring Amelia. At one point, Amelia even met with the bride's priest, who was going to marry them at his church. She remembers praying with him, alone on their knees, to help the future husband get over "groom's jitters."

Couples sometimes looked to Chloe to help them decide how serious their ceremony should be. Would it be all right to verge on a whoop-it-up New Year's Eve party? Or did it need to feel like a solemn church service? In such a role—part-operative, part-therapist, part-minister, part-grandma—she essentially helped settle questions that might never have arisen in the days of the village with its implicit, shared standards. Couples looked to her for the common knowledge they didn't feel they possessed or for some assurance that yes, they were doing it right. They had outsourced confidence in their own judgment.

> I had one couple who asked me if I thought it would be funny if they exchanged gum ball rings. Would guests be offended? I told them, "Hey, this is *your* wedding." Actually, I think they were afraid. Both sets of parents had divorced and they didn't want that to happen to them. So they wanted to keep it light, as a fallback. If the marriage failed, they could tell themselves, "Ha ha, we never meant it anyway." They wanted to keep it serious *privately*. In the end they decided against the gum ball rings.

On another occasion, she remembered:

> I had a groom whose last name was Cohen. The groom thought it would be hysterical to put a big *C* like a corporate brand over the fireplace. For the groom, this was a little inside joke he wanted my okay on. The guests would think, "Oh, Stewart chose this room because it had a *C* over the fireplace," without realizing *we* put it there. I said, "Sure, why not?" I was telling him, "It's a serious day. You're spending serious money. But it's fine to be playful."

But sometimes Chloe felt called to intervene more actively to persuade a bride to give up the idea of a venue or a dress that she thought she wanted, and accept what it was she "really" wanted:

> I had a young black doctor from a quite well-off Chicago family, and she was marrying another doctor. She told me, "I think I want a downtown loftlike venue over the water." I listened to her for half an hour and knew there was no way she would be happy with a loft. I showed her a loft here, a loft there. Then I took her to a fancy old hotel and she lit right up. She needed to be a princess.
>
> It was the same with her dress. At one bridal shop she had tried on a lot of knee-length cocktail-type dresses. It was getting late and the clerk was dying to go home. I told her, "I'm sorry; we can't go until my client tries on *that* dress." It was full, floor-length, princess waist. Then I told the bride, "We can't leave until you try on that dress because that's *your* dress." She tried it on. We all sat there openmouthed. Her mother burst into tears That's how we knew it was her dress.

The Promise of Legends

Chloe, who had long lived with a man without marrying him, said, "A lot of my brides and grooms grew up in shaky families. It really matters to them that this event be just right. My job is to intuit what to them will feel just right."

The high divorce rate in America—which surely saps the confidence of many young couples and may increase the urge to rely on professionals—can complicate a wedding planner's job. As one New York–based planner observed, "The WASPy Park Avenue people divorce so many times you can't keep track of who's in court with whom. And you don't want to put the father's new twenty-two-year-old wife at the table anywhere near his fifty-four-year-old ex-wife or she'll throw her crème brûlée at him." The divorced parents of one bride, Chloe recalled, were so bitter that "they hadn't spoken in eighteen years. The mother of the bride wouldn't stand anywhere near the father in the receiving line."

At the same time, that high divorce rate has paradoxically elevated the importance of the wedding ceremony itself. In a sense, the wedding has become a symbolic stand-in for what marriage was once believed to be. There, at the ceremony, one can imagine lasting happiness. One is surrounded by joyous well-wishers at an event that affirms a reassuring permanence that marriage in America can no longer promise. A certain market logic may underlie this displacement: "If we put this much money down," a couple may believe, "we've invested in something solid; we're going to last." ("In the men's bathroom," Chloe commented wryly, "there's always some guy who says, 'they're sure spending a lot of dough on this wedding; I hope they last long enough to pay it off.' ")

Laura and Trevor's wedding took place on the grounds of a majestic old mansion, bedecked with festive spring flowers. After the ceremony, a five-piece band struck up salsa music. A professional photographer roamed the clusters of guests, women in flowing pastels, men in summer suits, everyone lifting glasses in champagne toasts and exchanging celebratory hugs. Waiters scurried in and out of an enormous tent set up on the lawn with trays of food and champagne.

For this happiest of days, Chloe had developed a unique theme that she intended to represent the couple's love. "I always try to find a theme. I ask a couple to think about how they fell in love. They give me a casual story and I give it back as a theme." Laura's casual story, as she told me over lunch, was this:

> On a walk one evening after dinner, Trevor and I passed a small lemon tree loaded with lemons. I remarked, "I'd really feel like a Californian if I had a lemon tree." On Valentine's Day months later, I got a dozen yellow long-stemmed roses placed around a small lemon tree.

Picking up on this passing tale, Chloe later explained "I worked with lemons. I said to Laura, 'How about we make your story into the legend of the lemon tree?' She said, 'Great.'" So after the ceremony, guests filed past vases of yellow flowers into the wedding tent, where they discovered dozens of white-clothed tables, each with a glass centerpiece filled with wheels of sliced lemons. On a large gold-framed card to the left of each setting was an image of lemons, and printed in elongated Franklin Gothic font inside the card a story—proposed by Chloe, drafted by Laura, approved by Trevor, and edited by Chloe—called "Legend of the Lemon Tree."

> One Valentine's Day, a treat unlike any other appeared at Laura's door. Much to her surprise, she found yellow roses and fresh lemons surrounding a tiny lemon tree. She then remembered a long romantic walk during which she made a passing comment that California would really feel like home if she ever owned a lemon tree. Little did she know, Trevor had worked for days to find the miniature tree and drove many miles to collect the only one he could find. Touched by Trevor's creativity, throughtfulness, and perseverance, Laura has nurtured the tree and protected it. . . . The hearty tree will now soak up sunshine, bear fruit, and greet guests on the front porch of their new home.
>
> —Laura and Trevor

Legends—Pocahontas, Daniel Boone, King Arthur's court—grow slowly over centuries. They bind the generations who pass them down. They span cultures. But they are seldom self-consciously created. The legend of the lemon tree was meant to bind Laura and Trevor to each other, though it was linked to neither nation nor era. It was private, professionally organized, and, in a sense, purchased. But it warmed everyone's heart. In a country with the world's highest divorce rate, with Trevor's two small daughters from a previous marriage in their flower-girl dresses, the legend conveyed the idea of everlasting devotion.[6]

Long after the wedding, Laura was left with the practical chore of maintaining the "legend." As she playfully lamented:

> I had to keep up the lemon tree because now it was a legend. Well, first the aphids ate at it. So I got a spray. Then the deer chewed nearly all the leaves off, so I got a wire fence. Trevor and I are doing great, but, man, that lemon tree has had a tough time.

De-Personal, Re-Personal and Just Plain Personal

Composing the legend, buying the dress, tasting the cake: Laura, Trevor, and Chloe casually deliberated over how emotionally attached each of them should be to any given act. Laura and Trevor both hired Chloe, and they jointly paid her fee. But Laura actively entered into the experience of preparing to marry; with Chloe, she coauthored many parts of it. Trevor leaned back, focusing on the result, the final state of marriage itself.

Though both Chloe DeCosta and Evan Katz offered a professional service, they had opposite formulas for success. Evan trained his client to "put in the hours," brand herself, maximize her ROI, and mind the bottom line. He taught Grace to depersonalize, to think of herself as a shopper, and—as a "6"—a person shopped for. In contrast, Chloe helped Laura and Trevor feel unique, incomparable, anything but a number. Through outsourcing, they repersonalized their lives. Through packaging their lemon tree—a plant rooted in their earth, needing care, bearing fruit—the two (or three) were able to create a deeply personal moment.

Laura and Trevor's wedding was, we could say, an expression of their membership in the upper middle class. It is the essence of that class, as Thorstein Veblen speculated, to feel themselves to be, and display to others that they are, detached from necessary labor such as hoeing corn, cleaning house, hammering nails—jobs such as the young Edith Pratt did on the family farm in Maine.[7] But Laura and Trevor were outsourcing another kind of necessary labor—emotional labor. As their experience shows, a couple could significantly reduce what they had to care about and still feel the wedding was "theirs."

By hiring Chloe, Laura was saying, in effect, "To be emotionally involved in this event, I need to do this act (select a wedding dress, compose a vow), but I don't need to do that act (taste the cake, meet the photographer), and wouldn't think of doing other acts (sew the dress, bake the cake). I am emotionally attached to this act, but detached from that one." Or, "I'm emotionally attached to the person who performs this important act for me, or I'm not." As for Chloe, she took on the unstated job of getting Trevor more involved, so as to make the wedding more properly belong to the couple. So part of the hired specialist's job was to take over an emotional attachment to an act—to become anxious if the gold-framed lemon tree cards were not to the left of each dinner plate, to feel relief noting that they were. And part of her job was to give that emotional attachment back, so that Laura and Trevor could feel as involved *as if* they had set the cards there themselves.

It is not just that America has moved from a world of villagers to one of outsourcers. Along the way, we've also created a market in emotional states. Ironically, one of the feelings the market can sell us is the feeling of being authentically out of the market. Brought to us by the market, the legend of the lemon tree was meant to symbolize a place apart from that market—a place so intimate that only two people could call it their own. Paradoxically, it was Chloe with her professional eye who ferreted out the lemon tree tale and lifted it into a "timeless"—and intimate—symbol of love everlasting.[8]

Chapter 3

For as Long as You Both Shall Live

Couples therapy as we know it today has taken a new turn. The advice books of my grandparents' time posed solutions to marital problems as matters of wifely duty and personal character—patience, diligence, and thrift, for example. Absent from such books was the language of psychoanalysis, with its focus on childhood trauma, unconscious mechanisms of defense, and the family as a repressive system. Absent, too, was the scientific approach shown through proprietary love-predicting equations and algorithms developed by Match.com's statisticians or trouble-predicting records of marital exchange observed through a one-way mirror and mapped onto oscillating rates of heartbeats, sweating, and white blood cell counts in John Gottman's "love lab."[1]

By the 1920s, psychoanalysis was a growing fashion and social workers, physicians, and psychologists were promoting abbreviated and less costly versions of it. By the early 1930s, courses in marriage counseling and family relations were appearing in church outreach programs.[2] The American Association for Marriage and Family Therapy certified its first therapist in 1942—that number has now expanded to fifty thousand.[3] In 1980, an estimated 1.2 million couples were going to marriage counselors and 4.6 million were in individual therapy. Fifteen years later, four out of ten married couples received some type of formal counseling.[4]

Along with the psychotherapist came the new idea that it's fine, indeed advisable, to get help when one needs it, however often that might be. Rachael Stein embodied the dramatic shift in approach from one generation to the next. A recently widowed Los Angeles–based art professor, she was more than willing to turn to a professional for help when she needed it, something her mother would not have dreamed of doing:

> My mother was born into a tight-knit Jewish community in Lodz, Poland, and when she and my father immigrated to New York, she brought her old-world ways with her. She would never have gone to a therapist; for strangers to know your problems with your husband would bring a *shande* (shame) and lower your *yiches* (status). It would make you "a poor dear."

As Rachael remembered: "My mother and my older sister, Leah, had an old-world deal. My mother took in Leah and her husband and twin boys when Leah's husband was studying for his CPA. And when my mother's turn came, she expected to be cared for the same way." But Rachael, the younger daughter by twelve years, was a product of the New World. And her "deal" was with the market:

> When I married and decided to move to Los Angeles, my mother fell to the floor, howled at the thought that I was moving away and might not depend on her, or she on me. She'd have to depend on a stranger. But I'm all for hiring strangers. I've hired service providers all my adult life—including a fantastic therapist who became the bookends of my marriage.

"Bookends" to a Thirty-Two-Year Marriage

Fresh from her yoga class, Rachael walked down the steps of her stucco bungalow, which was surrounded by a blooming pink and yellow cactus garden. She shook my hand in a warm, direct manner and conducted me into her home. We sat down in her living room and I asked Rachael what had brought her and her husband, Roger, into couples therapy. Therapy itself was not new to her, she explained. She'd seen a psychoanalyst "for a hundred years" before she'd moved to Los Angeles. So going with Roger was a natural next step.

Their relationship had been fraught from the start:

> Roger and I had been friends for three years and office mates for two and each of us was married. I'd been separated from my husband and was seeing another man and Roger was in an unhappy twenty-year marriage to a severe alcoholic. One weekend we both attended a beachside company retreat where we danced together. Later we went for a moonlit walk and kissed. We said, "No, this can't be," but after just a few days we had fallen madly in love.

Not long after that, Rachael left her boyfriend and Roger left his wife and moved into Rachael's house. The couple now lived together with Rachael's two daughters, Abby (eight) and Becky (ten), and Roger's troubled thirteen-year-old son, Jeremy, as well as a dog and a cat. Rachael described a tense ménage:

> The girls shared one room, Jeremy had his, and we had ours. Then the girls began to quarrel terribly over who Jeremy liked best. So we gave our bedroom to Abby, and we slept in the living room, which meant we had no privacy. We didn't agree on how to raise the kids. We didn't agree on what to eat. We approached life so differently. If you asked Roger how he felt

about anything, he'd say "I have to think about that." If you asked me what I thought, I'd tell you straight out.

In addition to the challenges of a blended family, Rachael and Roger had to contend with their very different backgrounds. As Rachael recounted:

> Roger came from a gentle, learned WASP family from Tennessee who played music, sang, and read. They were poor but cultured, calm, and never shouted. He had a crazy sister but they always said in their soft way, "Oh, that's just Millie." I came from an immigrant family in the Bronx, very passionate, loud, and easily alarmed. We were constantly interrupting each other.
>
> My father was a hatmaker back in Lodz. They lived on the edge of starvation—potatoes one meal, potato skins the next, potato gruel the one after that. My parents loved America, but even here, we were never sure we were safe from harm.

In some ways these differences were a good thing: Rachael credited Roger with introducing her to nature—to Joshua Tree National Park, to Yosemite, to Mount Hood. But time and again, their temperaments clashed.

> We'd get halfway to the campsite and I'd ask Roger: "D'you know where we are?" And he'd say, "Not really, but we're on the right trail." And I'd say, "You don't *know* where we are?" He'd say, "Don't worry." I'd say, "What do you mean, don't worry?" I was always afraid of getting lost. I needed to feel the trip was all figured out. He never worried. He never felt in danger. He was sure of his place. I wasn't.

Deeply in love but unable to agree on what to have for dinner, how to handle the kids or plan a wilderness hike, Rachael and Roger "got into a lot of trouble," Rachael said, adding, "the marriage would not have lasted without Sophie. And I have to confess, it was always Roger who thought to call Sophie.' As Rachael described:

> Roger would feel I wasn't listening to him. He'd raise his voice and I couldn't stand that. So I'd say: "That's *it*! We've given it a royal try. I'm out of here."
>
> Roger would say, "Let's call Sophie."
>
> I'd say, "It's too late."
>
> He'd say, "I'm dialing Sophie."
>
> I'd say, "Forget it."
>
> He'd say, "She's on the line. We're making an appointment."
>
> I'd say, "No way."
>
> Roger would hand me the phone. "Sophie wants to speak to you."
>
> I'd take the phone and Sophie would say, "Rachael, Roger, and I have made an appointment for tomorrow at eight a.m."
>
> I'd say, "I have a class at nine thirty and need to prepare."
>
> Sophie would say, "Okay, come at seven."

At each visit to Sophie's office, Rachael and Roger sat in the same spots on the sofa, as Sophie described a series of practical techniques to help them speak and listen to each other. During periods of crisis they met Sophie twice a week and, at other times, once a month. When they felt they were communicating better, they said good-bye to Sophie, who always assured them, "I'm here if you need me."

When Rachael and Roger finally decided to marry, they invited Sophie and her husband, who, Rachel recounted delightedly, "danced at our wedding!"

The marriage careened between long stretches of "intense shared joy" and periods of crash and burn. Whenever they got stuck, Roger would call Sophie. Rachael would object. Both would take their places on her office couch for a booster on careful listening. This oddly stable arrangement continued for thirty-two years.

Then one terrible day, Roger was diagnosed with bone cancer. Their community of colleagues and friends came forward in the spirit of "just do." Rachael's daughter Becky set up a Web site, and friends signed up for various tasks. Jill brought weekly casseroles. Alice brought soups. Bill drove Roger to therapy appointments. George gave Roger weekly baths. But Roger's condition grew steadily worse.

For the three years that Roger battled his disease, he and Rachael paid weekly visits to Sophie's office. At first, he would walk in briskly; later he came in hobbling and finally leaning on a cane. As Rachael remembered:

> Roger asked the doctor how much time he would have if he stopped his medication. "Weeks," the doctor said. Roger thanked him and told me, "I want to call hospice."

Roger's decision to stop treatment prompted their last marital crisis. Weeping, Rachael recalled:

> I told Roger, "*Please* don't give up. We'll figure this out. If you have to be in a wheelchair, that's fine. Just please stay." He told me, "I've stayed this long only to be with you. I can't do this anymore. This isn't me. Let me go." But I couldn't. To *me*, weak and thin as he was, it was still him. And I couldn't let him go. So we called Sophie. He was so weak, he couldn't walk to her office. So Sophie came to our house and sat where you're sitting.

Then, as she had for three decades, Sophie helped Rachael listen. From her chair in their living room, she turned to Roger and said, "Please tell us what you want." Roger answered, "To die with dignity in the company of my family." This statement—the imminence of his death and his acceptance of it—broke Rachael's heart. She fell to her knees, took his hands, and implored him, "Roger, please don't leave. Please hang on." But Sophie told Rachael calmly, "Rachael, it's time to listen. Roger is telling you what he wants. It's not what you or I might want. It's what he wants. And he wants your help. You have helped him live a good life. Now he wants you to help him die a good death." To encourage her to accept this role, Sophie rose and repositioned Rachael's chair so that it was no longer across from Roger's but next to it. "That's where Roger wants you, by his side," Sophie said. And sitting by his side, Rachael told me, her face streaked with tears, "I could finally let him go."

One afternoon two weeks after Roger had called hospice, a week after he had stopped eating, as he was lying on his bed in the living room of his home, his wish was granted. His son, who had cared for him through the night, was asleep in the next room. According to Rachael, "Sophie must have known it was Roger's time to die because at a certain moment, like an angel, she quietly glided into the room. According to Sophie, it was time for one of their regularly scheduled home appointments, which Roger and Rachael had, in their crisis, forgotten, and so she knocked and came in. Both stood by Roger's side as he died. Minutes later Sophie left. Rachael called Roger's son to his father's side and phoned her daughters to come home.

Rachael had left the Old World—where family and friends met emotional needs—for the New World, where trained experts were paid to help in times of need. But though marriage-long therapy was a decidedly novel idea, there was something strangely traditional about Sophie's presence in Rachael's and Roger's lives. She had helped them get married, stay married, and end their marriage in peace. Although the relationship was one of professional to client, Sophie had brought with her the wisdom, patience, and authority of a village elder, and perhaps even of an ideal mother.

The End of the Therapeutic House Call

Most couples who make it into a therapist's office do not keep returning for thirty-two years, of course. On the other hand, the practice of consulting a therapist has become fairly routine. As one social worker remarked: "Today, going to a therapist is almost like going to the dentist." Indeed, a couple can get therapy before they marry, while they're married, and after they've broken up.[5] In their brochures, some practitioners compare going to the therapist to other things any sensible person does. One likened premarital therapy to "an inoculation" against divorce. Another called it the "training wheels" of marriage. Still others compared it to training for a career, launching a business, building a house, preparing to pass the graduate record exam, or even Driver's Ed. "The DMV has made sure to educate the American driver to prevent fatal car collisions . . . but how come getting married requires so little attention?"[6] Without therapy, one ad cautioned, a couple is just "winging it."[7]

With a staggering array of choices just two clicks away, modern couples never need to just wing it. Googling NetworkTherapy.com, a couple can go to "Find a Therapist" and under "session format" choose "Marriage." They can decide among such treatment approaches as Jungian, Gestalt, Behavioral, Christian, Existential/Humanist, Light Therapy, or Critical Incident Stress Debriefing. They can further refine their choices with such "practical specialties" as infidelity, life transition, self-esteem, and so on—as well as "demographic expertise"—Latino American, Middle Eastern, Pacific Islander, Military/Veterans. I talked with one Los Angeles–based therapist, currently establishing a national chain of therapy centers, who helps couples limit their use of technology (cell phone, Internet, TV) to increase quality time at home. Added to this variety is a wondrous array of mom-and-pop new age therapies—such as Julia's New Start Therapy, Sandra's Active Transformational Hypnotherapy, or Rachael's Bless Counseling.

Therapies of the twenty-first century might be based on psychoanalytic theory but they also look to empirical science—or "marital facts" as the psychologist John Gottman calls the information he derives from his "love lab." In the lab, scientists peer through a one-way window to study couples as they interact in a living room–like setting. Taking a leaf from Gottman's lab, the for-profit dating service eHarmony has developed its own laboratory in Santa Monica, California.[8] Their observation room is equipped with semihidden cameras that are trained on couples who are given various tasks such as "teasing each other." Observers rank the couples on the degree to which the teasing is bullying, critical, or good-natured.[9] And then, based on these sample interactions, advise them on whether or not to seek counseling—a decision many couples now look to the expert to make.

In 2006, eHarmony developed eHarmony Marriage, a "wellness program" to help its married couples stay married. Neil Clark Warren, the founder of eHarmony and a Christian-focused marriage counselor, called the program a "computer-mediated skills-based approach to therapy." As Warren wrote on the eHarmony Web site, "even the best marriages can benefit from a tune-up." The program, which lasted six to eight weeks and cost $150, began with a forty-minute online questionnaire, to be filled out by each partner separately. Topics included spirituality, family relations, trust, housework, and finances. The two sets of answers generated what Les Parrott, a psychology professor and one of the designers of the program, described as a report on the couples' "strengths and weaknesses." Based on that report, Parrott said, "the computer produces a marriage action plan that includes interactive video, exercises, articles, and resources."

But human beings were strangely absent. Responses generated a computer report. The report produced an action plan. And in the end, couples found themselves home alone. Perhaps for this reason the eHarmony program closed in 2009.

As Gian Gonzaga explained:

> The wellness programs didn't make money. There is room for products that help relationships stay well. But in a computer-mediated environment, you have to take care how you apply them. Interventions should be lighter, shorter, easier, not work—especially not for the men.

So wellness-seekers were redirected to eHarmony Advice—an e-bulletin board where one posts opinions, reads others' posts, and joins, the eHarmony ad claims, a "community that you can turn to 24 hours a day 7 days a week."

Finding other therapy programs online can be equally impersonal. One therapist, self-described Twenty-Five-Year Marriage Saving Expert Dr. Lee H. Baucom, asks potential clients to click through a series of harrowing options:

A. If he/she is threatening to leave you, click here.
B. If he/she has already left you, click here.
C. If you're thinking about leaving him/her, click here.

The choices continue through various scenarios—do you suspect that your partner has cheated on you? Have you yourself had an affair? Are you fed up with bickering?—and ends with a Free Instant Online Assessment.

Unwelcoming as it may be, couples therapy is increasingly delivered online. There are now nearly 750,000 sites for "online marriage counseling and over 100,000 for online relationship counseling." (eTherapistsOnline.com, a Web site with links to various therapists, offers the curious category "therapeutic therapy.") Based in Atlantic Highlands, New Jersey, DeeAnna Merz Nagel offers both "In Office and Online counseling"—the latter by e-mail, Skype, chat, and instant messaging. When she counsels couples by e-mail, partners take turns e-mailing her. She also offers therapy through client-improvised avatars, imaginary selves in the form of figures that appear on the Web site Second Life. She trains, consults with, and for a fee of $200 for the first year ($100 thereafter) "verifies"—that is, vouches for—other online therapists called "distance credentialed" counselors. Her own site features the friendly image of a porcelain coffee cup with a sugar bowl, and another of a welcoming couch and a box of Kleenex.[10] Dr. Nagel also offers therapy on Internet addiction—by e-mail.

How useful is such therapy? Even with the rise of many new forms of intervention, the American divorce rate remains the highest in the world. Indeed, through the 1970s, marriage therapy and divorce rose together. Divorce peaked in the 1980s, declining slightly since, to rest at nearly 50 percent. Harvard historian Jill Lepore has asked whether today's couples aren't an "endlessly exploitable clientele," trained by self-interested professionals to aspire to an ever-escalating standard of marital bliss. Perhaps, she suggests, therapists ignore the ordinary joys because there is no money to be made from the "unglamorous and blessed ordinariness of buttering the toast every morning for someone you're terribly fond of."[11]

The high bar set for marital happiness has resulted, perhaps, in more Americans waiting to marry or not marrying at all. Households headed by married couples sank from 78 percent in 1950 to 48 percent today. As one forty-something woman quipped, "I'm staying single to save myself the trouble of divorce," and, she might have added, the trouble of paying a couples therapist.

But if more Americans are deciding not to marry, they still experience the needs a spouse was once supposed to fill. One man resolved this dilemma by posting an ad on the Internet that read:

> (p/t) Beautiful, smart, hostess, good masseuse—$400/week.
>
> Hi there.
> This is a strange job opening, and I feel silly posting it, but this is San Francisco, and I do have the need! This will be a very confidential search process.
>
> I'm a mild-mannered millionaire businessman, intelligent, traveled, but shy, who is new to the area, and extremely inundated with invitations to parties, gatherings, and social events. I'm looking to find a "personal assistant," of sorts. The job description would include, but not be limited to:

> 1. Being hostess to parties at my home ($40/hour)
> 2. Providing me with a soothing and sensual massage ($140/hour)
> 3. Coming to certain social events with me ($40/hour)
> 4. Traveling with me ($300 per day + all travel expenses)
> 5. Managing some of my home affairs (utilities, bill-paying, etc., $30/hour)
>
> You must be between 22 and 32, in-shape, good-looking, articulate, sensual, attentive, bright, and able to keep confidences. I don't expect more than 3 to 4 events a month, and up to 10 hours a week on massage, chores, and other miscellaneous items, at the most. You must be unmarried, un-attached, or have a very understanding partner!
>
> I'm a bright, intelligent, 30-year-old man, and I'm happy to discuss the reasons for my placing this ad with you on response of your e-mail application. If you can, please include a picture of yourself, or a description of your likes, interests, and your ability to do the job.
>
> NO professional escorts please! NO Sex involved!
> Thank You.
> You can e-mail me at . . .

The man did not want to hire different service providers for each need but rather plucked services out of the *idea* of marriage and wrapped them into one tempting job offer.[12] Here on the far frontier of the New World, he chose to avoid marriage and working on marriage and went right to the shelf instead.

I have no idea who posted this ad, or whether the man found his nonwife. I shared the ad with my students in the sociology of the family class I was teaching. Some were shocked and some were not. "I haven't seen this ad before, but it's one jump beyond what I have seen," one student remarked, adding, "it seems like the man wants a wife without having to be a husband." Some speculated that the man was afraid of marriage, others that he was a control freak. Some imagined him as disabled, others as a predator. One female student confessed, to a wave of nervous laughter, "The salary looked good."

Meanwhile, in my own life, I was coping with my aunt Elizabeth, a woman who had had no therapy of any kind, dismissed it as stuff and nonsense, and would doubtless have benefited from it. But now she was languishing in the convalescent home and hated it there. With the physical therapist's kindly encouragement, she could slowly step forward, with her walker, first one foot, then the other. But the better she got, the more desperately unhappy she was to be there and the more determined to leave.

"I'll do fine on my own," she told me earnestly. This wasn't true. And besides, having appraised her condition, authorities at the convalescent home determined that they would not release her without my assurance of around-the-clock care. Maybe I could get a caregiver to be with her from 8:00 to 4:00, to feed and bathe her, and keep her company, I thought.

"I'll take full responsibility; you won't be legally liable," I remember saying to the chief administrator, whose face turned to stone. I could see the category I had entered by her resolute jaw: difficult family member.

"We cannot release your aunt to you without the guarantee of 24/7 care."

With no other prospects in sight, I checked out five nursing homes in the area, picked out the best, and, with heavy heart, wheeled Elizabeth in. She was plunged into the company of elderly strangers, some sunken into wheelchairs, clutching teddy bears, eating with their hands, mumbling to themselves, staring vacantly ahead. My aunt wept, and then started to go a little nuts herself. Nights she called out for her long-dead mother. She barked orders to no one in particular to "Take me home!" During the day, she sat in her wheelchair in the doorway of her small room, facing the exit at the end of a long drab hall.

"Just get me *home*," she pleaded each time I visited. "I'll be fine on my own."

That was not possible. However, after a near century of living like a church mouse, she had saved enough to pay for care. We found some useless, uncanceled checks quirkily tucked in an old telephone book. In fact, I discovered that bringing her home would cost less than the nursing home. I just had to find someone to be with her.[13] I began calling around for a live-in caregiver. I called a suspicious-sounding woman living in a trailer park off Route 4 who declined due to a bad back. I called a farmer's wife who needed the money but couldn't leave her ailing husband's side. I contacted all my friends and their friends, and their friends' friends. The search was on.

Chapter 4

Our Baby, Her Womb

As we drove into the vast parking lot at 10:45 in the morning, mothers in floral summer dresses and flip-flops, fathers in short-sleeved shirts, and girls in strapless tops and capri pants were slowly streaming from every direction toward the auditorium of the Holy Mission Baptist megachurch in Jackson, Louisiana. At the entrance, a young man in a dark suit passed out sheets listing "Events of the Day" and pointed parents with toddlers toward one door, older children toward another. I was led into a great auditorium filled with nearly five thousand seated parishioners facing three enormous screens. Looming above us was the projected image of two earnest singers in a loud and rousing vocal duet of "Jesus Lives," set to the 1960s tune "Celebration Time."

The singers moved on to "Christ Is Alive" and "The Empty Grave Rejoices." Parishioners were tapping their feet, rocking, bouncing gently in their chairs. A few stood. Hands clapping, hips swaying. Soon a dozen smiling ushers roamed the aisles, tossing in the air dozens of red, white, and blue beach balls for the audience to catch and pitch about the festive auditorium. When the music drew to a close, the Director of the Youth Ministry, dressed in jeans and a blue shirt with rolled-up sleeves, led us in prayer. He then called on parishioners to stand and shake hands with their neighbors, left and right. "Ask them, What's your favorite Beach Boys song?" Laughter arose. "I can't remember . . . 'California Girls'? 'Do it Again'?" "Now," the minister said, "ask the person in front and in back." More laughter. " 'Good Vibrations.' 'Fun, Fun, Fun' . . . I like that one, too."

This lighthearted ritual of greeting was part of the church's open-arms philosophy—one that had attracted Tim and Lili Mason, both born-again Christians. Before they married six years ago, they had been American nomads, moving several times each to new cities and, once settled in Jackson, from one neighborhood to another. The parents of both Lili and Tim lived in other states, and the couple knew neighbors only enough to "wave at." So it was through Holy Mission Baptist—which served 17,000 believers, Tim told me proudly—that they had discovered a community. In fact, soon after they joined the church, a facilitator proposed that they join a group of young couples looking forward to parenthood. To improve their marriage, they also signed up for church-sponsored marital counseling. All of it offered them a welcome relief from the lonely, restless lives they had lived before marriage and church, though this sense of community also felt, to Tim, somehow moveable. As he said cheerfully, "If we move again, we can find a satellite campus and still feel part of the same community."

Despite the thousands of people in the audience that Sunday morning, the pastor's message seemed directed specifically at Lili and Tim and their thwarted hopes for a baby. After describing the heartache of waiting for something that just didn't happen, the pastor told the biblical story of Sarah, the wife of Abraham, who found herself too old to conceive the child she yearned to have. She "foolishly took tools into her own hands," the pastor said, and talked Abraham into sleeping with her servant Hagar. When Hagar conceived a son, Sarah flew into a jealous rage and banished her and her baby, Ishmael. Abraham was, the pastor commented wryly, "a wimp for going along with Sarah's wild scheme," and now found himself in a fine mess. A murmur of appreciation for the pastor's frank remarks rose from the rapt congregation.

The message of the sermon was to "leave the tools in God's hands" and not, like Sarah, take them into one's own. Little could the pastor have known that two listeners in the front middle row had actually flown halfway around the globe to hire a "Hagar" to bear their child.

This was to be their biological child—the product of Tim's sperm and Lili's egg—implanted in the womb of a surrogate who lived in India. The science, the technology, the very idea would have been beyond the wildest fantasies of my grandparents, not to mention Sarah and Abraham. Yet Tim and Lili were not even venturing into the farthest reaches of today's reproductive possibilities. For a person can now legally purchase an egg from one continent, sperm from another, and implant it in a "womb for rent" in yet another. An Israeli entrepreneur who calls himself "Doron" in the 2009 documentary *Google Baby* assembles such parts of life for a fee. A client can even purchase the sperm and egg online, have them delivered in liquid nitrogen to a clinic in India, have them implanted in the Indian surrogate, and pick up the baby nine months later. Where, I wondered, was the human touch in all this—the spirit of the gift? I was visiting Lili and Tim to see how they were feeling their way along this part of the market frontier.

After lunch at a nearby mall, we returned to the Mason home through a quiet, leafy neighborhood of dandelion-free lawns, small ornate water fountains, and two-car garages. All was quiet except for the distant roar of a leaf blower and weed whacker down the street near a truck marked TOP TURF LAWN CARE. The elegant homes, the sculpted shrubs, the manicured grass, all spoke of a desire for order and control.

"I'm a talker," Lili began, handing me a tall glass of iced tea on a porch behind their spacious three-story redbrick home. A pretty, bright-eyed, petite woman, the daughter of Indian immigrants, and a computer programmer, Lili was wearing cutoff shorts, a white shift, and plastic sandals, an outfit she had worn to church earlier that day. "I'll tell you anything you want to know," she offered.

In recent years, Lili had suffered from osteoarthritis and scoliosis, and after a double hip replacement, her doctor advised her to give up on trying to bear a child. But physical problems were not, she offered, the entire reason why she had never had a baby. Like many working women, she had delayed the decision to conceive and, even now at forty, approached the idea of a baby with caution: "I was slow to really *want* a baby. I was never one of those women who knew from day one she had to be a mother. But I don't beat myself up about it."

When I asked Lili about her early years, she slowly tucked her lustrous black hair behind her ears and described, with surprising detachment, the painful memory of her father's relentless tirades ("You're filthy. You're a slut. You're no good") and her after-school job cleaning blood and vomit off the floors of mussed rooms in her father's small hotel. "He didn't want me to turn out like the women who stayed in his hotel. I used to cry, hit myself, pull my hair, and slap myself. There was a railroad track behind the hotel. I used to think about lying down on it. So going through all that, I learned to be numb."

Ironically, her father seemed to push Lili into the very nightmare he imagined himself protecting her from. In her teen years, Lili began experimenting with drugs and sex. "I'm a 'try stuff' sort of person," she said, "so I thought I could handle it. But I couldn't." After a series of boyfriends, four abortions, and one failed marriage, Lili found herself living alone in a high-rise apartment building in New Orleans, working a temp job as a file clerk during the day, flipping channels on her television at night, and accepting monthly checks from her worried parents.

"I was so depressed," she continued. But one late weekend afternoon, she switched the channel to a plain-talking spiritual adviser, Joyce Meyer, and that day, alone in her apartment, she "submitted to Jesus." Some while later, she moved to another apartment building and met Tim, also a recent convert, who told her he very much wanted a child. They married. With a brightened outlook, a desire to strengthen her bond with Tim and to be a good Christian wife to him, Lili began to try to want to have a child. "There's still part of me that says, 'Gaaaa . . . no!' But another part says, 'I'd like to do it for Tim.' Tim is the real *go go go* guy on getting a baby."

When I spoke to Tim later, he made no secret of his desire for a child. He was seated on the living-room couch, his leg in a full-length plaster cast propped up on a stack of pillows, the result of a recent fall in their backyard. Stocky, blond, with cherubic blue eyes, it was in a soft voice and slow measures that he described his day job managing warehouse shipments and Saturday afternoons coaching soccer and baseball. "I'm thirty-four and have gotten to a certain stage in my career," Tim said. "I want to devote the next chapter of my life to being a father." When he imagined being a parent Tim pictured quitting his warehouse job, while Lili continued to work, and after Lili got home in the evening, teaching guitar in his basement office.

Refusing to be disheartened by four years of fruitless effort to get pregnant, Tim turned to other possibilities. Before their marriage, he had assumed it would be easy for Lili to get pregnant. But after four years of trying, they turned to in vitro fertilization. For this, the doctor harvested Lili's eggs, combined them in a petri dish with Tim's sperm, in hopes of creating an embryo that could be implanted in Lili's uterus. But try after try, the procedure failed and costs mounted. After Lili's double hip replacement and her doctor's disappointing counsel not to carry a child, Tim started to research surrogacy.

> I was Googling around and found some articles online about this infertility clinic in Anand, Gujarat, that offers very inexpensive IVF and surrogacy. I gave it to Lili to read and said, "Tell me what you think." She read it and said, "You want me to go to *India* for a medical procedure? You must be out of your mind."

Lili's parents, naturalized Americans who had been born in India, had never heard of Indian infertility clinics. Nor had word of them come through the *samaj*, the local Indian community in Jackson that kept up on eligible marriage partners and local dowry prices. Instead, word came to Tim via Google. Lili remembered her response: "No way! I wouldn't be caught dead in an Indian hospital!" But Tim persisted: "I brought up online images of their modern equipment; it looked just like the IVF equipment the clinics have in Jackson."

Had they considered adoption? I asked. Yes, but only as a last resort. Had they thought of asking a friend or relative to be their surrogate? Tim replied:

> Actually, my brother's wife and the wife of a friend both offered. We weren't really entertaining the idea of my brother's wife as much as Betty, the wife of my childhood buddy. We're pretty close to them. I was overwhelmed that she offered us this huge gift and was excited to do it for us. They had to stop at one child for financial reasons and she'd enjoyed her pregnancy and wanted to go through it again.
>
> They also felt bad for us. My buddy is a fireman and he told us he goes on calls in bad neighborhoods at 3:30 a.m. or 4:00 a.m. and will see a toddler in the middle of the street. There are so many people with babies that just don't take care of them. And yet it's so hard for responsible people to become parents.

"Why not accept Betty's offer?" I asked. "It's the cost," Lili replied. "Insurance doesn't cover the cost of medically preparing me to produce eggs, the cost of preparing the surrogate's body to receive them, or the cost of the surrogacy itself." Tim continued:

> Then there's the cost of the psychological evaluations. Plus lawyer fees. Altogether it would come to between $20,000 and $22,000 just to try. Then if Betty got pregnant, there are labor costs. The total could come to $50,000. We'd obviously

> want to pay Betty, too. If we hired a stranger here in the States, that alone could range from $25,000 to $40,000. So the total bill could be $80,000 here—and that's if you have a normal baby. In India the total could be $10,000.

Lili and Tim earned a combined $172,000 a year. I asked them if they had considered moving to a smaller home to save money so they could pay for a surrogate in America. No, they liked the house and needed the basement for Tim's music lessons. The SUV? It was handy, and at least they didn't have two cars. Could they accept a gift, I asked Lili, from her well-to-do parents?

> My parents wouldn't hesitate to give us money. But now, at age forty, I have a fifteen percent chance of having it work with my egg and another woman's womb. I wouldn't want to spend their money for such a slim chance of success. Who goes with these odds? Do you invest in a stock with such terrible odds of return? No. Even if you have the money, it's not a wise decision.

So, despite Lili's hesitation, Tim e-mailed Dr. Nayna Patel at the Akanksha Clinic in Anand. She replied with a series of medical questions. Tim answered these, inquired further, and asked for names and e-mail addresses of references. Thinking over the events that had led them to Anand, still painfully fresh in their minds, Tim recalled: "She gave us the names of three couples, all of whom ended up with babies. We e-mailed all three and spoke by phone with two. They said sometimes you e-mail Dr. Patel and she doesn't answer and you have to e-mail again, or call late at night. She's very curt, but it's not a scam."

A few months later, Tim and Lili flew to India. "When we decided to go I began to feel, 'Hey, I really want this baby,'" Lili said. They checked into a small hotel in Anand. The next morning, they took an auto-rickshaw to the clinic, where Dr. Patel's amiable husband ushered them into her office.

Dr. Patel herself graciously greeted Lili and Tim and, after a short interview, drew back a white curtain separating the front of her office from two examining tables in the back. She asked Lili to undress and lie down. As Lili recalled: "When Dr. Patel examined me with the wand [a medical device used in pelvic exams], it felt like she was driving a stick shift around my abdomen: first gear, reverse. In the United States, a doctor might warn you, 'You'll feel a little pressure here or there. . . .'"

Lying on the same table, Lili prepared to have blood drawn. Tim described the scene: "There's no rain for ten months of the year in Anand. So the ground is very dry with big cracks in the soil, dust over the cars, rickshaws. So this blood-work guy comes into the clinic office with dusty feet." Lili added:

> He looked like a street vendor. He pulled syringes out of what I thought was a dirty camera bag. He entered the exam room with his rubber gloves already on. I thought, "What the heck is this?"

To collect semen, Tim was conducted to a room with a bed (he recalled grimy sheets) and a loose faucet hung over a dirty sink. "They tell you to wash your hands," another client who completed his task in the same room told Tim, "but my hands were already cleaner than that water." Lili was then sedated and the doctor retrieved two eggs, which were mixed with Tim's sperm in a petri dish. Five days later, an embryo formed. They were elated.

The Quiet, Thin Surrogate

The Akanksha Clinic houses the world's largest-known group of commercial surrogates. A baby a week is born there. Dr. Patel, the director, is especially proud of her clinic's attention to quality control (most surrogates live on a supervised high-quality diet, often in secluded dormitories) and efficiency (Akanksha encourages highly businesslike relationships between surrogate and client so as to facilitate the easy transfer of the baby).

When Lili and Tim arrived at the clinic to meet the surrogate into whom their precious embryo would be implanted, Dr. Patel handed them her profile. At the top was her name and under it:

> Age: 25
> Weight: 44 kilos
> Height: 5 feet
> Complexion: wheatish
> HIV: negative
> Hepatitis: negative
> Occupation: housewife
> Marital Status: married
> Children: one
> Cast [*sic*]: Hindu
> Education: uneducated

The surrogate, recruited by Dr. Patel herself, was ushered into the main office, her eyes fixed on the floor, as were those of her husband, who filed in behind her. As Tim recounted:

> The surrogate was very, very short and very, very, very skinny and she didn't speak any English at all. She sat down and she smiled. She was bashful and her husband, too. You could tell they were both very nervous. We would ask a question and the translator would give a one- or two-word response. We asked what her husband did for a living, and the age of their child, just to make conversation. I don't remember the answers. I don't remember her name.

Surrogates earn more money if they agree to live in the dormitory for the full nine months, which nearly all of them do. Tim continued:

> We asked whether she planned to stay in the dormitory or stay with her husband. She said she would live in the dormitory the whole time. Dr. Patel told us her husband would only be allowed to visit for a couple hours and in a crowded room, so there would be no chance they would have sex or that he would transmit any infection.

Lili remembered being nervous about meeting the surrogate:

> It was because of this Indian-to-Indian dynamic. Other client couples—American, Canadian—tend to react more emotionally. They hold hands with their surrogate. But to me, that's weird; we don't do that touchy-feely thing—especially not for services rendered. You know, "I'm so glad you are doing this for me, let me hold your hand." I'm a little bit rough around the edges anyway. But to me it's simple: This girl is poor and she's just doing it for the money.

But when Lili saw the diminutive woman enter the room, she did feel an urge to reach out.

> I didn't want her to think of me as this big rich American coming in with my money to buy her womb for a while. So I did touch her at some point, I think, her hair or her shoulder. I tried to smile a lot. Through the interpreter I told her, "I am very glad and grateful you are doing this." I explained that we'd tried to have a baby but couldn't. I told her not to worry for herself; she would be taken care of. I asked her about her own child. She didn't look at ease. It was not the unease of "I can't believe I'm doing this," but more the unease of the subordinate meeting her boss.

The surrogate and her husband asked Tim and Lili no questions about themselves. "I'm sure to them it's a pure business transaction," Tim said. "Payment for surrogacy could equal ten years' of salary in India. Still, if she'd been more cheerful, maybe we would have talked more."

The encounter lasted fifteen minutes. The second and last time the Masons met the surrogate, she was lying on a table preparing to have their embryo implanted in her womb. Lili stood by the table and held the surrogate's hand for about half an hour. A day later, Tim and Lili flew back to Louisiana. Two weeks after that they received an abrupt e-mail from Dr. Patel: "Sorry to inform you that Beta HCG of your surrogate is less than 2, hence pregnancy test negative. Herewith attached is the report of Beta HCG." In other words, the egg had failed to grow in the surrogate's uterus.

Had the surrogate been malnourished? Had the procedure been done correctly? It was hard to know. Dr. Patel recommended trying again with Tim's sperm and a donor's egg. Weary of the roller coaster of hope and disappointment, they asked about the chances of success. "Sixty percent," Dr. Patel responded. But she had told a television interviewer it was 44 percent, and still other gynecologists estimated 20 percent. "We couldn't tell what the real rate was," Tim said, adjusting his leg cast on the sofa.

But the Masons decided to take the next step. They agreed to purchase a donor egg that would be artificially fertilized by Tim's sperm and implanted in the womb of another surrogate. For this, Dr. Patel's clinic needed to locate the right donor.

Several months went by.

At last, Dr. Patel wrote to say that she had found an egg donor. She was already on her seventh day of medication, the doctor explained, to help stimulate egg production. But who was paying for the medication she was already on, Tim and Lili wondered. Other clients? Had they dropped out? If so, why? "It seemed strange, but we wired her the $4,500 she requested," Tim said. Egg donors at the clinic, Tim later discovered, received $100 to $500 per donation.

Lili and Tim asked to see a photograph of the donor so they could have some idea of what their child might look like. Weeks passed. No photo arrived. Lili called Dr. Patel. In the notes Tim kept at the time, the exchange between them went like this: "Doctor asked, 'If you don't like the picture, will you pull out of the egg donation?' We said, 'No, it would just be nice to see the picture.'" A day later, a photo arrived.

She was "small, thin, and fairly pretty," Lili recalled. Soon after, Dr. Patel implanted the donor egg fertilized with Tim's sperm into the second surrogate. (To increase the chance of success, the doctor routinely implanted about five embryos at a time, aborting fetuses if they numbered more than two.)

Two weeks later another dispiriting e-mail message appeared on Tim's computer: "Hello. Sorry to inform you that Beta HCG of your surrogate is less than 2, hence pregnancy test negative. Herewith attach the report of Beta HCG."

Tim and Lili never met their egg donor or second surrogate, nor did they see their first surrogate again, nor did they see the dormitory where both surrogates had promised to live for nine months. And when I asked them whether they would have kept in touch with their surrogate had a baby been born, both paused in slight surprise at the question. "I would have left that up to the surrogate," Lili said.

> If she had no preference one way or another, and just gave some polite answer, I probably would have sent some photos of the baby or a letter. If there had been no response, I'd probably have given up. She probably can't write. The Surrogate Profile Form said "no education." Even if she could write, I can't read Gujarati. It's probably a big cost for them to write letters. And who knows if they'd still be living at the same address.

Although Tim and Lili had no real interest in forming a friend- or family-like bond with their surrogates, it was not a sign of callousness or moral unease. They were caring people who faithfully tithed their income for the poor in India. They objected to any suggestion of exploitation and were disturbed to hear surrogacy mentioned in the same breath as the black market for organs. As Tim reflected:

> There are so many activists out there saying that "wombs for rent" are a violation of human rights. I think it's just a decision people make on their own. It's not the same as one person buying and another selling a liver on the black market in Mexico. These Indian surrogates are very poor. They may not be the people you drive by, living beneath a blue tarp by the edge of some Indian road. But they're not much above that. So why would you not want to help somebody out? What's wrong with that? If they have a financial incentive, that's fine.

Simply, Tim and Lili saw their relationship with the surrogate as a mutually beneficial transaction. They imagined themselves as outsourcers paying a stranger to provide a professionally supervised service. They hoped to establish a pleasant, temporary bond with the surrogate, to pay her, thank her, and leave. They sought to create the sort of relationship one might establish with an obstetrician or dentist. In the outsourcer ideal, relations are pleasant and honest, but the point of them is to facilitate the exchange of money for service. In the course of a modern day, the outsourcer manages many such relationships—with a babysitter, psychiatrist, physical trainer, for example—and can't get "entangled" with them all.

Tim and Lili's relationship with the Akanksha Clinic came to a decisive end after they received the last of Dr. Patel's cryptic, disheartening messages, and Tim declared the search for a surrogacy baby at Akanksha over. "We're now looking into adoption in Nepal," he said. To prepare for that, they took an adoption class that Lili said had transformed her thinking.

> When we were doing the surrogacy, I wasn't so aware of the mother-child bond. I didn't know a baby could recognize the voice of the mother who carried it. I guess I felt detached.

> But after we took the adoption class, I realized how important contact between the surrogate and baby might be, and so how important it was for me to feel connected to the surrogate. If you're carrying a child for nine months, and then suddenly it's delivered and gone, there would inevitably be a void. God didn't create our bodies to work with IVF and surrogacy. So I now think I would have wanted some relationship with the surrogate—for the sake of the child.

Everything for Sale

The international search for a baby immersed Tim and Lili in a globe-spanning stream of "medical tourists" for which India is a particularly popular destination.[1] Since India declared surrogacy legal in 2002, an estimated three thousand Assisted Reproductive Technology (ART) clinics have sprung up nationwide and are predicted to add, from 2012 onward, an annual average $2.3 billion to the nation's gross domestic product.[2] Advertisements describe India as a "global doctor," offering First World skills at Third World prices, short waits, privacy, and—especially important in the case of surrogacy—a minimum of legal red tape. The Indian government encourages First World patients to come to India by granting lower tax rates and import duties on medical supplies to private hospitals that treat foreign patients.

The fertility market is flourishing in the United States as well. Had Tim and Lili decided to purchase an egg in the United States, they could have entered the world of ads placed by fertility clinics and prospective parents in college newspapers, on Facebook, and on craigslist. In a 2006 study of more than one hundred advertisements seeking egg donors published in sixty-three college papers, Dr. Aaron Levine, a professor of public policy at the Georgia Institute of Technology, found that a quarter of these offered potential compensation exceeding $10,000. Guidelines issued by the American Society for Reproductive Medicine, the nonprofit arm of an industry group, take no issue with the commercial purchase of eggs but urge limits on their price. A client should pay no more than $10,000 for an egg, they suggest. But ads in newspapers at Harvard, Princeton, and Yale on average promise donors $35,000.[3]

The society also recommends that fertility clinics forbid clients from paying additional fees in return for special "traits" such as a gift for math or music. The society has no means to enforce its guidelines, however. With its Corporate Council members from Good Start Genetics, Freedom Fertility Pharmacy, Merck & Co., Pfizer Inc., and other for-profit companies with a financial interest in the matter, the society is unlikely to question the wisdom of placing reproduction on the market frontier. Dr. Levine discovered that for every extra one hundred points in a university student's SAT score, the advertised fee rose by two thousand dollars. And dozens of American clinics now offer would-be parents detailed profiles of the characteristics of sperm and egg donors. Xytex Corporation in Atlanta, Georgia, for example, provides potential clients a list of genetically coded attributes—including the length of eyelashes, the presence of freckles, and results of the Keirsey Temperament Sorter test.[4]

Students themselves found the fertility clinic ads unremarkable. One twenty-two-year-old Brown University undergraduate told the *New York Times* that she was shocked at first that they would target "what they were looking for, like religion, SAT score, and hair color." But like other things she was first exposed to in college, "the shock wore off." I asked one of my students at University of California, Berkeley, how she felt about ads for human eggs in the *Daily Californian*, the college newspaper: "Our tuition is rising," she said, "and we're less and less a public university that regular families can afford. I have friends who are looking seriously at those ads. I don't blame them."

Tim and Lili had themselves come to accept things that had once seemed unthinkable. In the meantime, they had placed their name on a waiting list, number 375, to adopt a Nepalese child and had settled in for a long wait. It might be a year or two. The minister at Holy Mission Baptist Church was right, they felt, sometimes waiting can be painfully hard. Still, Lili now saw meaning in the wait. "I need to work on my anxiety and anger issues. Maybe God is giving us time to truly prepare."

When I contacted the Masons a year later, Lili told me that the Nepal adoption agency had been accused of corruption and that several countries had pulled out, including the United States, through which they had put in their application papers. But Tim had gone online again and discovered a clinic in Hyderabad, which he visited with his father, leaving behind a check for $7,000 and a semen sample. "This clinic keeps trying with surrogates and donors for as long as it takes until one succeeds," he explained. "The next payment isn't due until a pregnancy is confirmed at three months. The total will come to $25,000, including the payment to the surrogate, the egg donor, the delivery, everything." The first donor's eggs yielded sixteen embryos, which were implanted in three tries over several months. The couple had recently learned that, perhaps due to storage problems, Tim's sperm had died and the clinic needed more samples.

Lili was resigning herself, it seemed, to life without a child. But Tim, "the upbeat spirit" in their home, as Lili described him, could not. His injured leg had healed badly, robbing him of much feeling in his left foot. This made it impossible to play soccer and took much of the joy out of coaching—another great love in his life. Perhaps for that reason, the wish for a baby loomed ever larger, and, cautiously hopeful, Tim was planning a second trip to Hyderabad.

Chapter 5

My Womb, Their Baby

Tim was right. Anand is dusty. I had come to India to visit friends, but was thinking about the downcast eyes and folded hands of the Masons' surrogate sitting that day in Dr. Patel's office at the Akanksha Clinic. What had brought her in? What was she feeling? The clinic guarded surrogate names, and the Masons had forgotten hers. But perhaps I could talk to other surrogates. I decided to try. I was joined on a flight from Mumbai to Ahmedabad by Aditya Ghosh, a journalist with the *Hindustan Times*, who had covered the expanding Indian surrogacy industry and had offered to come with me and translate. Together we made our way through the town by auto-rickshaw. The driver honked his way through the chaos, swerving around motorbikes, grunting trucks, and ancient large-wheeled bullock-carts packed with bags of fodder and slowly hauled by head-nodding oxen. Both sides of the street were lined with wind-tossed plastic trash and small piles of garbage on which wandering cows fed. The driver turned off the pavement onto a narrow, pitted dirt road, slowed to circumvent a pair of black-and-white-spotted goats, and stopped abruptly outside a dusty courtyard. On one side stood a small white building with a sign that read, in English and Gujarati, AKANKSHA CLINIC.

Two dozen dainty Indian women's sandals, toes pointed forward, were lined up in a tidy row along the front step of the clinic. After being greeted by Dr. Patel, the clinic's director, I followed an embryologist to a small upstairs office to talk with two women, Geeta and Saroj, who had both carried other women's babies. They entered shyly through a door that led from a large dormitory filled with closely set iron cots. Nearly all of the surrogate mothers who have carried the more than three hundred babies delivered at Akanksha since 2004 have lived in this dormitory or in two others nearby. Each facility has a kitchen, a television, and a prayer room. Small children are allowed to stay with their mothers, but older children and husbands are barred from overnight visits. Surrogates are not permitted to leave their quarters without permission and seldom do. This is partly because they try to hide their pregnancies from disapproving relatives, and partly because they are forbidden to sleep with their husbands during pregnancy. They are offered weekly English lessons (which few attend) and computer lessons (which more do), and they receive daily vitamin injections and nutritious meals served on tin trays.

Geeta, a twenty-two-year-old light-skinned, green-eyed Muslim beauty, was the mother of three daughters. One sat wide-eyed on her lap. Like all the surrogates, Geeta was healthy, married, had the assent of her husband, and was already a mother. As one doctor explained, "If the surrogate has her own children, she'll be less tempted to claim the baby she's carrying for a client."

"How did you decide to become a surrogate?" I asked Geeta.

"It was my husband's idea," she replied.

Her husband cooked *pav bhaji* (a vegetable dish) during the day and served it from a street cart in the afternoon and evening. He heard about surrogacy from a customer. "The man was a Muslim like us," she told me, "and he said it was a good thing to do."

> So I came to Madam [Dr. Patel] and offered to try. We can't live on my husband's earnings and we had no hope of educating our daughters. My husband says if we can afford to send our daughters to school and if they study hard, they won't have to end up as housemaids and depend on others for money. Today, daughters are better than sons—more studious, loyal, and compassionate. While I'm at the hostel, my husband is cooking and caring for our two older girls.

Geeta leaned forward, adding softly, "Besides my husband, only my mother-in-law knows what I'm doing." All other surrogates I talked to spoke of carefully guarding their secret from gossiping family and neighbors since surrogates were generally suspected of adultery—a cause for communal shunning or worse. So as to disguise their identity when photographers visited the clinic, they would don white surgical masks that covered all but their eyes. Geeta had even moved with her husband and children from her home village fifty miles away to one nearer to Anand. As one surrogate's husband remarked darkly, "People don't understand or approve, and they talk."

Geeta met her clients twice, the first time for fifteen minutes, and the second time for about thirty. "Where are your clients from?" I asked. "Very far away. I don't know where," she answered, adding, "They're Caucasian, so the baby will come out white." She had been promised five thousand dollars for delivering the baby, and, deposit by deposit, the money was placed in a bank account in her name.

How, I asked, did she feel about carrying a baby she would have to give up? "I keep myself from getting too attached," she explained. "Whenever I start to think about the baby inside me, I turn my attention to my own daughter. Here she is." Geeta bounced the chubby girl on her lap. "That way, I manage."[1]

Seated next to Geeta was Saroj, a heavy-set, dark-skinned Hindu woman with intense, curious eyes and a slow-dawning smile. Like other Hindu surrogates at Akanksha, she wore *sindoor* (red powder applied to the part in her hair) and *mangalsutra* (bangles), both symbols of marriage. She is, she told us, the mother of two girls and a boy, and the wife of a street vendor who earned one hundred dollars a month. She gave birth to a surrogate child a year and three months ago, and was now waiting to see whether an implantation has succeeded so she could carry a second—the genetic child of Indian parents from Bangalore. Half of Akanksha's clients are Indian, I was told, and half are foreign. Of the foreigners, half come from North America. Like Geeta, Saroj knew very little about her clients: "They came. They saw me. They left," she said flatly.

Geeta and Saroj were in seclusion for now. I asked Saroj, who had done this once before, whether the money she earned made her feel more respected once she returned home. For the first time, the two turned to each other and laughed out loud. Then Saroj said:

> At first I hid it from my mother-in-law. But when she found out, she said she felt blessed to have a daughter-in-law like me because she's never gotten this kind of money from her son.

In a study of forty-two Akanksha surrogates, Amrita Pande, a sociologist who lived nine months in Anand, found that over half described themselves as housewives; the rest listed such occupations as bank teller, farmer, cleaner, waitress, nanny, maid, and plastic sorter. Hindu, Muslim, and Christian, most had seventh- to twelfth-grade educations, five were illiterate, and one—who turned to surrogacy to pay the expenses for a small son's heart surgery—had a bachelor of arts. Over three-quarters of them lived at or below the Indian poverty line.[2]

Many of these women came to surrogacy through word of mouth, which was actively spread by recruiters who were themselves former surrogates. Many first tried making money by donating their eggs, five hundred dollars per operation. To donate eggs, women visit the clinic for weeks beforehand to receive injections of ovary-stimulating hormones. Then they are sedated, undergo a procedure that is uncomfortable nevertheless, and are released to go home. "Women are lining up to have it done," Pande told me. "I talked to one woman who had endured six or seven retrievals and was thinking about an eighth. She told me it was extremely hard to ride home in a bouncy auto-rickshaw hours after a painful procedure. Often after egg harvests, the women go on to become surrogates."

Acting as a broker, the clinic normally negotiates a fee with the client on behalf of the surrogate. Fees differ. One dismayed surrogate carrying twins for an Indian couple discovered that she was being paid far less—$3,400—than the surrogate sleeping in the next cot, who was carrying a single baby for an American couple for $5,000. Despite the jealousies that arose, the Akanksha surrogates were glad to share tales about an experience largely invisible to those outside it.

Anjali at Home

It was dusk.

Aditya Ghosh, Manju (a photographer who has worked with Aditya in the past), and I were on our way to visit Anjali, a twenty-seven-year-old commercial surrogate who lived in a village on the outskirts of Anand. As a Muslim call to prayer hung in the air, we skirted mud puddles along the ill-lit path through the village. Sari-clad women balancing pots on their heads, gaggles of skinny teenage boys, scurrying children, and shuffling elderly men proceeded along a path lined with brick, tin-roofed shacks and mildew-stained concrete homes.

Suddenly a man's voice pierced the dust: "Aditya! . . . Aditya!" A stocky figure approached. A warm smile. A quick arm wraps itself around Aditya. It was Anjali's husband, Chahel, who now led us along the pathway to his home where his wife was waiting to receive us, seven months pregnant with her second surrogacy.

"*Anjali!* We have guests!" he called out. Waving from the second story, Anjali beckoned us up. We shed our shoes and stepped into the family's bare living room. Two cots with floral bedcovers were flush against opposite walls, serving as seats. Chahel hauled in a white plastic chair from the kitchen. A television with a surround-sound system stood tall in one corner and behind it an array of small gold-framed pictures including one of the elephant god Ganesh, whose help worshippers invoke to overcome all obstacles. Along a bare concrete wall a ledge bore a row of large black-and-white photos. One was of Anjali and her two children playing in a stream, and two others were of Anjali, Dr. Patel, and the entire family inside Dr. Patel's clinic. Anjali, the *doyenne* of Anand surrogates, had been the very first surrogate to bravely show her face to curious newspaper photographers who periodically appeared at the clinic and challenged the shame attached to surrogacy. She was now trusted—unlike most others—to live pregnant outside the dormitory.

Married at sixteen, mother of two, she had come to surrogacy through misfortune. Seven years ago, her husband had been a housepainter supervising eight other painters. Mixed into his paint was a caustic ingredient, lye. After accidentally rubbing his eye with a paint-covered finger, Chahel discovered that his eye had become both painful and blind. He was rushed to a doctor who told him he needed treatment that cost far more than he as a painter and Anjali as a shopgirl could afford. Unable to borrow money from struggling kin, they went to the moneylender who charged—as is typical—an annual interest of 40 percent. They soon found themselves in debt, destitute, and ashamed, daily sneaking past neighbors to a nearby temple to eat charity meals.

It was at this point that Anjali applied to become an Akanksha surrogate. She tried to get pregnant for hire altogether seven times, miscarried once, and then carried a baby to term for an Indian couple for $4,000. She earned nothing for her failed attempts and miscarriage, but the $4,000 was more than Chahel could have made in a decade. Anjali paid a contractor to build a two-story concrete house, the first floor of which they rented to another family. With the rest of the money she enrolled their nine-year-old daughter and seven-year-old son in private school. Returning to surrogacy, she failed to conceive four times—each time given shots of powerful hormones—before becoming pregnant again. But this time she negotiated the unusually high fee of $8,000.

Shuffling in her house slippers into her new kitchen, Anjali returned with a tray of teacups, sat down, and asked, "How much does it cost to go to medical school in America? My daughter wants to be a doctor," she explained. When she learned how expensive it was, she asked Aditya, "Are the surrogates in Mumbai paid more than in Anand?"

"Yes, more."

"So I'll come to Mumbai," she replied. "Give me the addresses of those doctors." Then, perhaps mindful of her own eagerness, she added, "It's not for me, but for a friend. . . ."

In fact, Anjali's practical approach was hardly surprising. Throughout the surrogate process, she had been instructed to remain emotionally detached from her clients, her babies, and even from her womb—which she was asked to imagine as a "carrier." Further, it was for the services of this carrier that she was paid: $115 on the first month, $115 on the third, $1,250 on the fourth, $115 on the seventh, and $2,750 on delivery. Anjali had done an extraordinarily personal thing—given life to the child of another woman. Paradoxically, during the snowstorm in Turner, my aunt Elizabeth's rescuers had done a far less personal favor—hauling in an electric generator—in a far more personal way. From every conceivable perspective, my aunt and her rescuers, on one hand, and Anjali and her foreign clients, on the other, stood at opposite ends of a broad spectrum. Elizabeth's relationship with her neighbors was face-to-face, rooted in the same land, lore, gossip, and religion, involving little direct exchange of money. Anjali's transactions with her clients were cursory, businesslike, and spanned differences in language, culture, ethnicity, nation, and, most of all, social class.

Before we left, Aditya asked Chahel: "Will Anjali be a surrogate again?"

"No. No. Twice is enough! This is the last time I'll let her do it. Does a man want his wife to do this? No. I am a man!"

"Yes, but the money is good, isn't it?"

"I am a man!" Chahel insisted as we approached the door.

We took our leave, thanking Anjali and Chahel, giving them small gifts, and making our way back along the dirt path through the village. We crossed the railroad tracks and walked in total darkness along the edge of a busy street without sidewalks, a jumble of cars, clopping donkeys, and pedicabs streaming past. After a while, Aditya asked Manju, "Do you think Anjali will do it a third time, even if Chahel doesn't want her to?"

The two mulled it over.

"I think so," said Manju.

"So do I," Aditya replied.

Although Tim and Lili were able to imagine the poverty of Indian surrogates, they had no sense of the emotional challenges they faced, especially that of retaining their dignity. Tellingly, dormitory gossip among the surrogates targeted those who were "too practical" about their job. Amrita Pande found, for example, that Anjali was roundly criticized by the other surrogates who felt that she had become too driven, too strategic, and too materialistic. She had her fancy new house, her children in private school, her stereo, her DVDs, and she still wanted more. They all needed money and they were all renting their wombs to earn it. But as a matter of dignity, the surrogates felt there were limits; their bodies were not just moneymaking machines. Granted, there was little talk among them of surrogacy as an act of altruism, and many admitted enjoying aspects of their nine months of dormitory life. "Ice cream, coconut water, and milk, every day—and they are paying for it!" one surrogate told Pande, adding: "I think I deserve it for all I am doing right now."[3]

Nonetheless, they drew a firm line. Yes, they had babies for money, but they strongly resisted the idea that materialism had suppressed their motherly feelings. As one put it, "We will remember our babies all of our lives." So some surrogates condemned Anjali for carrying babies only for money, and for being therefore "like a whore"—a dishonor they all feared. Poignantly, even surrogates desperate for money took pride in not becoming *too* money-minded, and in feeling that they were giving the gift of life.

"Was It My Baby to Give or Was It Bought Before I Gave Birth?"

A week after my visit to Anjali, I was accompanied by Alyfia Khan, another *Hindustan Times* reporter, on a visit to another fertility clinic, this time on a pockmarked street in Mumbai. Together we headed to Dr. Nandita Palshetkar's office to meet with Leela, a lively twenty-eight-year-old deli waitress who, six months earlier, had given birth to another couple's baby. Like other surrogates, Leela desperately needed money. But whether because she was not directed to detach from her baby or minimize contact with her clients, or because of her outgoing personality, Leela's experience seemed a world away from that of the Anand surrogates—far less alienating

Leela's black hair was drawn back from her open face into a long braid, which bobbed cheerfully about her back. Dressed in a bright pink sari, she smiled broadly and leaned toward me, eager to talk. How had she become a surrogate? I asked.

> My father died young, so my mother raised us three girls on her wages as a maid. She was too poor to offer a dowry when my older sister married. And after the marriage, my brother-in-law's family hounded my mother mercilessly for money because my brother-in-law wanted to buy a motorbike. One day while my sister was in the kitchen, her husband doused her with kerosene, lit her, and burned her to death.[4] Looking at my sister's glassy eyes and burnt face, I vowed I would never be poor.

At age eighteen, Leela married a waiter at the deli where she worked and had two children with him.

> I didn't know he was an alcoholic until after we married. My husband ran up a four-thousand-dollar debt with the money-lender, who sent agents to pressure us to repay it. They yelled and knocked on our front door and made my life hell. We had to lock the door and couldn't leave the house for work. I decided to act. I heard from my sister's friend that I could get money for donating my eggs, and I did that twice. When I came back to do it a third time, the doctor told me I could earn even more as a surrogate.

The genetic parents paid her well, she felt. "Was she able to pay off her husband's debt?" With lowered eyes, she replied: "Half of it."

For the last few months of Leela's pregnancy, the genetic parents arranged for a maid to come to her home in Mumbai, and, unlike all the other surrogates I spoke with, Leela openly bonded with her baby. "I am the baby's *real* mother. I carried him. I felt him kick. I prayed for him. At seven months, I asked the doctor if I and two other surrogates could celebrate *Godh Bharai* [a ceremony to honor the in utero child]. We had sweets. We took photos. Yes, he is mine. I saw his legs and hands on the sonogram. I suffered the pain of birth. To this day I feel I have three children and one of them I gave as a gift."

The baby's genetic parents, Indians from a nearby affluent suburb, presented Leela with a "lovely new sari" for *Godh Bharai*, and continually reached out to her:

> The genetic mother sees me as her little sister and I see her as my big sister. She held my hand during the delivery. When the baby was born, she said, "Look how beautiful our child is." Afterward she helped me back and forth to the bathroom. They telephone me every month, even now, and call me the

baby's auntie. They asked if I wanted to see him. I said yes. They brought him to my house, but I was disappointed to see he was long and fair, not at all like me.

Although a friendship of sorts arose between the two mothers, Leela's doctor, like Dr. Patel, discouraged it. "I deleted their phone number from my cell phone list because Madam told me it's not a good thing to keep contact for long," Leela says. "But that's okay. What we had is more than enough for me."

Most surrogates at the Akanksha Clinic had little contact with their clients and wished for more. Many imagined that their clients were concerned about the details of their pregnancy and were grateful for clients' all-too-rare check-in messages. Unlike Leela's client, those at the clinic could be very businesslike. In fact, three surrogates woke up after cesarean deliveries to discover their babies gone. Two years later, one of them, whose clients had been very friendly up until then, still hasn't gotten over it. "They just took the baby and ran. They never said thank you or good-bye."[5] Another wondered: "Was it my baby to give or was it bought before I gave birth?"

After giving birth, surrogates are not allowed to breast-feed the baby to avoid enhancing their attachment. Those who got to hold the baby before giving it away reported strong feelings. Another surrogate, named Sharda, said: "When the baby cries I want to start crying as well. It's hard for me not to be attached."

As a topic, the surrogate's attachment to her baby and client arose again and again in unexpected ways. For example, after Anjali's baby was born, and the joyous Canadian genetic parents traveled to India to claim it, Anjali—a devout Hindu—made what was, to her, a horrifying discovery. As she later told Aditya over the phone, "My clients were Muslim! I am a Hindu. For nine months I carried a Muslim child. I have sinned! They gave me a lot of money, but all my life I must live with this sin. It was a huge mistake. I could have waited for other clients." For nine months, Anjali had thought of herself as a carrier with little regard for the identity of the baby inside, much as Dr. Patel had instructed her to do. But now, she realized how much it mattered to her that she was carrying a Hindu baby. Another surrogate told me she would refuse to carry a baby for gay clients, but in a separate interview her obstetrician confided, "If I have gay clients, I don't tell my surrogates."[6]

One Delhi-based Hindu surrogate agreed in a written contract with her Sikh clients to visit daily, for the nine months of her pregnancy, the Sikh Gurudwara Temple in Delhi and there listen, for the spiritual sake of the fetus, to chanting from the Sikh holy book. The clients even hired a maid to tend to the surrogate, instructing the maid (the surrogate suspected) to make sure that she went to the temple every day. She was a Hindu surrogate carrying a Sikh baby. But she confided to an interviewer, "Secretly I prayed for the baby to my *own* Lord."[7]

Parvati, a thirty-six-year-old Akanksha surrogate, learned, after the fact, that in signing her contract (which was written in English), she had signed over the right to decide whether or not to abort a baby. At Akanksha, surrogates were usually implanted with many eggs, and when three or more survived, Dr. Patel routinely aborted the "extras." When Parvati found she was pregnant with triplets, Dr. Patel told her that one had to go. Distressed, she told Amrita Pande:

> Doctor Madam said that the babies wouldn't get enough space to move around and grow, so we should get the surgery. I told Doctor Madam that I'll keep one and Nandinididi (the genetic mother) can keep two. After all, it's my blood even if it's their genes. And who knows whether at my age I'll be able to have more babies.[8]

Against Parvati's strong wish, Dr. Patel aborted one fetus.

Geeta, Saroj, Sharda, Parvati—all might seem like victims of hypercommodification, a twenty-first-century, female service-sector version of Marx's "alienated man." They were paid for their labor. To get paid, they had to agree to terms that severely limited their say over various aspects of their pregnancies, which, in turn, whittled down their autonomy, their selfhood, and, because of this, their capacity and desire to relate to the baby they carried. The less they related, the more like a vessel they felt, and the less they were able to see themselves as giving a gift. The surrogate who awoke from a cesarean birth to discover the baby gone had no sense of "giving" the baby to her clients. The clients took it. It was already theirs. From the transfer of money on, the Hindu surrogate carrying the Sikh baby was also—in the clients' eyes—carrying their private property. Each Akanksha story was different, but in nearly every one commerce—and the ethos of production, control, and efficiency that went with it—dampened the spirit of the gift.[9]

As did the effort to undermine any possible bond between surrogate and baby. Dr. Patel, for example, required that the egg inside the surrogate must not be her own. In addition, she instructed surrogates to think of their wombs as carriers, bags, suitcases, something external to themselves. The surrogate had no say about whether or not to abort an "extra fetus" or have a cesarean section. At Akanksha virtually all births were by C-section, ostensibly to "reduce infection" but perhaps also to sedate the mother and reduce her memory of the birth.[10] The clinic maintained a policy of no breast-feeding, and a surrogate had no legal right to see or say good-bye to the baby.

The women at Akanksha had experienced pregnancy both as mothers and as surrogates. And there was a difference. This difference did not reside in the fact of surrogacy, according to most people I talked to. As one Mumbai-based gynecologist put it, "surrogacy can be a beautiful thing." Rather, the difference had to do with giving birth in or outside Akanksha's culture of mass production. It reminded me of the contrast between early capitalism—where a worker owned his shop, controlled his tools, and took personal pride in his craft—and late capitalism—where a worker labored on a factory assembly line, monitored by efficiency-minded managers.[11] The new Indian fertility clinics were for-profit "factories," and Dr. Patel aspired to be the Henry Ford of surrogacy. "There may be surrogacy clinics all over the state, the country, the world," she told Amrita Pande, "but no one in the world can match our numbers."

Given the poverty propelling the women into surrogacy, it is not clear whether they were free agents in an open market or exploited workers in a reproduction factory.[12] The surrogates themselves seemed to see it both ways. Some sported the rhetoric of "free choice," setting aside their dire options. Despite her terrible predicament, Anjali, for example, claimed to be the proud author of her fate. Another surrogate, who got pregnant twice, once with one child and the second time with twins, had very clear objectives: her Israeli clients had promised to buy her tickets to Israel, where she hoped to land a lucrative job and send home remittances.[13] But most surrogates, as Amitra Pande found in her fieldwork at Akanksha, described their "choice" as *majboori* (a compelled, involuntary act). One broker, hired to recruit surrogates, hung around an abortion clinic, where he could waylay women who'd recently aborted a child they could not afford to keep and draft them into surrogacy. Other brokers preyed on women's fears of being bad mothers—unable to pay dowries or school fees.

However they saw themselves, surrogates paid a heavy price in emotional labor. For it was by no means natural or automatic to feel as detached as they were required to feel about the baby growing inside them.[14] They worked at their detachment. As Saroj put it not too credibly, "If someone puts a precious jewel in my hand, I don't covet it as my own." Others sought to reinforce their detachment with various rationales. "With children you never know," one said, "kids can leave you in the end." One who had girls of her own talked about how girls were more loyal and helpful than boys, and so she had no need or desire for more children of her own and no desire for the boy she carried.

Akanksha has become a model for other fertility clinics emerging in India and other countries. Indeed, a certain competition between them for market share seems to be in progress. In *One*

World, Ready or Not, William Greider describes a "race to the bottom" that unfolds as entrepreneurs seek cheaper and more pliant labor and customers seek cheaper goods and services.[15] At each stage of the race, the company finds workers willing to accept lower wages somewhere else, and at each step, workers' rights dip lower. Some observers fear a similar race to the bottom in the production of babies.

That race is already under way, Amrita Panda observed, in India: "With so much publicity, and promise of money, you see mom-and-pop infertility clinics opening up all over Delhi." According to Dr. Thankam Varma, medical director of reproductive medicine at a well-known hospital in Chennai there are now over thirty thousand infertility clinics in India.[16] Many large clinics receive U.S. clients via channels set up with American clinics, such as the Los Angeles–based Planet Hospital, which links treatment with "fertility tourism" to exotic Indian temples.[17] New Life India, like other bigger clinics, also recruits women from Georgia and Ukraine to travel to India and have their white, blue-eyed eggs harvested for sale.[18]

Smaller clinics are getting in on all this, too. Sponsored by drug and medical equipment companies, national conferences on assisted reproduction, once held in major cities, now take place in more provincial Indore, Jodhpur, Cochin, and Guwahati. "With so many new clinics springing up and no regulation, I worry about a proliferation of quacks," Pande noted. To save costs on the expensive IVF medium, 21 out of 43 small clinics in one recent study even organized test tube conception in batches.[19] Following the dynamics of global capitalism, will Thai entrepreneurs set up clinics that undersell those in Anand and Mumbai and other smaller clinics such as these? Will Cambodia set up clinics that undersell Thailand?

In response to commercial surrogacy and the economic logic that might take hold, the nations of the world are, like individuals, trying to draw the line. And at the moment, they seem highly confused about how and where to do that. In Saudi Arabia, surrogacy was permitted between two wives of the same husband, though this has now been banned. Israel has legalized commercial surrogacy, and whether provided by public or for-profit clinics, the state pays for it—though only for heterosexual citizens. In Spain, commercial surrogacy is illegal but egg donation is not. The laws in most countries around the world ban commercial surrogacy, although the practice sometimes goes on. Only four countries in Western Europe (Finland, the Netherlands, Belgium, and the United Kingdom) have explicitly legalized nonprofit surrogacy.[20] The United States is a legal patchwork—a 2007 study found that seventeen states and the District of Columbia had passed laws on surrogacy, some to ban it and others to approve and regulate it.[21]

In the midst of evolving legislation, the complexities of surrogacy itself have evolved as well. A PBS documentary, "Surrogacy: Wombs for Rent?" documented what occurred, for example, when clients hired a surrogate but then felt buyer's remorse. A Los Angeles–based surrogate named Susan Ring agreed to carry a child—twins, as it turned out, from a father's sperm and a donor's egg—for the married couple who hired her.[22] But, "when the intended mother handed me the ultrasound photos of the fetus," Susan reported, "I thought that was odd." Then she found out the couple was having marital difficulties. Just weeks before she was due to give birth, Susan asked the parents what they planned to do, and the wife replied, "No, what are *you* going to do?" When the twins were born, Susan recalled, "no one was at the hospital." The divorcing couple planned to put the babies into foster care and never paid the surrogate. In the end, the surrogate, herself a single mother of two, heroically hired a lawyer to gain custody of the legal orphans. Since she was not the genetic mother, her case was at first denied. She appealed and, after three months, won. She then placed the twins into the loving hands of adoptive parents.

Susan Ring, the Indian surrogates, and their clients all find themselves in uncharted market territory. Some fiercely resist the market ethos. Others circumvent it, while still others earnestly embrace it. Most Akanksha surrogates tried to blend submission to the factory-like rules of the clinic with pride in providing for their own children. And birth after birth, the delivery room handoffs from poor women to richer went smoothly—for the most part. Before I left, I asked a kindly embryologist, Bhadarka, whether the clinic offered surrogates any psychological counseling. "We explain the scientific process," she answered, "and they already know what they're getting into." Then, looking down and stroking the table between us, she added softly, "In the end, a mother is a mother, isn't that true? In the birthing room there is the surrogate, the doctor, the nurse, the nurse's aide, and often the genetic mother. Sometimes we all cry."

Chapter 6

It Takes a Service Mall

In early twentieth-century America, one aspect of intimate life occasionally outsourced by the upper class—paying a wet nurse to suckle one's baby—was the subject of a cultural storm. Many turn-of-the-century ministers and doctors scolded mothers from the pulpit or in print for hiring wet nurses. At a 1904 Congress of Arts and Sciences meeting in St. Louis, Missouri, the founder of American pediatrics, Dr. Abraham Jacobi, asked his audience, "What are we to say of the refusal of well-situated and physically competent women to nurse their children? I do not speak of the four hundred [top socialites]. I mean the four hundred thousand who prefer their ease to their duty, their social functions to their maternal obligations, who hire strangers to nurse their babies." Meanwhile Boston wet nurses, many of them poor immigrants recently off the boat from job-starved Ireland, were alternately denigrated as "one part cow and nine parts devil," or praised as a welcome "traditional" alternative to the worrisome new baby formulas just going on sale.[1]

More than a century later, when I sat down with April Benner in the breakfast nook—wallpapered in a cookies-and-teapot design—of her suburban Los Angeles home, much had changed. Most parents trusted the formulas on the supermarket shelf, and no one was working as a wet nurse, but outsourcing child care had flourished into a massive, multifaceted industry.

Having talked to love coaches, wedding planners, and surrogates, I was hardly surprised to find that many of the tasks once considered "the heart of a mother's job" were now given over to paid help. April herself had engaged a nanny who "believed in Penelope Leach," and had also hired a consultant who helped her find the right summer camp, a bicycle trainer, a kiddy chauffeur, and a lice-lady for when her boys returned from school with itchy heads. She was a fan of outsourcing in every realm of life. Therapy for herself and her husband, Martin, was a "no-brainer," essential to keeping "all channels open" in their relationship. To a depressed friend, she recommended a closet organizer; for a lonely widow, a dating service. Overall, she was a savvy and apparently unambivalent shopper in the service mall.

A lithe, blond woman of thirty-five, April was dressed in gray sweatpants, a burnt orange jersey, and a gray cable-knit sweater. As she half-opened the door, she sprang to grab the collar of a wiggly yellow Labrador puppy. "He kisses everyone. No restraint, so refreshing. Come in!" Now working from home doing tax returns for a national tax consultant agency, she told me how she had insisted on providing breast milk for her boys despite the long days she used to put in at the office. As she recounted:

> In my twenties I worked feverishly in corporate public relations. Long hours. I earned a lot. I got promoted. And when my first son was born, the firm was launching a big project. So I took breast pump, bottles, cooler to the office and expressed my milk in the lady's room. It was the closest I could get to breast-feeding, which I was dying to do, because, at that point, I didn't have the time to be with my son.

For a period, breast milk became a symbol for the mothering she couldn't manage. When her second son was born, her husband, Martin, was still putting in long hours at his law firm, but April had cut back to thirty hours a week working out of her—she pointed at her pocketbook—BlackBerry.

While relieved to have more time at home, she also felt "fidgety."

> I scaled back on work to devote more time to my kids, and I thought it would solve my problem, but I'm struggling. I feel like I'm plodding along, not really excelling, and anxious about that. That makes me a less good mom.

April's struggle to reconcile the drive to excel at work and the need to be a "relaxed mom" may have influenced her response to the array of family services before her. While they held the promise of boosting her shaky pride as a mother, they also held the potential to undercut it. She thought of herself as a devoted mother; in the greater scheme of things, that came first. But—crediting the productivity gurus whose best-selling books she'd devoured in business school—she wanted to focus on what she was best at, and she wasn't sure that was motherhood.

> I apply to myself the same logic my company applies to itself. If it's a better use of the world's resources to make cars in China, then everyone will be better off if we build cars in China, and specialize in what we do better than they do—like inventing technologies. I apply that idea to my personal choices as well. What am I good at? I ask myself. Tax strategy. So I want to outsource everything except what I'm best at. I'm always asking myself: What can I outsource? Hopefully not *me*!

It was odd, April felt, to apply to her life a logic that economists apply to nations but "it sort of made sense," whether you were filling a specialized niche within a global division of labor or a specialized niche at home. This way of thinking had one important advantage: it made it easier to outsource tasks once considered integral to a woman's role and to the family. As April explained, "I don't invest my identity in the stuff I hand off. I'm not a fantastic cook, so it's no problem to order in or eat out."

At the same time, she worried she might be going too far.

> My self-esteem rests on excelling at that one thing—being an ace on the U.S. tax code. I don't value myself for much else. So I worry: What if I'm laid off? Do I know how to value myself for doing the things I've outsourced, let alone remember how to do them?

Some weeks after our first meeting, April's focus had shifted somewhat. Martin was now working "flat out," and she had taken up full responsibility at home. April was still working some, but she had redirected her energy: for the moment, home was her business. In fact, she proudly showed me a printout of a fifteen-page PowerPoint presentation entitled "Family Mission Statement." On the first page, "Family Goals," she had written:

1. To love each other
2. To spend time together
3. To teach the children to help others
4. Be world citizens

Then came a series of family photos: the boys on the beach in enormous sunglasses mugging for the camera; the boys in red baseball caps, sandwiches in hand, looking over their shoulders toward the camera from a picnic table; her husband, Martin, arms looped around his beaming parents; the nanny playing tug-of-war with the dog.

April appeared to be bringing the corporate approach of defined goals to her mission of family management. Given the family's $150,000 income, she could draw as much as she liked on the expertise of the service mall, but as I began to discover, her desire to do so was not without complication.

Sitting at her breakfast nook, I showed her a series of Internet advertisements that I had collected, services used by people I'd interviewed or read about. I asked her what she thought about each one. We began with an ad for a "nameologist"—a person who is to help new parents choose the right name for their child. "Why are Jeffs, Brandons, Mikes, and Mary Anns always struggling with impatience, restlessness, and lack of discipline," the ad for Maryanna Korwitts, nameologist, read. "Why do Marks and Stephanies seem to lack confidence, while Joes and Julies chatter a mile a minute?"[2]

"Didn't parents use to name children after relatives? In Africa, don't relatives name children?" April mused. "I'd never dream of consulting a professional to name my kid." But she added, "Maybe the nameologist is right about Jeffs." She was joking. But through the joke there was some curiosity about what a professional might really have to say.

"Don't guess," Korwitts warned, "about what a name will do. Find out before you put the name on your child's birth certificate." Korwitts believed that a name—the sight and sound of it, the initials, and possible nicknames—"designs" the child's personality. "Garth" encourages sports. "Zeta," "Cannon," and "Ford" foster art.

Korwitts claimed that applying the "energetic science of names" could stave off a newborn's unhappy future. This could be accomplished in two one-hour phone conversations for a fee of $350, in which she would help a client:

> Find out which names encourage weight problems, attention deficit disorder, and fear of intimacy, poverty syndrome, and addiction. Also learn which names stimulate leadership abil-

ity, financial reward, creativity, and satisfying soul-mate connections.

Does a "science" of names touch, in the new parent, a nerve of self-doubt? Are parents overcome by an excess of choices for names, as they sometimes are by an excess of choices for goods and services? Do the names suggested by family and friends seem passé? April was as curious as I was to understand the spirit in which a parent might pick up the phone. But for herself, she didn't take Korwitts seriously: "For three hundred fifty bucks, I could drink some great wine and come up with some names: Vintage, Sauvignon Blanc, Beaujolais. . . ." We moved on.

"How about hiring a baby planner?" I asked April. For fifty to one hundred dollars an hour, you can hire a walking up-to-date Consumer Report on every item and service available for babies: green bassinets, efficient breast pumps, slings versus chest-huggers, chemical-free cloth diapers versus "hybrids," and more. April felt such a person could be useful but "you have to ask yourself if some companies train planners to tout their stuff. So then you have to research which planner to hire."[3]

What about other tasks that would once have been kept in the family but for which a modern American parent can hire a specialist? Here are a few:

- Safety-proof an apartment or house (install safety gates, cord-free window coverings, fireplace barricades, covered electrical outlets; check chemicals and car seat belts)
- Teach baby sign language
- Train babies to sleep through the night
- Train toddlers to stop thumb sucking
- Potty train a child
- Pack a child's school lunch, including personal note
- Drive a child to after-school games and lessons

- Control a child's temper
- Teach table manners
- Teach bicycle riding, baseball, Frisbee throwing
- Locate an appropriate summer camp
- Locate friends for playdates
- Plan a child's birthday
- Organize a child's photo album
- Shop for a child's birthday gift

April had an ambivalent response to this profusion of services. Since she believed a person should focus on an area of expertise and outsource all other tasks to specialists, surely the same division of labor should apply to a child's needs, with each discrete job to be done by an expert? That way, we could all live in a more efficient, skill-based world, and also focus on what we are best at.

But April couldn't bring herself to apply this principle to every aspect of parenting. She found herself drawing lines, based on nameless feelings, between what should be outsourced and what should stay in her hands. Potty training was one such area. In the ads we saw, a parent could either contract for potty training as part of a coach's overall package or as a stand-alone service. The costs ran from an "$800 Quick & Ultimate Pack" by Adriana's Services with "optional nannying," to a $17 e-book from "Joanne, the Potty Trainer" that could be downloaded to a parent's smartphone. Over-the-phone coaching can run from 75 cents to $1.25 a minute. Such training, the ads promise, could help prepare a child for preschool or camp while saving $80 dollars a month in diaper bills. It could even, one ad observed, help parents enjoy stress-free shopping and cleaner-smelling kitchens.[4]

Like a number of advertisers, Joanne at thepottytrainer.com disparaged the nonprofessional and "outdated" village lore of elderly grandparents, hurried doctors, unknowledgeable babysitters, or hyperclinical psychologists. At the same time, Joanne claimed to base her own expertise on instinct: "I have a beautiful gift and a way with kids. I did not learn it. I was born with it."[5] On potty training, April felt that:

> We should all be able to get help if we need it. On the other hand, potty training isn't just a task. It conveys a big message to a little kid: "My body is good. I'm proud to learn how to control it. It's important to me that you see me when I do"—all that. So I want Martin, or our babysitter, or me to do it. It's my child, after all.

When it came to a professional party "animator" to enliven a teenage party, she drew a similar line. An "animator," according to a 2003 *New York Times* article about Lonnie Hughes, spreads infectious fun at a party for a fee. Dressed in formfitting black shirt and pants, Hughes "regularly spends his weekends dancing with 13-year-olds in braces and formal wear at bar mitzvahs from Great Neck to TriBeCa" in the New York City area. Wealthy parents can even hire multiple "interactive motivators" at $100 to $300 an hour for an event. For Michael Beck's bar mitzvah at the Fenway Gold Club in Scarsdale, New York, for example, his parents hired "seven motivators in tight black outfits from Total Entertainment," a New Jersey company; without them, *Times* journalist Elissa Gootman asked, would "12-year-old Stephen Purcell have made his way to the lighted dance floor?"[6]

"My boys are too young for all that," April said, by way of response. "But when they're older, I'd rather they learned for themselves what to do when a party gets dull."

Sweeping her eye over the ads, April remarked, "A lot of them are just-in-case. Okay, the nameologist, the animator—that's over the top. But the potty trainer, the thumb-sucking specialist—if I got stuck, I'd give one a call, and I'd recommend a friend do the same." She could understand parents trying to give their children a good head start in a competitive world; she was trying to do that, too. On the other hand, she said:

> You have to ask yourself, are these needs kids have or are they needs these professionals are making up? I always wonder. And if you outsource all these tasks to a different specialist, your kid is going to feel like the car you take in for the tune-up, oil change, wheel rotation, lube job. How will he remember his childhood? Appointment, appointment, appointment. . . .

Did American parents always put such great faith in family experts? At the time my grandparents married, home economics classes were just beginning in high school and college to teach young women how to cook, sew, clean, budget, decorate a home, and raise a good child. Deriving from a late-nineteenth-century domestic science movement, and promoted by the American Home Economics Association, such courses established the idea that homemaking was a science and full-time motherhood a profession like any other. Much as their husbands practiced professions outside the home, which called for advanced training, so mothers practiced a profession of their own inside the home—the thinking went—and needed a similar advanced training. The leading expert on how to become a scientifically informed mother, according to Rima Apple, author of *Perfect Motherhood*, was the physician.[7] "Mothers left alone," turn-of-the-century books and pamphlets insisted, "were incapable of raising their children healthfully." In those same years, the clergy, until then the obvious resort of mothers in need of advice and help, were beginning to lose out to secular experts.

Today, when seven out of ten American mothers work outside the home, such scientific standards are still in demand. If anything, the standards have become more exacting. Expertise in them is not found in lesson plans for the stay-at-home mother but in services a working mother can buy. So if experts know how to raise children better than we do, how do we feel about our own amateur efforts? I asked April.

> That question just came up. All the second- and third-graders in our school district are supposed to do a special report on the historic California missions of the Catholic Church. They're supposed to build little replicas. A few years back, parents hunted down the materials themselves. We'd go to Jimmy's Art Supply downtown and buy oak tag for the roof, yarn for the trees, green paint for the garden.
>
> Now Jimmy's has a special section with *kits* that have precut foam board, trees to glue onto the mission grounds, a model railroad, and grass for the native grasslands that are supposed to surround such missions. There's one kit for Mission Dolores, another for San Juan Bautista. You buy it, take it home, glue four walls together, put on the roof, stick in the trees and grasses, and take it to school.

"So what are the kids learning?" April wondered. "That the store-bought mission makes the kid's homebuilt mission look crude. The trees around Jimmy's Spanish missions stand straighter. The roof fits perfectly. The windows are all the same size." Now, as she saw it, the parents ran a risk if they didn't buy the kit:

> You may be a parent who says to her kid, "Build the mission out of things you scrounge around the house." But then your kid is embarrassed to walk to school with his homemade mission.

Compared to a typical parent, April thought, experts were like Jimmy's missions—they held up higher standards. The specialist-trained, diaper-free, ex-thumb-sucking four-year-old might, indeed, gain an extra step up in life. The coached child might throw a better ball. The child trained by an expert biker probably would ride a steadier bike. Parents eager to help their kids succeed at a wide range of things or simply get ahead were now surrounded by services that saved time, claimed better results, and generally raised the bar on every facet of "village" parenting. "That's the good side," she said.

> But they cost money, and we end up dumping advice from family and friends as if it were worn-out stuff, ready for the trash heap. We constantly need to go out and buy new stuff. Nothing's ever enough.

There was another problem as well. "They say we should ask the experts and hire help so we can relax, but," April mused, peering out the window at her upper-middle-class neighborhood, "who's relaxing?"

> Take us. We buy takeout. We have a nanny. We pay for enrichment classes. And we're still frantic. I don't know anyone—including me—who comes home from work, having outsourced house care, laundry, cooking, and child care, and then enjoys a cocktail with their partner for an hour looking at their lovely backyard garden and chatting. That 1950s scene? No one.

Does the recent rise of parenting services resemble the earlier advent of home appliances also designed to save time? I wondered. As Kathryn Walker and Margaret Woods found in their classic 1976 study of homemakers in Syracuse, New York, washing machines, dryers, dishwashers, and other appliances did not actually increase free time. The average homemaker spent the same eight hours a day on housework as she had before she owned such appliances, only now she spent longer hours shopping, arranging for household repairs, and paying bills.[8] Today's parenting services, April felt, didn't save time either: "I still feel inside a whole world of whipped up, overbusy parents, and whipped up, overscheduled kids."

While the service mall relieved tired and busy parents of some time-consuming, difficult tasks, it also devalued amateur family efforts—April's son making his own lopsided Spanish mission, the teenager stepping onto the strobe-lit floor without the animator's extended hand. By comparison, they seemed less impressive, more a source of worry and shame.

Making Up for It Somewhere Else

Like Grace Weaver, who outsourced some tasks to the love coach but also drew a boundary, April felt the need to balance outsourcing with some activity that reaffirmed the idea that she was authoring her own life, raising her own kids. If she was going to hire experts in some part of her life, she wanted to compensate by "getting back to basics," as she put it, in others. "The kids are so cooped up, scheduled, aimed. Sometimes you just feel like you need to give them more rope, and you need more yourself as well."

"Looking around, I discovered a farm with nine horses and a man named Don who gave riding lessons a mile from our house," April explained. "Don taught the kids to ride. Then we got to grooming the horses." In the course of things, Don, a widower, became a good friend, and when he was stricken with cancer, April's family took him in while he underwent treatments and twice a day drove out to feed and water his nine horses and clean the barn. "You do a lot of things in your life," April said thoughtfully, her finger circling the rim of her coffee cup. "That's the one we feel the gladdest about."

I spoke to April's husband, Martin, by car speakerphone a week later. He was driving to the farm, April at his side, the boys in the back. "We love going to the stables to take care of the horses," he said. "They're like family." I asked him how he had managed to help with the horses and still work those killer hours at the law firm:

> I get up at three thirty, put on my sweats, drive to the farm, water and feed the horses and clean up the barn from four

a.m. to five a.m. I drive home, shower, dress, and go to my law office by six a.m. Actually, I shovel shit at Don's. Then I shower, dress, drive to my law office, and shovel shit there.

Back in her breakfast nook, April elaborated, "I do the afternoon shift. Weekends, we're all out there. One time the whole family walked all the way there and back."

This wasn't just another activity; it was, at least on April's part, a quite conscious strategy—of counterbalancing. She described a moment at the barn:

This one very hot day the water troughs were really low. There's no nearby running water. You have to drag hoses to the troughs. The troughs were mossy, so I said, "Okay, boys, we've got to clean the troughs before we fill them." When we drained the troughs, the water created huge, muddy puddles over patches of dried manure. The boys ended up soaked to the bone. They made mud pies. Then they began a mud house, then a neighborhood, then a city. After hours my oldest, covered head to toe in mud, said, "Mom, this is the best day of my life."

April had outsourced many activities that her mother—a generation back and a step less affluent—had done herself (child care) or done without (kiddy chauffeur to games). At the same time, she riveted her family's attention on one goal—caring for the horses—that called for their collective exertion, sacrifice, and fun. All this infused more than a touch of village into their pressured lives—and not just for her family. By stepping in when Don was sick, they extended the village to him as well.

Like April, others struggled, too, to defend against an expert-standards-oriented way of life, creating out-of-time moments that felt almost homemade as a way of taking their life back into their own hands. One working mother who had, as she put it, "child- and house-care coverage from 7:00 a.m. to 5:00 p.m." for her five-

and ten-year-old, organized "weekend stay-at-home camping trips." "We challenge the whole family to live without electricity from 4 p.m. Friday to Monday morning. We unplug the house. We set up the Coleman stove on the picnic table and sleep in the backyard. We use the toilet but we set the rules so we can't turn on the light to get there. The kids talk about it all the time."

Others didn't so much compensate for loss as invest symbolic value in objects or activities that represented home—the intimate life they felt had been sacrificed to the market. For a surprising number of the people I talked to, a new stove was a particularly meaning-charged object. As one woman recalled:

> One of my happiest memories is standing on a stool in my pj's, stirring popover batter with my dad on Sunday mornings. I have that association with stoves. I love stoves. And I love our stove and our new convection oven. It cuts the time you have to spend cooking. The sad thing is, we don't use it very often.

I was reminded of a real estate broker's description of how prospective buyers explored the homes she showed them:

> The first room they go to is the kitchen. . . . And in the kitchen they imagine the family all together. They want to know about the stove and oven and countertop, but when I check back, I find they barely use them.

A new oven, a new countertop, a kitchen remodel, these can become important substitutes, symbols of a happy family gathering. In the same way, an airport-shop gift for a child can represent, to a traveling parent, time with a son or daughter at home. Two-income families actually give their children more gifts than single-income families, even with the same disposable income, suggesting that parents may be trying to substitute a gift they can give for another that, at the moment, they can't.[9]

After recounting her adventures at the horse barn, April

walked me to her front door, her lively lab by her side, and left me with this parting thought:

> It won't be long before Jimmy's is selling Swiss Family Robinson kits, with CD and video produced by a get-away-from-it-all coach. These days we need experts to tell us how to get away from experts. But you know, I think I'll skip that one. My hands are such a mess from making mud pies.

Chapter 7

Making Five-Year-Olds Laugh Is Harder Than You Think

My grandmother had four children, the average for 1900, including my aunt Elizabeth. Birthday photos show squinting boys in squashed hats and girls with fixed smiles sitting, arms folded, at a table on the front lawn. A birthday was loosely planned around a family sit-down with a cake baked by either my grandmother or an Irish maid, Mary, who was hired the year my aunt Elizabeth was born and who lived with the family for thirty years.[1]

More than a century later, in the upscale San Francisco neighborhood of Michael and Anastasia Haber, parents regularly engaged Sophie, a birthday planner, to ensure a day to remember. Sophie helps organize the guest list, puts on the treasure hunt, and paints cat's whiskers on four-year-old faces. She brings along an orange-haired, big-nosed clown, Spotty Joe, who does magic tricks. As Anastasia recounted:

> Kids walk into a birthday party these days and ask, "Where's the coordinator? Where's the itinerary?"—because Sophie hands them out. It's what kids around here expect. Afterward, they write Sophie these sweet thank-you notes:

> Dear Sophie, Thank you very much for the fun birthday.
> Love from your friend,
> Harrison.

Or even

> Dear Sophie,
> I was wondering how you are today.
> Love, Maya

Sophie was probably wonderful. Michael granted her that, but he had been dead-set against hiring a planner for his daughter's birthday. To him it had felt over the top, a "status thing." And it gave kids the idea that they couldn't create their own fun. He had been perfectly willing to hire other services to help with the kids—a nanny, a tutor, a piano teacher—but a birthday party? Couldn't a parent at least do that? Why thank Sophie? Why not thank Dad?

We were seated on the spacious living-room couch, two plump dogs, Rufus and Dufus, nipping each other at our feet. An energetic, fit forty-eight-year-old, dressed in a blue turtleneck and brown slacks, Michael Haber leaned down to scold the dogs, who continued nipping, unconcerned, a state he took with good humor.

Michael and Anastasia were private equity fund managers whose firms had sent them for several years each to Hong Kong, Paris, and most recently to a small town outside Geneva. I had already talked with Anastasia about many things, including her husband's "faith in the global free market"—a topic that at first seemed completely unrelated to the issues raised by hiring a birthday planner.

Talking about his three daughters, Raquelle, Marcela, and Beatrice, his face softened. "They're *amazing.*" He described their interests, quirks, and dreams before turning to the question of how, as a highly pressured businessman, he made time to be with them:

> My wife works full time and I'm in the air a third of the time—Hong Kong, Salt Lake City, New York. So we have a weekly housecleaner, a full-time nanny, and a dog walker. We hired them because we need time with our kids and each other, not because we want to show off to the neighbors. I'm so thankful we can afford it.

Neither Michael nor Anastasia grew up with domestic help. But, he said: "We don't feel guilty about having help, not like Anastasia's radical sister in Oregon. We just need to live our two-career lives, and we treat those we hire warmly and fairly, like the employees I hire in my firm."

Michael used to take care of things at home himself. "When I was a bachelor," he told me, "I rented a house, rototilled a vegetable garden, and tended rose bushes. But roses take endless maintenance. They get aphids, they get one disease after another. It was a big hassle. And complicated. I'd never think of doing a thing like that now."

When he married Anastasia, they held a ceremony he described as "so low key you could barely notice."

> We hired a part-time minister who sold industrial machinery on the side. I'm scared of wedding planners and luckily our three daughters aren't the wedding-planner types. . . . Well, I'm not sure about the middle one. She's joined a sorority at the University of Texas. We might be in for it there.

After they had children, Anastasia hired a gardener to tend their small backyard plot once a month and a series of child-care workers. "We had a very nice woman who tragically lost her only two sons at Jonestown," Michael told me.

> Then we had Guadalupe, who only speaks Spanish, which I don't speak (Anastasia does), whom we found through Anastasia's sister. We had a live-in nanny named Melba, a lovely

> woman in her fifties from Detroit, a trained nurse who owned a gun; she wanted a pleasant job where she didn't need to carry it. We had Kula from Greece. Anastasia knows them all better than I do.

In addition, Anastasia hired someone to take out Rufus and Dufus while they were at work and to board them when the family went out of town. As Michael talked, his voice rose.

> I saw a girl walking six dogs one Saturday. *Saturday.* Why do people even have dogs if they can't manage to walk them on Saturdays? Or Sundays? Why would they hire someone to do it when they could do it themselves? Why *have* a dog?

Why have a dog? Why have a wedding? Why have a child? These questions often arose, whether explicitly or not, when middle-class, time-pressed people considered outsourcing intimate, personal tasks. To the suggestion that he hire someone to buy his holiday gifts—a growing niche service—one of my interviewees responded incredulously, "Why give a gift if you don't choose it yourself?" Of a hired photo-album assembler, another asked, "Why keep a family photo album if you aren't going to pick and label the pictures yourself?"

And this is how Michael used to feel about birthday parties. "Why have one," he had said to Anastasia, "if you're going to hire a stranger who doesn't even know your kid to plan it?" But then something happened that changed his view. It was three years ago, but to Michael, Anastasia, and their youngest daughter, Raquelle, it was like it happened yesterday.

Michael had been traveling a great deal and Raquelle's fifth birthday was approaching. "All of her school friends hire these party planners," he said to his wife. "I don't know why they do it except to show off. Some things parents should get off their duffs and do themselves, like organizing their kid's party. We should do it ourselves." "We?" Anastasia had replied. "Okay, me," Michael had said. "*I'll* do everything. It's simple enough. And Raquelle will love it."

Michael wasn't trying to counterbalance an overserviced lifestyle with some new back-to-basics activity nor was he taking a general stand against the market's intrusion into family life. He just wanted to snatch back a single small task from the service mall—one he didn't think should be on offer in the first place—and in the process emphasize his role as an involved, if itinerant, father.

As a child, Michael had had only one birthday party and the memory of it was painful.

> We were dirt poor. My father pressed pants in a factory. My mother worked in a shop. Later, they both ran a small grocery store, then a small bakery. My grandmother brought me up because my parents worked six days a week. The big toes and second toes on both of my feet are deformed because my shoes were always too small, and my parents delayed getting me larger ones as long as I could bear it. We lived in a bungalow the size of this living room.

His grandmother and parents raged at one another constantly, and in their small quarters there was no escape. It was to his bone-weary parents that Michael, then eight, appealed. Might he have a birthday party like his better-off schoolmates? They said yes:

> Twenty children came and we had little sandwiches and cakes my father had baked. We played in the backyard. But all I remember was how exhausted my parents were. I never had another party.

Now, Michael was happy to be living, as he put it, the American dream—financial success, a loving wife, and beautiful children. But such dreams were fragile he felt:

> America is held together by a toothpick and a dream. Society is constantly shaken up because we don't stay where we are. We move. Then our children move, and move again. Our marriages break up. Our generations live apart. There's a lot of anxiety for business to cash in on, and here in America they do.

Michael compared America to the small town in Switzerland where he and Anastasia had lived for eight years in the 1990s:

> People had lived in that place since the thirteenth century. They thought of the town as theirs, and looked after it because it was. Our kids could go anywhere because there were always people watching out. For them it was a big shock to come back to the States. Here each family is on its own. Couples move from place to place, like we do. No one feels part of anything larger. It's like we're a collection of bits and pieces floating in a vast sea.

With the sense of community gone, Michael felt, "stuff and services filled the void." Party planners like Sophie might be nice, but they also took over a space the family had abandoned, and, like a number of others I talked to, he felt torn about that. Anastasia mostly agreed with Michael: "In the U.S. we live in a culture of want-want-want, buy-buy-buy, dump-dump-dump."

Neither Anastasia nor Michael wanted to live all their lives in a Swiss village. On the other hand, they worried about raising children without a community around them to help ward off the constant pressure to want, buy, and dump things. To be a good parent, they both felt they had to fend off a certain amount of commercialism. One way to do this was to build up your own family traditions. At least that's what Michael was thinking as his daughter's fifth birthday approached.

He sent out Evites to Raquelle's friends, Anastasia recalled. He ordered a cake and bought a pin-the-tail-on-the-donkey set with blindfolds. He blew up balloons. He twisted and hung pink and white streamers from wall to wall. He planned a few games and decided to provide the entertainment himself, dressing in a broad-brimmed hat, khaki shirt and shorts, and tall leather boots, like the character Crocodile Dundee. After the ice cream and cake had been served, the moment arrived. Before an audience of seven little girls (he later recalled twenty), Michael made a dramatic entrance, whirling his hat and stalking back and forth. He talked of fierce crocodiles, jumping kangaroos, of cuddly koala bears in the gum trees of the Australian desert. Then, after five minutes, he ran out of things to say.

In a bemused tone, Anastasia recounted:

> Michael had no plan for what to do next. Worse yet, the children thought his outfit was odd and his accent not all that funny. They began to stare at his knobby knees. Then they began to fidget. Then the whole thing fell apart.

Michael remembered Raquelle's birthday with dismay.

> There must have been over twenty girls. And the party dragged on and on. Do you know how *long* two hours is? I didn't know it would be so bloody hard! The girls needed constant organizing and entertaining. You have a quick two seconds to engage them. It's like being a continual stand-up comic. If there's any gap, they break into little groups. It nearly killed me.

How did Raquelle respond? She said, "You're not as good as Spotty Joe."

At birthday parties the girls were used to a planner briskly directing them from one game to the next and the next. Left to themselves, they felt lost and fell into confusion. Michael continued:

> When I couldn't hold their attention, the kids scattered in every direction, and the parents had to put down their wine-glasses to deal with them. I'm sure they were tired, so not very grateful to me either. Most of them hire planners and probably didn't want me to start any backyard do-it-yourself movement. They were probably thinking, "That'll teach him!"

A neighbor, Reena, had watched the event closely from the kitchen door. Afterward she drew Michael, still in his Crocodile Dundee outfit, aside. "Michael," she told him, "leave it to the experts. They know what five-year-olds think is funny. They know games five-year-olds like. We don't. Don't embarrass yourself. Leave it to them."

In the weeks that followed, Michael was first baffled, then ashamed. Slowly he began to feel that Reena was right. Professionals did know more than parents about what five-year-olds think is funny. He should have left it to Sophie.

Building Home Life Here, Destroying Companies There

Michael worked as a private equity fund manager for a company that specialized in "asset stripping," breaking up businesses on the verge of failure—or just not profitable enough—and selling off their assets. For ten years, Anastasia had done the same job, but now, as a financial advisor to nonprofits, she saw that whole line of work in a new light: "A lot of people don't understand that if they park money with an investment firm, some money manager may, on their behalf, take over and asset strip some little company they've never heard of," she told me. Anastasia thought it was fine to asset strip a badly managed company in a big city because laid-off workers could find similar work elsewhere in the area. But to asset strip a company factory that was the economic heart of a small town? Why would a person with Michael's love of family and community do that? She wondered:

> Michael is always saying America is a land without community, and so people turn to shopping to fill that void. But then a while ago he talked about wanting to asset strip a Virginia-based vacuum cleaner factory and of us moving there while he did it. That's what a lot of private equity funds do these days. They buy up shares in a company, take on a lot of its debt, and then break it apart, which means firing a lot of people. It's called "cleaning up" the company. The company closes down and the inventory is sold to X, the buildings to Y, the intellectual property to Z. Small businesses go under. Neighborhoods disappear. Families break up.
>
> When Michael wanted us to move to that small town in Virginia while he asset stripped the company, I said: "Are you out of your mind? How can you tell yourself 'I've created a lot of net worth for investors,' when you know you've disrupted all these people's lives? And you want us to *live* in that community *as* it's torn apart? Send our kids to school there? Have these fired workers as our neighbors? Our friends?"

Anastasia saw the contradiction between Michael's striving to resist the encroachment of the market into his own home by running his daughter's birthday party while at the same time leading the charge of the market as it destroyed other communities and families. She saw the same contradiction among Michael's colleagues at the equity fund:

> They value education, hard work, and good friends. They feel bright, creative, cutting edge. They don't think of themselves as making money; that would be crass. If an asset strip is clever and legal, they admire it. But what's the effect of what they do? That's what I find troubling about the world I used to work in.

When I spoke to other couples in the financial world about Michael's "schizophrenia," as Anastasia put it, many shrugged with tilted head in a gesture of helplessness and recognition: "It might not make sense, but that's how it is. What can you do?"

In the end, the Habers did not move to Virginia. In this case, Michael listened to Anastasia: save the village. But in his own home, Michael succumbed to the market.

> If you're going to have a party and you don't live near a beach or park, and the child is five or less, and you have a bunch of kids for more than an hour, they will start smearing cake on the walls and each other. I thought I could do it. But I was wrong. It's really best to hire an expert.

Michael knew to respect a superior product and for the five-year-old set, Sophie's party-planning service trumped his Crocodile Dundee. That was the way the market worked. So he saved the factory in Virginia but gave in to the market competition at home.

Many of the people I spoke to shared Michael's desire to snatch back a familial role they felt slipping away. One woman hired an interior decorator to help her redesign her living room. The decorator urged her to buy and hang on the wall a large gilt-framed imitation eighteenth-century-style portrait of a country squire in a curled wig. "I realized that was *his* idea of a nice living room, not mine. Nice guy, but I thanked him, paid him, and did the rest myself." A busy male executive, whose assistant had sent birthday flowers to his mother on his behalf, said, "When my mother got the flowers, she asked me what kind they were. I didn't know. Daisies? Roses? I was embarrassed. I figured I'd do it myself next time."

A professor relayed yet another story:

> The wife of a colleague had just given birth to a new baby. They had set up a gift registry at Babies "R" Us, so I went to my computer and clicked on the registry. There were about a

> dozen choices. I didn't want to pick the most expensive, since I don't know the couple that well. But I didn't want to be cheap, so I didn't choose the least expensive thing either. I aimed for something in the middle, gave my Visa details, and that was that. But then I felt strange. I hadn't visited the baby. I hadn't gotten in the car. I hadn't looked over toys or baby clothing. I hadn't wrapped the gift or written the card. I didn't deliver the gift. I hadn't even called to congratulate them on the birth! A month later I couldn't remember what the gift was, only how much it cost. So I bought some little plastic measuring spoons, got in the car, and paid the family a visit.

The decorator, the assistant, the online store—all were there to guide, to help, to save time. And in each case, customers wondered, is this act mine or yours? Does it express me or you, or me through you? In each case, the client outsourced a personal act and then tried to recover some aspect of the act as a personal expression of him- or herself. Largely unremarkable in the day-to-day flow of middle-class life, these moments nonetheless stand out as minor signals of distress, signs that something doesn't feel right, that a line has been crossed.

When I asked the professor how she felt about the gift registry, she reflected:

> It seemed like an automatic Visa-to-baby gift. It eclipsed me. I felt cheated—and maybe guilty—that I'd done the whole thing so fast in order to get back to my work. Mainly, it made me sad to miss out on the feeling of giving a gift.

Like Michael, she felt called to buck the system to recapture some sense of an authentic act.

In the end, Michael felt that he had failed. But what did it mean to fail? In my final interview with Anastasia—she had since left the financial field and was happily enrolled in a professional cooking school—she reflected back on the birthday party: "At first I was embarrassed. Then it seemed hilarious. But you should hear what Raquelle thought of it." Now age eight, she told me cheerfully over the phone: "I remember Daddy went all out. That's just like him. I'm so lucky to have a dad like that."

Chapter 8

A High Score in Family Memory Creation

Driving from the airport to a town outside Minneapolis, it seems as if, in the soft light of a spring afternoon, I pass through a lesson in rural poverty and wealth in America. First come rambling, disheveled farmhouses, rusted mailboxes, rubber-tire rope swings, and old pickups, then expansive fields of early corn that give way to skirts of lawn encircling hilltop mansions. I turn at a sign that reads JOHNSON'S FARM, actually a twenty-acre settlement of affluent homes, an upscale version of the farmland-to-suburb transition in process all around my aunt Elizabeth's home in Maine. I stop at an iron gate at the bottom of a great hill, step out of my rental car, and ring the gate-side buzzer.

A child answers. "Hello? . . . Mommy, it's the lady."

The mechanical gate slowly swings open and so begins my visit with the Hart family, clients of "Family360"—a parenting-evaluation service highlighted by the *New York Times Magazine* in their 2002 survey of America's "ninety-nine most innovative ideas of the year."[1] It was, and still is, an unusual addition to the parenting industry.

Created by LeaderWorks, a management consulting firm based

in Monument, Colorado, Family360 was started by two men, one an executive coach at Lockheed and the other a human resources expert at Merck. The service offers to coach busy executives at such corporations as General Motors, IBM, Honeywell, Goodrich, and DuPont on how to become better fathers. When told about it, April Benner and Michael Haber expressed surprise. "What will they think of next?" April had laughed. Michael became lightly sarcastic: "What a clever business inroad into an anxious market," he'd said. "Why didn't I think of it myself?" So who, I wondered, would embrace Family360? And what did they get out of it? These were the questions that had brought me to the outskirts of Minneapolis.

Family360 was based on a corporate prototype called Management360, wherein one or two consultants—or coaches, as they also call themselves—evaluate an executive through a series of interviews with his secretary, boss, coworkers, and clients. (The company's brochures/Web site featured only male clients.) The consultants gain a "360-degree view" of the manager, analyze the data, and draw up PowerPoint presentations to describe executive performance in categories such as "develops innovative change strategies," "identifies potential problem areas," and "initiates timely responsive action plans."

Family360 brings these ideas home. With the consultant, the client-dad convenes a meeting of the family—wife or partner, children, mother and father, stepparents, stepchildren, sisters and brothers, grandparents, and, if there is one, nanny. Each family member is handed a pencil or pen and a fifty-five-item questionnaire, or the father can himself read the items aloud. For example, "pays attention to personal feelings when communicating"; "says 'I love you' often enough"; "solves problems without getting angry or keeping silent"; "works hard to provide food and a home for the family." Everyone in the family then rates the father on a scale of 1 to 7 for each item. The numbers correspond to a value that the father is advised to write out on a large pad of paper set on an easel:

1. Needs Significant Attention
2. Needs Some Attention
3. Almost Acceptable
4. Acceptable
5. More Than Acceptable
6. Strength
7. Significant Strength

After family members record Dad's scores on 3 by 5 cards, he collects everyone's answers and later, privately, calculates his average for all fifty-five items. The family then reconvenes for a group discussion and the father is asked to reflect on his "personal and family inhibitors," as the consultants call them—that is, anything that might a lower a score, such as "treating family members like employees" or "not leaving time for personal conversations."

With the help of the consultants, the father then creates an "Action Plan" drawing on a list of "best practices" spelled out in a Family360 work booklet.[2] These practices include suggestions to:

> "Listen to uplifting or classical music during your drive home to get your mind in the proper spirit."
>
> "Stimulate communication during dinner. Put preselected questions on (or under) the dinner plates of family members."
>
> "Inventory family members' strengths."
>
> "Audit your family conversations." For this "you may want to enlist the aid of another family member."
>
> "Keep a pad of paper and envelopes in your briefcase or pocketbook. Write a short, personal weekly letter to each family member, even when you are not traveling."

> "Motivate yourself to eliminate poor listening and problem-solving behaviors. For example, if impatience is something you are trying to improve, offer $10 each time you are caught raising your voice or showing a lack of patience."

> "Cut out articles from *The Wall Street Journal*. . . . Bring the articles to dinner and have each member of the family read the articles and discuss."

Other "Action Items" include apologizing—an act described as elevating a spouse or child to the role of "personal coach or consultant," or simply showing respect. "If I treated people at work the same way I treat my wife," one client told the consultant, "they'd fire me."[3]

Armed with company-provided bar graphs and pie charts of fathering "behaviors," the consultants then help the dad implement his Action Plan. In what they describe as a "hard-hitting, personalized change management session," they specify ways the corporate father can maximize his "high-leverage" family activities. He can join a family game night by speakerphone while on the road. Or he can go for a walk with his child every day, "even if it's only to the end of the driveway." Such activities take little time, the team points out, but get good results. A father can even create "communication opportunities" while doing dishes or waiting in line with a child at a store.[4]

Crucially, the advisers propose ways for a man to increase his score on the 7-point "Family Memory Creation" scale, a scale based on the idea—or perhaps fantasy—that a father can engineer the memory his children have of him. The more high-leverage behaviors he performs, the higher a dad's memory score, and the richer his family "portfolio." The creators of Family360 envision all this as a starter service, to be followed by other paid services—which target more specific family problems and open the possibility of the perpetually monitored family.

In its corporate-speak way, the service is trying to deliver the basic and poignant message that families need time and attention. So far, so good. But what took me aback was one basic assumption embedded in the company's approach. "Today's tough organizational climate demands the most from employees," reads the service's online ad, "including ever-increasing amounts of their time, energy and commitment." Family360 takes that "tough climate" as a given. Being a better father doesn't require rethinking the "ever-increasing" hours or travel time a high-stress job might entail. Like so many army chaplains, the Family360 coaches help executives cope at home so as to more smoothly settle into the corporate trenches.

Child-rearing advice books in J. Porter's day—generally written by men and addressed to women—featured a father supervising his wife in her full-time devotion to the children.[5] Expert advice from psychologists, educators, doctors, philanthropists, and reformers likewise focused exclusively on mothers.[6] But the twenty-first-century American ideal increasingly features the "sharing husband" and the "involved dad." In the modern two-paycheck home, a dad is expected to flop onto the couch to read aloud *The Three Bears*, help a child build a block castle, and notice when the baby's diaper needs changing. And this ideal stands in modified form, even if the wife doesn't work outside the home. Unfortunately, over the last decades, men's hours of work have remained long, while their jobs have grown less secure. So the notion of the happily involved dad inevitably conflicts with ever more anxiety-provoking demands at work—a conflict that Family360 tacitly resolves. The answer to market pressure outside the home? Market thinking inside it.

Family360 in Action

I drove up a steep hill to a majestic three-story, white-pillared home overlooking six acres of freshly cut green meadow. The front door opened before I rang the bell, and Faith Hart, a short, blond, blue-eyed forty-three-year-old full-time homemaker, stepped forward. She was dressed in a golden cable-knit sweater and she wore small diamond stud earrings. While shy in manner, she spoke in the steady, soothing voice of someone who handles complex situations well. I could imagine her as a CEO, the calm center of a bustling enterprise. She walked me through a hall into a spacious, comfortable living room and out a glass back door, past a pool and tennis court, to a vegetable garden, chicken coop, and a view of distant hilltop estates beyond. After we dropped my overnight bag in a poolside guest room, she explained:

> Peter and I are lucky to live here, but we were very happy when we were dirt-poor, too. When we were first married we were *so* broke we used to go to the card shop and point to the cards we would have bought each other if we'd had any money. In those days, I made everything. I baked all our bread. My mom gave us wheat and we used a friend's wheat grinder. I was in awe of the churchwomen who made their own clothes, canned all their fruits and vegetables. I wondered if I could ever measure up to them, but I learned. We were saving our pennies, but we loved feeling self-reliant, too.

Faith and Peter went on to have seven children, and the family was very close-knit—partly through joint worship in the Mormon Church, and partly through Faith and Peter's strong efforts to counteract the instability caused by Peter's many job moves. "We've lived here just three years," Faith remarked, "and we've moved seven times in twenty-one years of marriage." Most recently they had moved for Peter's latest job as an executive with a large clothing company.

Faith invited me to a cup of tea in their living room, where the walls were covered with family photographs, large and small. Mantelpiece images in many other homes I'd visited proudly featured children one by one—at graduation, on a ski slope, in a sports team lineup. Here, in picture after picture, the Harts were a tribe, a flock. In one large photo, on a gloriously sunny day, the two parents and seven children are squinting into the sun in front of the St. Anthony Falls Bridge in Minneapolis. In another, they are gathered before a Christmas tree.

Faith had homeschooled three of her children, including her oldest daughter, Trisha, for fourteen years. Now, the two oldest were away at college and Faith was still homeschooling five-year-old Amber, who, after we settled on the living-room couch, approached us to share her new poem about a tree that fell on a house.

Faith had offered to let me follow the family for a full day. Before I arrived in the early afternoon, she had completed Amber's lesson plan and prepared a casserole for dinner. Her fifth-grader, Bianca, had returned from school, and the two children were mixing batter to make tops and bottoms for ice-cream sandwiches, a favorite "Family Night" treat. Leaving Bianca in charge of Amber, Faith drove with me in her minivan to fetch seven-year-old Brett from his Cub Scout meeting, circled back to collect Bianca and Amber, and headed off, with four of us in tow, to fifteen-year-old Randy's lacrosse game. "It's a logistical nightmare," Faith told me proudly, "but we try to have the whole family go to each child's games."

As we approached the bleachers on this chilly afternoon, an older couple in parkas and scarves began waving from their seats—Peter's mother and her husband, John. They, too, tried to attend all the games. So seven of us were now seated on two rows of benches under warm blankets in the barely filled bleachers. Ten minutes later, spotting us from below, a man waved and bounded up the steps: Peter.

Lean and athletic in a blue button-down shirt and pullover, Peter kissed Faith, shook my hand, sat down, and, hands on knees, intently scanned the field for number 16 in a blue jersey. "I've made eighty percent of my daughters' four p.m. swim meets. And

I'm about there with Randy's lacrosse," was the first thing he said before calling down the field: "Go, go, *go*!"

While players jogged forward and back across the field below, Peter described his work schedule to me:

> I work sixty hours a week. I have employees who are in England. So I wake up in the morning at five thirty, I read my own personal scriptures or sometimes step out for fifteen minutes to our nearby church. I briefly check my e-mail before we start Family Prayer at six thirty a.m. Then I spend another twenty to thirty minutes on e-mail. And then, before I go to bed, I'll look at my BlackBerry for fifteen to twenty minutes. I leave the house at seven a.m. and get home at seven p.m. So these are twelve-hour days—
>
> Hey, Randy! *Way to go*—
>
> On the weekend I'm always checking my e-mail. I'm rarely off the clock for large periods of time.

The family was just as tightly scheduled. Before getting the kids off to school, Faith and Peter often tried to attend a short, sunrise service at their nearby church—which provided inspiration for their lives, guided their activities, and offered them community. Each weekday morning the entire family dressed and came downstairs for Family Prayer, held in a small room that they used for a household chapel, from 6:30 a.m. to 6:45 a.m. This was followed twice a week by back-to-back half-hour piano lessons: 6:45 to 7:15 for Amber, 7:15 to 7:45 for Bianca, and 7:45 to 8:15 for Brett. After the last child's lesson, the kids filed out the door and into the minivan to be driven to the nearest school bus stop.

At the end of the day, the family regrouped for dinner. Once a week they had Family Night, a time for prayer, family business, and a scripture lesson. I found a seat in the circle as Peter started:

> Dear Heavenly Father, we thank you that we can have this Family Night tonight, we thank you that we could watch Randy's game today. The team won, and we pray that Randy's neck injury heals. . . . We wish Neil and Trisha could be with us . . . but thankfully they are in college and doing things to realize their full potential. . . .

"Okay," Peter said, "family business?" A hum of talk rose from the children, like an orchestra tuning up. When was Tae Kwon Do? What about Peter's two tickets for a Vikings' game? "Can I come, too?" Sylvia, fourteen, asked.

> PETER: How about you, Randy?
> RANDY: I have a dance that night.
> PETER: Is it a church dance?
> RANDY: It is a church dance.
> PETER: Okay.

And so it went, through talk about what First Corinthians said about bodies being "a sacred temple of God" and the need for people—he looked at his sulking teenage daughter, Sylvia—to dress modestly. They moved on to why kids dress Goth or even cut themselves (because they're unhappy), before Peter returned the conversation to Corinthians. According to the teachings of the Mormon Church, Peter was the head of the Hart family, its guide, its final word. But though he clearly ran Family Night, he took interruptions and challenges in good spirit, laughed at the byplay, and combined his serious purpose with a flexibility that revealed a more modern style of fatherhood.

After the circle broke up, Bianca and Amber brought out their freshly baked cookies. Everyone scooped ice cream onto them and ate their homemade, drippy sandwiches while comparing favorite flavors of ice cream. When the dishes were cleared, Peter and Faith and I sat down at the dining-room table.

The Authority of the Company

I'd long wondered why watching a child compete at sport has become the quintessential American parenting act. But that aside, I was looking at a man in motion twelve hours a day who made it to 80 percent of his son's lacrosse games, who focused lovingly on the lives of his children, who, along with Faith, gently enforced their child-centered rules—television limits of three hours per week per child, no cell phones or dating until age sixteen—who conducted Family Night with authority and warmth. The time had come to pop the question: Why would this man pay Family360 consultants two thousand dollars to help him become an even better dad than he already was? As Peter explained, Family360 had originally come to him.

> I'd participated in a lot of 360 evaluations at work. I'd heard good things about Family360. I actually knew and trusted one of the guys that started it. And I'd had a terrible relationship with my dad. So when I was approached, I said "yes."

His reasons were personal:

> My own father never came to one school event in my entire boyhood—middle school, high school, college—not one. Not my swim meets. Not my baseball games. Not my football games. He saw me swim *once* in my whole life. I was an All-American in college. He never saw me at the NCAA Championships. I played golf tournaments in high school and college. He has never seen me play.

Faith added:

> Peter's parents divorced and his father remarried. When his father's second wife spoke proudly of her children, Peter's dad never said anything about him. One time, Peter's sister piped

> up, "Hey, Dad, did you know Peter won a national championship in swimming?" His Dad said "No. . . ." "Did you know he was valedictorian when he graduated from business school?" His Dad said, "Oh, really?"

Single-mindedly devoted to his own career as the head of a military academy, Peter's father ignored all accomplishments that were not strictly academic. A bright child, a gifted athlete, but struggling perhaps with dyslexia, Peter could never catch his father's eye. "All I remember is my mother in the bleachers in her waitress's uniform, cheering me on."

Peter was seven and his sister nine when his parents divorced, and his mother began working two jobs to support the children through what Peter recalls as grim years:

> After the divorce, Mom put me in KinderCare before and after school—which I *hated.* It was a jail. There was constant staff turnover so no one knew who I was. I sat on a mat. Or I put my head on my desk. I remember hanging on to the gate watching my mom drive away. I was in a holding pen until the bus came for school.

Peter's father made weekly phone calls and paid monthly child support (although his payments didn't rise along with his salary or the cost of living). He went on to marry for a second, third, and fourth time, and his mother married twice more:

> Come. Go. Come. Go. For the first twenty-two years of my life, that's what I saw. I resolved that when I got married, I was *staying* married. Although it's not that I wanted my parents to stay married. They fought and yelled horribly. My sister and I used to cry ourselves to sleep in bed listening to them.

The Mormon Church presented Peter with a different vision of a father—the Holy Father—one who listened. The church also awarded Faith a respect for traditional homemaking that she found lacking in wider society. The church filled a great need for them both, offering a refuge from mainstream American culture. But, again, what did Family360 add to the mix?

For Peter, it added an aura of workplace efficiency to the role of fatherhood, a discipline almost like religious practice, with its step-by-step ladder to success at home. The Family360 evaluation sheet was like a report card. It told him where he stood, the highs and lows of his "behaviors" in relation to Faith and the children. For his marriage to Faith, the report read:

Rater Category: Spouse

Highs:
Demonstrates Love
Fun and Humorous
Is kind toward family when they do wrong

Lows:
Partnership/Respect
Kindly respects differences of opinion
Encourages everyone to participate in decision

Suggestions (to work on the lows):
Involve a "family coach" to audit speech
Schedule a service week with activities
Give service as part of family time

Rater Category: Children

Highs:
Says "I love you" enough
Support
Sense of Purpose

Lows:
Communication/Listening
Problem Solving
Openly talks about important things

Suggestions:
Implement "Rewind and Replay" [e.g., make a greater effort to understand what others are telling him]
Hold a brainstorming session for answers
Use commute to mentally prepare for home

So how did Peter implement the consultant's suggestion to "use commute to mentally prepare for home," I asked.

> It's true that I come home agitated. But the consultant gave me an idea for how to come home more calmly. He told me, "When you drive home, why not imagine a worst-case scenario. The house is trashed. Everyone is gone." So when I do come home and find everyone there, I'm grateful. There's a little mess, so what?

Overall, the highs far outnumbered the lows, giving Peter a 6.2 out of 7—an A—for his behavior as husband and father. He was delighted. In an uncertain world, the score was clear and high. Peter's father may have aced his academic tests, but Peter was acing the one test his father had flunked.

Perhaps Peter's high score accounted for the fact that on this family at least, the influence of Family360 seemed minimal. Outside of the discussions that I initiated, I heard little about the 1–7 scores, efficiency-minded "high-leverage activities," or flowcharts of parenting behaviors. But what is striking is the enormous respect for market ideas that pervaded the whole exercise. Peter put a high premium on the measurable over the intuitive, the quantifiable over the organic. He welcomed his family members' comments on his behavior as a father but relied on a corporation-minded expert to judge him. The market validation of his parenting seemed to him superior to any he might come up with himself.

And therein lies the paradox of Family360. On the one hand, the program helped men improve their domestic lives. On the other, it brought the company, its lingo, its mental categories, its scales and graphs, right into the heart of the home. Just as the love coach Evan Katz escorted eager singles into the dating marketplace, Family360 took families into the world of corporate management. Both mingled the languages of home and business. A dating coach I talked to advised a lovelorn client to become the "CEO" of her love life by, among other things, appointing three friends as her "board of advisers" and offering a financial incentive to the first one to get her a hot date. In the same way, Family360 advised men to climb the corporate ladder of fatherhood and to perceive child rearing as a management issue, subordinate to the iron-clad demands of the corporation itself. As with professionally organized birthday parties and store-bought Spanish mission models, the focus was on results, not on the journey toward them. In a family, ideally speaking, the acts that deepen bonds constitute the very essence and purpose of intimate life. In the company mindset of Family360, however, those acts are reconceived as good "behaviors" and high-yield investments. The market comes home, not simply through a paid service, but through the great reverence for a business way of imagining life.

Before leaving the Harts, I asked Faith to comment on Peter's record of "Family Memory Creation"—a category measured by Family360 even though the score was not broken out. I was interested in whether she felt it was possible to deliberately manufacture a memory of oneself. Memories leap about, after all, twist and cast long irregular shadows in a child's consciousness in ways quite beyond anyone's will. Psychotherapists speak of magnified "screen memories" behind which lurk years of unremembered life. Could the very idea of making memory be a Family360-made fantasy of familial control?

Faith reflected:

> You have to intend things. If you go with the flow, life drifts. I remember my dad always falling asleep in front of the golf game on television. He didn't try very hard with me, and that's what I remember.

Peter agreed. "You *can* create memories. My dad created a terrible one." Both Faith and Peter saw it as their task to make sure that the memories they intended and the ones they created were one and the same. I wondered. Fifty years from now, Peter's youngest daughter, Amber, may most vividly recall the yellow pencils, 3×5 cards, and fifty-five-item questionnaires, wondering what grade the man from the company gave daddy on the job he was doing at home.

Chapter 9

Importing Family Values

Alice and David Taylor weren't looking for the latest miracle in reproductive technology or the best expert advice on how to raise their daughter, Clare. They were looking for someone to give Clare the time and care their work lives prevented them from giving her themselves. A Google software designer, as was her husband, Alice took four months off after Clare was born, and was then ready to go back to her job in Mountain View, California. The workday was demanding. Alice and David usually left the house at 7:00 a.m. and returned around 6:30 p.m. The waiting list for Google's Kinderplex child-care center was long and the monthly fee had recently risen beyond their budget, from $1,470 to $2,300. And wouldn't Clare get more individual attention, the Taylors reasoned, if they hired a loving nanny to care for her in their home? Through lucky word of mouth, Alice had found Maricel Santos.

The Taylors felt like good employers:

> Maricel is undocumented and poor. We pay her well—and I know she sends the money back to her family in the Philip-

> pines. Here she's like part of our family. She's helping us, but, given their poverty over there, I like to think we're helping her.

They were extremely pleased with Maricel's care of Clare:

> She's so cheerful, relaxed, patient, and affectionate. We thought we'd have Clare in preschool by now, but she's thriving with Maricel. Clare loves puzzles and Maricel will sit with her by the hour and not zone out. Now me, I can't do that very well. I'm a get-it-done-fast person and I get fidgety and impatient. But Maricel is amazingly patient. Honestly, hour after hour, all day long, I don't know how she does it.

Arriving home tired from their nine-hour workdays, and eager to spend time with Clare themselves, Alice and Daniel checked in with Maricel briefly each evening about Clare's nap, meals, moods, activities—the headlines of her day. As for Maricel herself, they knew a bit about her current husband, her finances, and Redwood City home—topics Maricel would occasionally bring up—but nothing about her life in the Philippines. They didn't want to seem nosy, suspicious, or judgmental, and frankly they were exhausted in the evenings. Besides, they felt they grasped the essentials of Maricel's background. Alice told me reverently,

> In the Philippines, they put family and community first. They all live in the same village their ancestors lived in. They carry on its traditions and help each other. They aren't going nuts chasing the almighty dollar the way we Americans do. They really live their family values, and community spirit. That's why Maricel is so patient, relaxed, and loving with Clare. It's in her bones.

When I asked Alice about relations in her own family, she replied:

> My parents live in Chicago. My husband's parents live in New York and Charlottesville; his folks are divorced and remarried. So we're all spread out. They're all wonderful people, mind you. One's an engineer like us, one's in finance, and one's a high school math teacher. But they're all as go-go-go as we are. So Maricel fills that big hole in our lives.

How did Maricel's story compare to Alice's view of it? I wondered. Three miles away, alongside an eight-lane freeway parallel to a row of factories, lay a surprisingly serene street in a tidy neighborhood in Redwood City, California. On the spring day I first visited Maricel, I passed a man leaning under the hood of a black pickup. A nearby cluster of young men in backward baseball caps, arms folded over their chests, chatted in Spanish on the sidewalk. Hearing a bell, they glanced across the street at an older man pedaling a large three-wheeled bicycle, a square glass cotton-candy machine hitched to its front. Schoolchildren heading home ran after it, stopped, clustered around the man and, one by one, took off with their wands of pink cotton fluff.

On each side of the street, fences marked off one small plot of neatly clipped lawn and freshly painted bungalow from the next. Maricel's fence was wooden, white, about five feet high and interrupted by a formal arched gate at the entrance. In front of the neighboring house, a scalloped span of wrought-iron fence lined the sidewalk with small, iron balls topping the crest of each curve. In front of the next was a tall, no-peeking, reddish wooden model. It was as if a fence salesman had dropped by with all of his samples. Whatever the style, the homes, the vehicles, the fences in this blue-collar suburb all seemed to guard a hard-won American dream.

"Would you like a soda?" A friendly, short, dark-haired woman of forty-two, Maricel peered at me through white-rimmed glasses as I sat down on her small living-room couch. She wore gray slacks, a pink sweater, and, hanging from a chain, a golden cross. She placed a chilled can of Coke and a glass on the table in front of the sofa, and sat down shyly facing me. She gestured toward a large television opposite the sofa and told me how faithfully she followed Oprah. She had, she began, learned from the weeping confessions on the show that it was all right in America to get difficult matters off your chest with strangers—and sometimes easier than with those close to you. She folded her hands in her lap and began in slightly broken English:

> I'm the second of seven. After my sister was born, my mother had three stillborn babies. Then me. I think they were afraid I'd die, too. Now that I'm grown, I see that's why they didn't dare get attached to me. It helps me to understand how they acted . . . because they didn't love me.

A neighbor had come forward while she was young:

> Our neighbor was actually my *nanay* [Tagalog for "mommy"]. She hugged me. She gave me medicines. When I was sick, I moved next door and lived with her. When Nanay visited the countryside, she took me with her. Sometimes, my mother punished me by not letting me go to her house. I feel more love for her than for my mother.

Still the norm in the Philippine countryside, Maricel told me, such informal adoptions were less common in the midsized town in which she grew up. Regardless, her mother had fostered Maricel's bond with Nanay, and regularly sent her padding back and forth to borrow garlic, tomatoes, special dishes, tools, and to carry dirty laundry over and fresh laundry back. For some of this—including the care of her daughter—Maricel's mother had paid Nanay, a neighborly, tacitly long-lasting version of the arrangement the Taylors had with Maricel.

As much as she loved Nanay, Maricel resented feeling excluded from her own home.

> I felt like I wasn't part of my family and I was very upset about it. My mom disciplined me if I didn't do what she said; she pinched me on the leg—we call it *sipitin*. She didn't hug or kiss me even when I was sick. She scolded me if I came home late or talked back.

Maricel's father worked as a night policeman, slept days, and delegated the raising of their seven children to his wife. She looked to Nanay to raise the young Maricel, and to Maricel to care for her still-younger siblings. Overwhelmed by responsibility, Maricel eventually dropped out of school and eloped with a man who made a good living selling raffle tickets. The couple moved into a fancy apartment and soon had two children. Maricel got a job in retail and hired a nanny and a maid to help out at home.

But in the economic downturn of 1998, Maricel's husband's raffle business collapsed and he turned to gambling. "We fought like a typhoon," she recounted. And when he suggested she earn money as a lap dancer in his sister's bar in Japan—"I was so ashamed!"—she decided instead to join the stream of migrant workers heading for the United States. Leaving behind her husband, fourteen-year-old son and ten-year-old daughter, who were staying with her mother, she traveled to the United States on a tourist visa. "I didn't cry until I sat down in my seat on the plane," she recalled, "It was like a death."[1]

In Maricel's first job in America she earned $700 a month. Within a year, working twelve hours a day as a live-in nanny, her monthly salary rose to $1,000. She also received free food and lodging, though no medical insurance, paid vacation, or sick time. Still, the money was good. "Back in the Philippines, I was embarrassed to be just a nanny, and I still don't tell friends there what I do. But here I admit it because, however they do it, Americans are proud to earn money."[2]

All the while, Maricel dreamed of bringing her children to America. But to do that, she had to become an American citizen. The first step was getting a green card and an easy way to do that was to marry an American. One evening, she recalled, "I went to a dance hall called The Shaboom, and met Janek. He's smart and nice, and Catholic like me." Shortly thereafter, Maricel divorced her Filipino husband and married Janek, a Polish carpenter who agreed to a green-card marriage. "But," she added, "after the eighth strong Polish beer plus vodka, it's 'fuckin'' this and 'fuckin'' that." Still awaiting her green card, Maricel brought over her children on tourist visas to "visit" her and Janek. But, appalled by Janek's drinking, the children departed after six months, her daughter back to the Philippines, and her son to a shared apartment in a city an hour's drive away.[3]

"They Think I Love the Baby Like in the Philippines"

Maricel's main source of happiness became Clare, the three-year-old American child she was paid to care for.

> I'm the one Clare sees in the morning, I'm the one she talks to all day, and I'm the one who gets her ready for bed. Her parents work long hours and don't give enough time to Clare. If I were them, I'd work seven or eight hours, then come home.

Maricel loved Clare, and that love grew out of various different needs. First, there was Maricel's loneliness. "I missed my kids. So taking care of Clare was like taking care of my own child." Then, there was Maricel's isolation. The Taylors' house felt cold and silent, "like a cemetery." Also, she said, "I didn't talk to anyone. My English wasn't good and I didn't drive. And in America, you don't know your neighbors. People say hi and good-bye and that's it. I look out the window. No one's home. I'm in prison in their large cold house. Sometimes I cry really hard. My only salvation is this baby. I survived because of the baby."

Ironically, it was within that large, cold house that Maricel finally began to feel like the mother she had neither experienced nor been. "Before, in the Philippines, I was so busy and had so little time for my children," she reflected. "I'm a better mother with this baby girl here in America. She loves me. I call her mine. I dance with her. I say goo-goo and ga-ga. I feel like I'm a small child again. I can have fun!"

The Taylors believed Maricel was practicing the natural routines of motherhood typical of life in an "ancestral village." But to Maricel herself, her love for Clare seemed as much a product of her adoptive country. While the Taylors assumed that Maricel both enacted and revered her "authentic" Filipina upbringing, the indigenous tradition she most studiously embraced seemed to be the one she absorbed weekday afternoons watching Oprah.

> I learned that it's good for families to say "I love you." To hug and kiss. I never saw my mother and father kiss or hold hands. I never heard my mother say "I love you" to anyone. In the Philippines it's rare for a parent to say *mahal kita* [I love you] to a child, especially among the poor, like we were. I never said it to my son or daughter. But my cousin in San Jose, he and his wife say "I love you, Paul. I love you, Stephanie." I like that. I wanted to start doing that with my kids.

In weekly phone calls to her daughter, Maricel tried to take the plunge. One day just before hanging up, she told her jokingly, "I love you!" "I felt so embarrassed," Maricel recalled:

> The next call I said it seriously and added, "I want to hug you." My daughter didn't say "I love you" back to me, because she's shy and she didn't grow up saying that. But now every time I call my daughter, she says, "Okay, Mom, I love you, too. I want to hug you." Even in letters. The next thing is to tell my mother I love her.

Whatever the Taylors imagined, in reality they were paying their nanny to assemble on-site the social parts—time, financial security, a yearning for companionship, and exposure to a TV-mediated ideal of emotional expression—to create the love Maricel gave little Clare.

Ripples on a Global Sea

The unforgiving demands of the American workplace impose penalties that reach far beyond the American home. With every Maricel in the wider world also come stories of separation. One nanny I interviewed left three children under the age of eight in Sri Lanka; another, her ailing son in Mexico. A 2003 UNICEF-UNDP (United Nations Development Project) field office survey of three states in Mexico—Zacatecas, Jalisco, and Michoacán—reported that a third of households with children in each state were without both father and mother.[4] A 2003 study of domestic workers from Mexico and Central America working in California estimated that 40 to 50 percent left children behind, usually in the care of grandparents or aunts.[5] According to a 2008 UNICEF report, a quarter of all Filipino youth today have been left behind by a migrating parent.[6]

In her book on left-behind children in the Philippines, Rhacel Parreñas reports that after their wives leave, husbands of migrant mothers often become less rather than more involved with their children. Taking their wife's departure as a virtual divorce, and imagining children as a mother's responsibility, many fathers set up second homes with new partners in distant villages and raise other sets of children. (Filipinos often refer to female migration as "the Philippine divorce.") Meanwhile, the children are left to wonder why their mothers went away.[7] For many years, the Philippine government—like the British in early twentieth-century Ireland—encouraged emigration, since remittances from overseas workers were second only to the electronics industry as a source of national income. However, as the country began to face rising rates of school failure, depression, and petty crime among the children left behind, the Philippine government urged mothers of very young children—though not childless women—to find work at home.[8] But to this day, private maid-training schools dot the islands, and emigration—for a quarter of its paid workers—continues undeterred.

Foreign-born women make up about a quarter of America's nannies and maids. (In Massachusetts, they make up two-thirds of the maids and a third of the child-care workers; in New York, more.)[9] And they are part of a larger global flow of female care workers. One group migrates from Central and South America to the United States and Canada, a second, from South Asia to Hong Kong, South Korea, and Japan. A third group travels from South Asia to the oil-rich Persian Gulf, a fourth one from Africa to southern Europe, and a fifth one from Eastern to Western Europe. Experts estimate that about half are undocumented; I talked to one who never answered her employers' front door for fear of encountering the INS.

Some women are pressed to migrate by the need for food and shelter, others by a desire to better educate their children and improve the lot of their families back home. The lives of many in the global South bear the brunt of neoliberal economic policies. Announced as reforms intended for their "long-term benefit," such policies press poor countries to tighten already well-cinched public belts and open their markets to overseas goods, which often outsell local products and put small farmers and craftspeople out of work. Meanwhile, in the North, the rise of women's employment, the ever-longer hours of the middle-class workday, and the dearth of public services have spurred the search for immigrants' services.[10]

In the eyes of their employers, the actual stories of the Maricels of the world are often replaced by mythic ones. In the global South, people live more authentic and relaxed lives, Alice Taylor felt. "Maricel and her family enjoy a way of life American-born people don't have anymore. Maybe we used to, a long time ago, but now we have to pay for it." It was as if Alice had displaced her nostalgia for the slower-paced life of America's village past onto a life she believed was still going on today somewhere else. Other versions of the "happy peasant" fantasy held by other well-meaning employers draw a similar curtain over the fractured lives of the many Maricels around the globe.

While I was talking to the Taylors and Maricel and others like them, I was also continuing my own desperate search for a live-in caregiver for my aunt Elizabeth. Miserably unhappy in the nursing home, she would sit slumped in her wheelchair at the doorway of her small room, with her pocketbook on her lap. The home would not release her from its jurisdiction without proof that I had arranged around-the-clock care. I'd gotten partway there.

A kindly neighbor told me of an experienced caregiver named Shirley who could take Elizabeth during the day but couldn't live in. I hired her to fetch Elizabeth from the nursing home at 10:00 a.m., drive her weekdays to her home on the hill, and return her to the nursing home at 5:00 for dinner and sleep.

These visits produced mixed results. Riding in the car, Elizabeth whooped and hollered. Once home, she began to use her walker again, moving around the rooms, reclaiming each photo, her wingback chair, and the view from the window of trees, grass, her beloved hill. Her appetite came back. Her mental outlook improved. But at 4:30, when Shirley talked of returning to the nursing home, she would balk, threaten, sulk, and only relent when reminded of the next day's visit.

"Your aunt is adjusting very poorly," a grim-faced head administrator informed me at a meeting I was summoned to in the nursing home. "Days at home, nights with us here; it's a bad arrangement. It confuses her," she said sternly. "Your aunt needs to stay here full time."

She was right about the poor adjustment, but wrong about the solution. In daily cross-country calls, I tried to coax my aunt to hang on until I could get someone nice to live with her.

"We just have to do this for a while longer, until I can find someone to live with you. Can you hold out?"

"I don't need anyone to live with me, thank you. If ever I do, you'll be the first to know."

I heard from a friend of a friend about a soft-spoken Filipina in Chicago who was looking for work. She was willing, sight unseen, to brave five feet of Maine winter snow and live in and care for an elderly woman who didn't believe in paying someone to take care of her. The woman in Chicago had a nice voice on the phone. But she turned out to be half the size and weight of my aunt and probably couldn't catch her if she fell. She also lacked a green card, and I already had enough trouble on my hands. I called an eager-sounding young man, described the setup, the money, the job, including toilet assistance, and he never called back. I called a friendly cheese-maker who worked at a local organic grocery story and needed extra money and a place to stay. But she had five cats, was deeply grieving the loss of a sixth, and ultimately declined. I would have to cast my net wide.

Chapter 10

I Was Invisible to Myself

Earthen pots of cheerful red and white tulips lined the stairs up to the Los Angeles apartment of Rose Whitman, household manager. A thirty-seven-year-old blue-eyed storybook beauty with chiseled nose, rosebud lips, and a musical voice, Rose conducted me, in the manner of a skilled maître d', past her daughter's parrot squawking from its hallway cage, and sat me down in her cozy living room. From her kitchen she fetched a silver tray set with what she called a "proper English tea": a small pot of warmed milk, a middle-sized pot of hot water, a large pot of black tea, freshly baked scones, butter, blueberry jam, napkins, cutlery, and plates. I felt transported into the elegant parlor of a member of the English gentry, settled in an islet of calm, grace, and dignity. It was exactly this sense of security that Rose strove to offer her affluent clients. And given her own financial woes, dissolving marriage, and mounting tensions at work, it was precisely this calm and safety that eluded her.

The Evan Katzes help people find love. The Chloe DeCostas help them wed. The Family360 evaluators help them parent. And household managers like Rose Whitman help well-to-do families run their homes. Trips to the vet, a child's math homework, car repairs, hairdresser appointments, airport pickups: through a string of such tasks, the Roses of the world become the nerve center of the homes they are paid to serve.

A key part of her job, Rose explained, was to be unseen. Yes, she was around her clients and the house all day, but if she did her job correctly, they should scarcely notice her. While she took on a great many personal errands, success in doing them involved leaving her employer feeling autonomous and accomplished, almost as if the employer had done them herself. No matter how dependent on outsourcing, Rose's clients wanted to feel independent. They wanted to be like the yeoman farmer, the self-made man—those American icons of self-reliance—even when their households included a maid, a nanny, a gardener, a personal assistant, and a Rose. Perhaps there was a sense of discomfort, even shame, at the delegation of very personal tasks. Even for the rich, the important thing is to be an adult and depending on another to pick up one's socks harks back to being a child. Evan Katz described himself as "everyone's dirty secret." One personal assistant told me, "My client doesn't like to admit to others that I work for her." A life coach said, "My first job is to congratulate my client on the courage it took to come to me." Casually accepting one's invisibility seemed to be an unmentioned part of many such jobs.

What was it like to enhance an employer's sense of self-sufficiency while enacting one's own self-effacement? As I sat with Rose, drinking tea, she began to share her story:

> I was trained as a nanny in England and graduated with the Best Nanny Award. In England it's a respectable profession. You're paid a salary. In the U.S., it's a job people think anyone can do and you're paid by the hour. You get more money in the U.S. but more respect in England.

Rose had been proud to be a nanny: "Society needs what I do—which is to care for kids and help give them a warm home."

But being a household manager was something else. Rose described the difficulties of working for Norma and Judd Brown, a wealthy New York couple, and their four children, David, 13, Joshua, 11, Diane, 6, and Stephanie, 4:

> I began working for the Browns as an infant nurse. But it didn't take long to sense the chaos in their house. The three older kids prowled around at night and tried to climb into bed with Norma, leaving her exhausted. The house had no center, no schedule; it was in total disarray. I started by tucking the kids back into their beds at night. After a while Norma hired a nanny for the baby and children, and I became the household manager.

The Browns paid Rose well, eighty thousand dollars a year. But the downside of her high salary was that, as she put it, "they think there's no limit to what they can ask." She arrived at the Brown house at 7:00 a.m., left at 5:30 p.m. and commuted an hour each way. She had been doing this for five years and for most of her waking hours she was within eyesight of one or another member of the Brown family. Yet she said:

> I'm invisible to them. I'll be in a room bustling about and they won't be aware I'm there. I'm sensitive to moods, and if I sense tension, I disappear. Mostly, though, I'm in the room and they don't see me. Neither do their guests.

Norma routinely asked Rose to shop for gifts, wrap them, and sign cards for birthdays and Christmas. As Rose described it:

> She gives me parameters like "red polo shirt for David, size eight." I get it and sometimes I get something else I think she'd like and return it if she doesn't. The Christmas gift tag fixed on the gift bears my penmanship. At first I tried to imitate Norma's handwriting but then gave it up. It's hard—and

> sad—because I remember my parents always wrote out tags on the Christmas gifts in funny large block letters, "SANTA," as if Santa were barely literate. It was their big joke.

Rose also substituted for Norma at her children's school bake sales, soccer games, and doctor appointments, and there she was invisible in a different way.

> I drive the kids to their piano and tae kwon do lessons and root for them at their soccer games. Sometimes I take them to doctor and dentist appointments, keep notes, and report back. Now that the older two kids are at boarding school, I meet them at the airport when they come home. I volunteer at the younger kids' schools on behalf of Norma. I bake cookies for Diane's school's bake sale, lay them out, and sell them. The last time I wrapped each cookie with cellophane and a red bow. Sometimes I see mothers' eyes dart around looking for the *real* mother. A lot of those mothers know me but talk to me only to ask about Norma. I've been to some events at the kids' schools where a majority of us behind the tables are hired staff.

Sometimes, Rose said, the children couldn't or wouldn't truly see her, either:

> A child might not look up from his iPod, or answer a question I've asked. One time, I asked the oldest boy to clean up his room and he said, "I don't have to. It's your job to clean it up." I had to call in Norma to get that straightened out.

Other personal assistants I talked with felt similarly invisible. One overheard someone exclaim to her employer, "What beautiful flowers!" and was pleased to hear him remark, "My assistant takes care of every detail." "But," the assistant confided, "if he's talking about tracking down a rare Rothschild wine that I found for him, he takes credit and I'm out of the picture." Another assistant expressed surprise at what her client allowed her to do or see: "My employer has me buy his condoms from the drugstore and the next morning I find them used on top of his bedside wastebasket. In his mind, I don't have eyes."

Rose wondered whether she had colluded in her own erasure. She recalled when she had worked in England as a live-in nanny for titled employers years earlier:

> I remember Sir Alfred saying, "Rose, it's so lovely having you here because when you're with us, it's as if you're invisible." He thought he was complimenting me. At the time, so did I. I remember saying, "Thank you very much, sir." Isn't that frightening?

The Brown Family

Having heard Rose's side of the story, I wondered how her employers, the Browns, saw the situation. So I visited them at their luxurious oak-shrouded mansion in Westchester County. A uniformed maid answered the door, led me through a hallway, eyes downcast, toward a living-room chair where I might sit. A while later, Norma Brown lightly descended the stairs and conducted me past a dining-room table already set for an evening's dinner for fifteen, to a backyard glassed-in gazebo overlooking a glittering pool. As I sat down, I spotted two attendants—one of them Rose—walking single file toward us, carefully bearing large trays of cookies, fruit, and freshly made lemonade.

Norma was a youthful forty-five, with coiffed dark blond hair and solemn, hazel, searchlight eyes. She was dressed in a light pink cotton polo shirt, slacks, and inexpensive tennis shoes, as if the mansion, the pool, the liveried servants relieved her clothes of any need to tell the story of family wealth. A former financial analyst, now the full-time wife of a real estate millionaire, Norma had five hired helpers and told me, in passing, "I may well need more."

Unlike the Benners and Habers and most couples I talked to, the Browns were not a two-career couple who hired help to make more time for work and family. Norma stayed home, but she was still very "stressed out." In addition to her four children, she was in charge of managing the family's extraordinary life style, lavish entertaining, and endless home improvement—the pool, the pool house, the gazebo—as well as the upkeep of other homes. Norma's job was status display, and it depended on outsourcing. But outsourcing took work: hiring, supervising, paying, firing, and, in general, managing a large staff of servants. It took time. She had to mediate jealousies between cook and maid. Mornings, she had to come downstairs fully primped to meet with the architect on the five-year house-remodeling project. She had to call and e-mail the staff that maintained the Browns' other residences in England and France, and call the skipper of their yacht, *The Ballyhoo,* which bobbed about, empty eleven months a year, in the Gulf of Mexico.[1]

Norma struggled against the stereotype of the rich housewife who "didn't do anything," an image that paradoxically made her feel invisible, too:

> People think I'm sitting here eating bonbons, but I'm not. I have an MBA from the Wharton School of Business. I worked for eight years before we had kids. We're lucky to have resources, but raising four kids is a lot of work. I've brought all the skills I learned as an MBA and manager to the job of mother. I treat it like any professional job—the financial side, the technology side, the people side; I'm a *professional mother.*

Leaning forward on the gazebo couch, Norma added that she was not to the manor—nor to professional motherhood—born:

> Growing up in my family was a lot like living in a labor camp. I was the next oldest among my eight siblings in a poor, rule-bound Ukrainian family in New Jersey. We worked all the

> time. And if my mom found a spot on a skirt or a wrinkle in our pants, we got the belt. I was the nanny to my younger siblings, so I didn't want to *ever* be a nanny again.

Now Norma employed a nanny for her children. But with a maid and a household manager in the house, she felt that her husband, Judd, had little sense of what she did all day.

> My husband earns the money, and he respects earning money. We agreed that I would stay home but he doesn't value—or even see—all I do at home. It wasn't until his therapist reminded him that I had an MBA that he began to show more respect.

Rose told me she thought that having outsourced so much of the work in the house, Norma secretly felt anxious that she wasn't being "productive" like everyone else.

> So she busies herself with this or that project—a bookshelf re-sort, a family photo album, an antique chair repair. Her projects lie in permanent piles around the house, always half done. I think the piles are a way of saying, "See, I *do* have something to do."

Norma described herself very differently—not as a person who'd outsourced herself out of a job, but as a skillful and proud manager:

> I've heard many stories of nannies who are kept like virtual slaves. I knew I was never going to do that. You pay your help fairly, and you treat them fairly. When you do, they tend to go out of their way for you and you for them. You have reciprocity with both paid staff and friends. With friends, reciprocity comes from loyalty; with paid employees it comes from money.

How well did she know her employees? I asked Norma. She answered: "My philosophy is not to pry." Because Rose's work took her around the house and deep into Norma's life, and Norma didn't "pry," Rose knew far more about the Browns than they knew, or were curious to know, about her. Over our "proper tea" in Rose's flat, she had offered a canny assessment of the Brown marital dynamic:

> Norma and Judd made a deal. Norma told Judd, "I'll give up my professional life to be your supportive wife while you climb to the stars. But in return, I get to hire help." That's where I come in: I pick up from Norma what Judd passed on to her. It's a hand-me-down job. She agreed to it happily, I think, but secretly she feels abandoned.

As Rose described it, her job was not just to manage the household but to provide emotional support for Norma.

> Norma's getting *no* appreciation from Judd. So she feels isolated. We, her hired helpers, are the only people she sees all day, but we can't make up for what she's not getting from Judd. She's disappointed about that.

Judd didn't see Norma. Norma didn't see Rose. And Rose, it turned out, had a hard time seeing herself.

On the Other Side of the Service Curtain

Three years before Rose began working for the Browns, she had been married—her second marriage—and happily staying home to raise her daughter, Joy. Then, in an economic downturn, her husband, Everett, lost his $70,000-a-year job as a property manager and, after a frantic search, ended up with a job that paid him $40,000. At the same time, their daughter was revealing herself to be highly gifted in music and math. Rose yearned to enroll her in a local private school. But the yearly tuition was $16,000 and "out of the question" for Everett. Raised by a Depression-scarred father who saw the world in price tags, Everett began to panic over ever-smaller expenses. As Rose recounted:

> Everett would tell me, "We can't afford to eat out. We can't afford to go on vacation. We can't afford to buy Christmas gifts." It got so he couldn't spend money at all. I'd say we need this or that, and Everett would immediately counter, "We can't afford it." At Christmas, he picked up a box of chocolates they handed out at his office and gave it to me as a present. For a number of years, he bought me no gifts, even for my birthday. Not even a card. Finally I said, "Bloody hell you can't afford it! A book of poetry? A bottle of perfume? I am not a woman who needs luxury." I'd say, "Please just give me a card because it's important that Joy understand the value of giving." I felt humiliated and ignored. In the end, I had to buy my own Christmas gifts and put them under the tree because I was adamant that I have something to open on Christmas morning.

Each time Rose criticized Everett's hyperfrugality, he withdrew further. Then one day he said, "Rose, you've had five good years raising Joy. You need to go back to work." To settle the issue and send Joy to private school, Rose took the highest-paying job she could get—eighty thousand dollars a year—working for the Browns.

> But the Browns felt that if they paid me this much, they could ask me to work ten-and-a-half-hour days. After an hour-long commute, at 6:30 each night, I'd find Joy the last child standing at the after-care door. It broke my heart.

This went on for four years. When Joy was nine, she would come home from school each day and call Rose at the Browns' to tell her she had fed the parrot, hadn't turned on the TV, and was writing another poem. "I was in agony," Rose said.

To avoid Rose's ever-sharper tongue, Everett began staying later at the office, leaving Rose to come home each night to a messy house, an empty refrigerator, and a bare dinner table. "Sometimes Everett would take off with Joy to do something fun and leave me to clean up." Rose felt increasingly discounted as a mother:

> I began to feel like a money machine. The only thing Everett valued about me was my paycheck. He didn't care about my need for rest. All that mattered was that I get in the car at 6:30 a.m. and head back to the crazy Brown household. Everett couldn't see how desperate I was for sleep.

Given her exhausting days, her anguish at neglecting Joy, the mounting dishes and laundry, every problem became magnified:

> Everett snored. So I couldn't sleep with him. I moved myself upstairs to a tiny room surrounded by boxes and files, just to get the sleep I needed to go back each morning to the Brown chaos. I was depressed. I put on a lot of weight. Oh, I can't tell you. . . .

Rose asked Everett to see a specialist about his snoring, but he said, "No. It's too expensive."

Meanwhile, demands were escalating at the Browns'. Norma had asked Rose to empty the contents of an enormous walnut cabinet onto the dining-room table so that the cabinet could be moved to the hall.

> I emptied it and carefully lined the dining-room table with rows of china cups, saucers, dinner plates, salad plates, dessert plates, soup bowls—so I could remember how to put them back in their original order. The nanny was out sick. Joshua and Diane were milling about and bickering. Workmen were traipsing in and out of the kitchen. The cell phone was ringing with callbacks on the kids' dental appointments and the school fund-raiser. Norma was in a great tizzy and I was trying to calm her down as well as I could. So I cleaned out the

cabinet. The workmen moved it. I put back the dishes exactly where they'd been and left for the day, wiped out.

That night at home, Everett complained about Rose's boxes of memorabilia that he said were everywhere. "But they were just in the attic and garage and had my life story in them," she said. To cap it all off, early the next morning, Rose arrived at the Browns' to discover all the cabinet's plates, saucers, and glasses in total disarray on the dining-room table, sideboards, and scattered on the surfaces in the kitchen. In the middle of the night, Norma had changed her mind about moving the cabinet, padded down to the dining room, and undone Rose's work. Rose snapped. "Norma didn't realize how much of *myself* I was sacrificing to tend to her," Rose said. "Here I was rearranging her beautiful house while my own life was falling apart."

Given Rose's growing misery at home, I wondered whether she didn't wish she could outsource her burdens as Norma had done. Did she ever envy Norma her staff of five? I asked. "Sure," Rose answered, "but the people who rise in my profession know how to manage envy; employers don't like being envied, so it's something we control or don't feel." Other house managers I spoke to often struggled not to compare the cost of a luxury item in their employers' house with the modest cost of a badly needed item or repair at home. As one remarked, "It's hard being exposed to my client's ugly fifty-thousand-dollar wood carvings every day, knowing that each one could pay for my girlfriend's student loans."

Rose did envy Norma her money, though not her marriage or life. But the lack of money wasn't what distressed her most. Mainly she felt depleted. "I asked myself: what does it mean to give and give and give until you run dry?" Rose felt there was only one place left to retreat:

> My bed. I'd say, "Bed, you are the greatest. Your only role is to comfort me and put me to sleep. You're always waiting for me. Change you, flip you, that's all you ask." What a refuge!

Soon after we met, Rose decided to quit her job at the Browns'. But Norma, smarting from the blowup over the walnut cabinet, got there first and fired her.

What Invisible People See

Rose and I kept in touch. A year and a half later, newly divorced and relocated in Santa Barbara, California, she drove me in an old red sports car to a small cottage on a vineyard outside of town. It was Rose's day off from her new job with a different family and we were on our way to visit Becka Mellon, a friend and personal assistant to a vineyard owner. Becka had been helping Rose recover from her divorce and Rose was lifting Becka's spirits after a rough two-year stint caring for her depressed mother and irascible father, both now deceased. We were quiet for a while before Rose remarked:

> I always thought I'd be a caring stay-at-home mom, like my mother. But that was never an option in either of my two marriages. Instead I ended up doing caregiving as a career and then coming home to do more caregiving—wrung out and invisible at both ends.

Who, I wondered, could she call on? Since her divorce, Rose had sometimes turned to her mother and sister, but even more to three close friends: "My three dearest women friends are the only people to whom I'm not invisible. That's because they're personal assistants and nannies." She continued:

> They all work long hours and say that nothing gets done at home. If your own home starts to slip because you're keeping other people's homes together, you realize that actually we all need help. But employers seldom realize that about the people who work for them because we're invisible to them.

It was to this sisterhood of single, female, invisible personal assistants that Rose looked for comfort:

> There used to be older aunts, grandmothers, female cousins who held things together. Now women like me turn to single friends. I know a group who are all single—some widowed, some divorced—and who live in a small town in the country. One of them was diagnosed with breast cancer. In her last days, the women were with her. They brought flowers, sang songs, took turns giving her massages. She died inside a loving ring they drew around her. We should all have a community like that.

Rose and I found our way to Becka's small cottage tucked behind her employer's winery. As we sat around a table, near a wall of flowering wisteria abuzz with bees, I asked them both what they saw that they imagined their clients could not. They laughed in unison. Clients don't grasp what it is they outsource, they felt. As Becka explained:

> A lot of my clients have been thirty-something dot-com executives and they talk very fast. *Rata-tat-rata-tat-rata-tat.* "Call Jim at the office . . . tell him we need the order by eight a.m. tomorrow. . . ." [She snaps her fingers—snap, snap, snap.] So I call Jim's office. I'm friendly with his receptionist. I talk to Jim himself, answer questions, and make sure he's got the message straight and is in a good mood about it. I respond to any hesitancy or resentment I sense in his voice. I'm patient. My clients outsource patience to me. And once they get in the habit of doing that, they become impatient people.

Could it be, I wondered, that we are dividing the world into emotional types—order-barking, fast-paced entrepreneurs at the top, and emotionally attuned, human-paced mediators at the bottom? Talking one's way past the protective layers of a top executive, teaching a child to tie her shoelaces, feeding an aging parent, walking a recovering patient down a hospital ward, waiting with a child in a doctor's office, meeting a teen arriving on a long-delayed air flight—all such acts call for patience, tact, sensitivity, qualities far removed from the bottom line.

Rose and Becka compensated at the bottom for a deficit of patience at the top. Rose didn't simply accomplish the tasks assigned to her; she created a smooth, calm emotional landscape through which her clients could glide unfazed. It fell to Rose to apologize to the saleswoman after Norma spilled red wine on an expensive gown lent to her to try on at home. It was Rose who gave airport hugs to thirteen-year-old David returning from boarding school, and conveyed Norma's love to him. It was Rose who gave Norma's regards to the bake-sale committee and who patiently sold cookies that she, herself, had baked for Norma's children. In such moments, Rose was required to enact Norma's better self, while holding her own feelings in check.

Compared to purely physical or mental labor, the performance of such emotional labor is hard to see. But it nonetheless takes its toll. After all, Rose was regularly in situations in which the essence of her job was to transfer sympathy to people who felt anxious, neglected, or distressed. Rose did that on behalf of Norma, who—whether she thought of it that way or not—had effectively purchased the right to keep her distance from anyone who might have unnerved, irritated, or upset her. Unwittingly, Norma had outsourced sympathy itself.

I continued to follow Rose for several years after the Browns fired her and she left Everett. For a brief stint—at the time of our visit to Becka—she worked as a household manager, then as a personal assistant. Then she took up a job directing a small non-profit preschool program. She raised funds. She brought in pots of fresh red and white tulips. In an effort to get families more involved with their toddlers, she initiated "Dad and Me" walks and "Grandma mornings." She extended the program to children living in shelters and on the street. Most important, she counseled parents to slow down. If Italian cocks could initiate a slow food movement, Rose thought, why couldn't she start a slow parenting movement? In a world that was outsourcing patience, maybe you needed a movement to take it back. Parents took notice. One enthusiastic young mother exclaimed, "You know that film *The Horse Whisperer*, about a man who could communicate with horses? Rose, you're the *mother*-whisperer." And why not a father-whisperer? She was on a roll.

At last, Rose was visible.

Chapter 11

Nolan Enjoys My Father for Me

One Saturday morning, Joann Mills and her two children, Peter and Alice, threaded their way past a row of Nepalese Forgiveness flags, a display of gem-studded rings, silver gongs, rows of flutes, crimson carpets, and a cluster of men dressed in striped pantaloons and flat hats with coins dangling from them, to claim front-row seats before an outdoor stage. They were there to watch two diminutive, almond-eyed *Bharatnatyam* dancers, wearing ankle bells, pleated red silver-bordered skirts, and bands of white flowers in their gleaming hair. The traditional Nepalese dance they would perform was part of an outdoor celebration of *Losar,* the Nepalese New Year, in San Jose, California.

As Joann later explained to me:

> I've taken the kids to the Festival of Lights, the Divine Mother festival, and *Losar* every year. We're not religious, but I like what the Buddhists teach—acceptance and care. The kids love the food and Alice loves to get henna designs on her palms. My father's caregiver, Nolan, first took us, and now she—and the festivals—are part of our life.

When the dancing was finished, we feasted our eyes on intricately designed red scarves, had a Nepalese spiced-lentil lunch, and returned to Joann's home, where we tucked into a kitchen nook to talk. Joann described a bond with Nolan Barai, the Nepalese caregiver for her disabled father, that was as loving, appreciative, and relaxed as the relationship between the wealthy Norma Brown and mother-whisperer Rose Whitman had been cool, detached, and strained. With a no-nonsense shake of the head, Joann, a lanky forty-five-year-old with a freckled face and short, wavy auburn hair, reached into her slacks pocket to turn off a ringing cell phone so that we could speak uninterrupted. A trained economist and happy late-in-life mother of two, she described how Nolan had slipped into her life:

> We'd gone through a lot of scary girls from Kansas and Iowa to help care for the kids. One was on marijuana. Another was manic-depressive. We had a testy au pair from France, then a great one from Norway. Come, go, come, go; it was hard on the kids.
>
> She laughed as she recalled how she found Nolan:
>
> I was talking to my best friend in New York. I told her, "Laurie, I'm desperate. I'll try anything." She told me, "Joann, don't worry. My manicurist has found someone for you, a friend of hers."
>
> "Your *man*icurist?" I said.
>
> "Yes!" She was emphatic. "I trust her completely, and her best friend has a wonderful Nepalese care worker who has a great sister out in San Jose." So through my best friend's manicurist's friend's caregiver, I found Nolan right here in California!

Joann marveled at the workings of these intersecting female grapevines—her own network of upper-middle-class big-city professionals stretching from San Francisco to New York and Nolan's world of nannies, maids, and elder-care workers reaching from Kathmandu and Minneapolis—the city to which she first immigrated—to New York.

Joann initially hired Nolan for sixteen dollars an hour to take care of her children after school until she and her husband returned home from work. Both Joann and her husband, Randall, had all-consuming jobs. He was the chief pulmonary physician in San Jose's largest hospital, and Joanne managed a local bank with a staff of seventy, oversaw thousands of transactions a day, hired, trained, monitored, and sometimes fired employees.

Their lives went along smoothly until one terrible morning when Joann's eighty-three-year-old widowed father was felled by a stroke. He was placed in intensive care, then recovery care, then in a convalescent home. Joann cut back her work hours, visited her father daily, and worried: what next?

I Can't Get Over It

Joann's account of her father's stroke seemed matter-of-fact at first:

> My father was an economist, like me, a professor, a writer, a very bright man. My mother had died twenty years ago, so he'd been alone for some time. As time went on and the kids grew up, little by little, my father developed dementia.

Then her voice wavered:

> Then he was diagnosed with primary progressive aphasia. He can't speak. But he can remember. So he's locked inside himself. It's not treatable. It's upside-down Alzheimer's. In

> Alzheimer's you lose your memory first, then your speech. But since my father can't talk, he notices if the nurse forgets to wash him, but he can't tell her.

With tears streaking down her face, she continued:

> He still remembers who I am. He remembers Peter and Alice. But he doesn't smile. He's emotionally detached. I've quizzed the doctors endlessly. They say he probably sees life as a movie without an emotional sound track. I don't know if he even enjoys being with me or not. His face is completely blank. All he says is "yes" and "no." I have a terrible time visiting my dad.

Joann recalled happier years when she was the most important person in her father's world and he in hers:

> We were very close. After we lost my mother, all he had was me. We used to banter and joke an hour on the phone every day. We used to love to disagree. He was a rabid Republican. I'm a liberal Democrat. We'd argue about every bill before Congress. We had a great old time. Now he's without mind and . . . we can't talk on the phone anymore or really at all. He has no . . . feeling.

Joann found herself both grief stricken and inexplicably angry:

> In my mind I'd reproach him. How can you get sick like this? Why not heart disease? Cancer? Arthritis? If you had these at least I could still talk to you.

Still she kept trying:

> I just chatter. Maybe some words get through. I can't tell. I had the kids take him out to the garden. He used to touch the

> flowers. But then he stopped. Now we have him come for dinner, but he doesn't speak. He doesn't *feel* anything being with us. It's hard to bear.

Had she ever thought of moving her father in with her family? I asked. Joann paused to compose her answer:

> I love my father. I want to take care of him. I feel terribly guilty, but I can't have my father live with us. Early in our marriage, my husband and father would get into big territorial fights over me. And the stairs are too much. He'd fall. And honestly, it's torture for me to be around him.

One day Nolan suggested, "Why don't I visit your father in Sunshine Manor?" And that's how Nolan's new job as a "less disappointed, less hurt, less agonized" Joann began. "Nolan cuts his hair," Joann said. "She bathes him. She dresses him. She takes real pride in him. He looks great, better now than when I was taking care of him. She really likes him. That's worth a million dollars to me. She cares for my father as he is, not as I want him to be."

Nolan didn't have to forgive Joann's father for his backward Alzheimer's. It was enough, to her, to make him comfortable, and she took genuine pleasure—Joann felt—from the small moments of bodily connection: a lift out of the tub, a rub on the back, getting the part in his hair right. In Joann's eyes, Nolan's job was not simply to keep her diminished father company but to enjoy caring for him in a way Joann could not.

Not until two friendships—one between Joann and Nolan, the other between Nolan and Joann's father—began to blossom, did Joann realize how relieved she was of anguish and guilt at not enjoying time with her father, and how grateful she felt to have discovered someone who could convey her love. Nolan didn't shop for gifts or sign holiday cards for Joann. But she felt empathy for Joann and her father, and sad for the lost bond between them.

To that she added memories of her own ailing father cared for by a sister-in-law back in Nepal.

Nolan did a better job of caring for her father, Joann felt, than she did herself. Indeed, Joann felt less skilled and practiced at handling many issues that came up at home than she did handling almost any problem at the bank:

> Compared to Nolan I have a much more jumpy, get-it-done-yesterday personality; it's what made me a good manager. Patience, relaxation, empathy—these have almost been bred out of me. I'm a feeling person, but to be a good manager you have to limit your empathy. You have to shorten your attention span and reduce patience to meet hard deadlines. It sounds strange but I had to go looking elsewhere for the qualities of a great care worker. Nolan is gentle, peaceful, and attentive to my dad. That's why I appreciate her so much. She is another me, or rather a different me, a stand-in for the me I wish I could be.

Nolan came as close as is possible to doing Joann's most intimate emotional labor for her.

Friend of a Certain Kind

I wondered about Joann's feelings toward Nolan. "Is Nolan a friend?" I asked. "A friend of a certain kind," she answered. "I recognized right away what a great person Nolan was—compassionate, intelligent." Then she added:

> I knew I had to make her feel involved. After all, first she had my kids, then she had my dad all day long in his apartment. So I guess befriending her was a way to get her involved. But it wasn't a cold, calculated strategy. And it turned into

> something far stronger. We adopted each other. I feel I'm in her hands and she feels she's in mine.

To be considered "part of the family" is, for a hired caregiver, a well-known double-edged sword. It can mean both greater than usual consideration (shared meals, holidays, and birthdays)—and far less (underpayment, overwork, disregard for life circumstances). A number of employers who think of hired caregivers this way imagine work contracts as too formal, too "un-family-like," and so avoid clarifying the terms of employment. But along the way, Joann drew up a contract with Nolan specifying pay, hours, sick leave, vacation, and health insurance. Rather than chill their relationship, the contract set out what, by agreement, felt fair to each, and formed a baseline from which to gauge extra favors—which freely flowed between Joann and Nolan in the spirit of the gift. Given the low status of care work, Joann's approach was unusual.

Indeed, many caregivers I spoke to described working in a legal never-never land, and many employers feared to sign contracts lest they turn a personal bond into a coldly legal one. I was reminded of the painful experience of a nanny I met at the National Association of Nannies in Herndon, Virginia. Delores was fifty-two years old and had cared for an eighteen-month-old baby from birth and "fallen in love with him." Delores's employers, navy office workers, paid her sixteen dollars an hour for a live-out job in suburban Virginia. The pay seemed reasonable, she felt, but the hours—7:00 a.m. to 6:00 p.m.—left her "with no other life." She didn't know what to do about it. At the conference a speaker told her rapt audience of some two hundred nannies, "I know most of your employers don't offer contracts, but you should ask them for one specifying pay, time of payment, hours, social security, health benefits, and severance if they let you go."

Inspired by the speaker, Delores returned home from the conference and proposed such an agreement to her employers. When I called to ask how the conversation had gone, Delores reported, "My employers froze. They said I must be taking care of their

One way in which we respond to the market's encroachment on intimate life is to laugh at its more absurd expressions. Our laughter tells us what feels "over the line," at least for the moment.

match.com

Match.com has something for everyone. Whether you're looking to meet Asian singles, gay & lesbian singles, divorced singles, or even Buddhist singles, single parents, or single doctors, Match.com has what you're looking for. So what are you waiting for? Head to Match.com today to take advantage of this opportunity to meet the person you've been searching for your whole life.

jazzed™

As a member of Jazzed, you'll be able to take advantage of proven conversation starters that make it easy to reach out to other singles. For instance, find out about their secret talents. Or what they can't live without. Or about the funniest thing that ever happened to them. Our custom search engine uses sophisticated algorithms to highlight members who are most interesting to you.

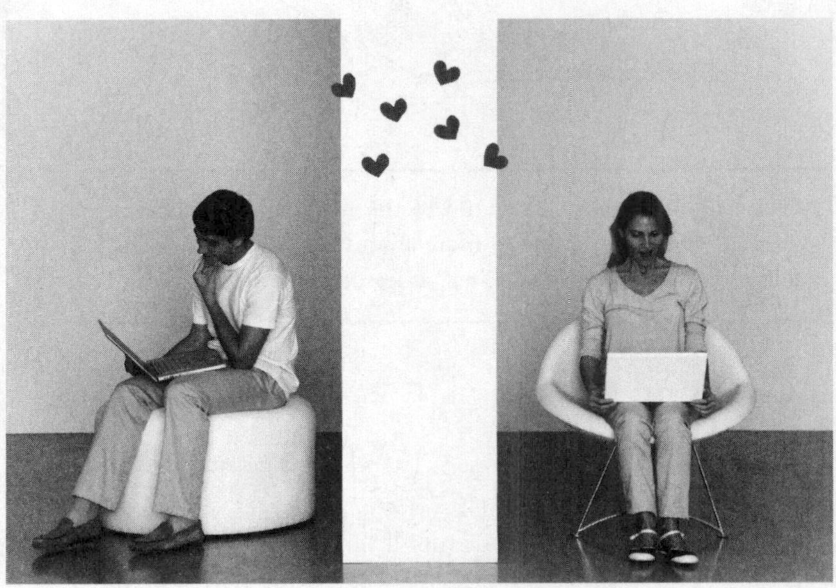

Services that help us find love, marry, and stay married are not new, but today the market provides services that reach deep into the heart of our emotional lives, guiding clients on what and even how to feel. Acts that were once intuitive or ordinary now require the help of paid experts.

The Heart Bandits

Marriage Proposal and Romantic Event Planners

The Heart Bandits are a marriage proposal and romance concierge consulting service. Our mission is to ensure that when you ask the most important question of your life or interact with the most important person in your life, it goes perfectly by providing you with ideas, consultation, research, full-service coordination, and flawless execution. Your fiancée will tell the story of how you proposed over and over for the rest of her life. Make sure it is a good one!

Courtesy Michele and Marvin Velazquez

MARRIAGE SUCCESS TRAINING ™

Give yourselves the best wedding present you'll ever get by attending Marriage Success Training. A quality marriage prep/premartial counseling program like MST is the single most important investment you can make in the long-term success of your relationship according to the latest marriage research. (It's also perfect for those couplets trying to decide whether marriage is right for them. Deciding whether to get or stay engaged? Click here.)

http://www.stayhitched.com

© Lynsey Addario/VII Photo

Perhaps the ultimate encounter between the market and intimate life is commercial surrogacy. The surrogate's experience, the parents' connection to the birth—every aspect of this service raises difficult questions about hiring others to perform personal acts.

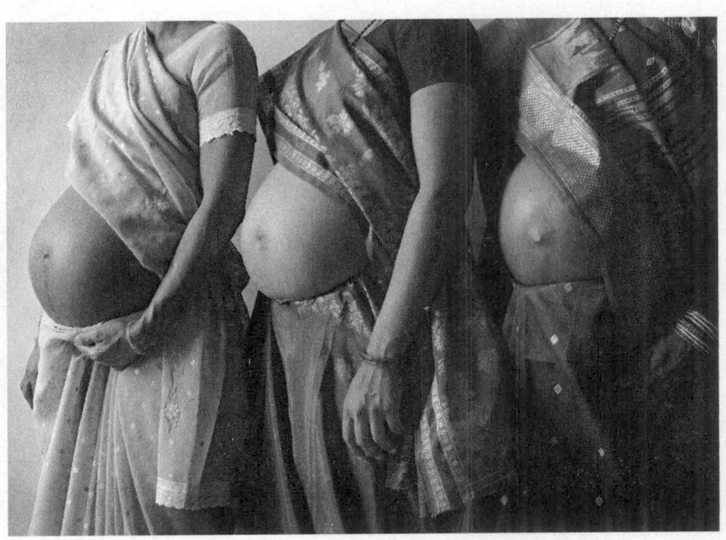

© Stephanie Sinclair/VII Photo

"Just wait until your nanny gets here."

Whether bearing a child, naming a child, or raising a child, Americans today are struggling with the limits of outsourcing, searching to determine how much is too much.

"Tell your assistant it's perfect."

Rent a Grandma is your one stop agency for all your quality domestic staffing needs. Our Grandmas are carefully screened mature women who are only the most professional, experienced staff and meet the standards you would demand for your own "Grandma". Rent a Grandma sets a standard unequaled in the industry. Our agency carefully screens and background checks each applicant. You can trust our Grandmas. Plus, our Grandmas don't text or tweet while they are watching your kids!

rentagrandma.com

Many market services offer to fulfill our fantasy of an abiding friend, a jolly grandmother, and a relaxed mother. But market language and values can also be applied to homes as they are. A family coach can teach a busy father to increase his "high-leverage" activities with his kids and so enhance his "family portfolio."

RentAFriend.com has Friends from around the world available for hire. Rent a Friend to attend a social event, wedding, or party with you. Hire someone to introduce you to new people, or someone to go to a movie or a restaurant with.

Hire a Friend to show you around an unfamiliar town, teach you a new skill or hobby, or just someone for companionship. You can view all of the profiles & photos on RentAFriend.com right now for free! Enter a United States or Canadian zip code below (For all other countries click here) or to learn more about RentAFriend.com click here.

Rentafriend.com

MAIL-ORDER MOMS

Want a mom who'll let you stay up as late as you want? Who'll let you watch anything on TV? I'm waiting. Box 7291.

HOMEWARD BOUND AERIAL SERVICES

- AERIAL ASH SCATTERING -

"Honor & Affordablity for your Loved ones..."

N372HB

A GREEN Company

WHAT ARE PEOPLE SAYING?

"Thank God for Ash Scattering and Homeward Bound. Our mother Beverly is home with our Lord"

- Mrs. Smith

http://ashscattering.org/

The most profound personal experiences may become something we purchase—especially when customs linking us to generations past have lost their meaning.

http://www.alwaysrememberedgravesitemaintenance.com
/alwaysrememberedgravesitemaintenance/Welcome.html

baby just for the money. I must not really love him." To her dismay, after ten days of agonizing confusion, they fired her.

Nolan and Joann signed their contract over a bowl of Nepalese *thenthuk*—red lentil and turmeric soup—not as a substitute for mutual respect, but as an expression of it. If Nolan spent more than the allotted five hours a day with Joann's father, Joann quickly offered to pay and Nolan proudly refused. Every so often, Nolan brought over delicious Nepalese dishes and Joann bought fresh daikon and cilantro to go in them, plenty for Nolan's family of five. Joann gave toys to Nolan's five-year-old granddaughter. They remembered birthdays. They shared jokes.

Joann helped Nolan prepare for her driver's license test and wrote a letter of recommendation for Nolan's daughter applying to college. She added:

> I helped Nolan's mother and second daughter fill out immigration papers. When Nolan's daughter's visa to enter the United States was denied, I spent hours on the phone with the American Embassy visa office in Kathmandu. I have a manager's voice. She got the visa.

The two women lived in separate worlds, but Joann had become fascinated with Nolan's.

> Nolan isn't going to talk with me about E. L. Doctorow's *Homer and Langley*. She doesn't read the *New York Times* cover to cover. But I hear tons of breaking news about the latest immigration scandal and lots of hot Nepalese gossip.

A paradox underlay this friendly trade. The more Nolan "gave from the heart" instead of counting dollars, watching the clock, and sticking to the contract, the less the time she spent with Joann's family seemed like a job. And the more essential she became to Joann's family, the higher her "market value" rose. Now Joann's friends were asking, "Where did you get *her*?"

Employment with friendship, work with play, Joann merged these with more warmth and talent than most employers I talked to. She had sought someone to enjoy her father as she wished she could. Among the gifts she received was entry into Nolan's world, her *thenthuk* soups, her immigration gossip, her *Bharatnatyam* dancers, her *Losar* festival.

Joann was not, like Michael Haber, the birthday-party-planning dad, trying to seize back a role she felt had been taken from her. And unlike April Benner, who cleaned the horse barn with her family, Joann wasn't trying to "get back to basics" as a counterweight to a super-outsourced life. As Joann saw it, Nolan was part of her "basics." She had come to love the person she hired to do some loving for her. To her friends, the way this had worked out looked like "good luck," the right "find." But it was far more: a fair and compassionate balance of market arrangements and village "just do."

So how common is the sort of friendship Joann had with Nolan? In her study of fifty caregivers, nannies, au pairs, and the women who hired them, University of Wisconsin sociologist Cameron Macdonald reported that only one out of five created true partnerships.[1] Among the many caregivers and clients I spoke to, only one other relationship ran as deep as that between Joann and Nolan. A single mother recounted:

> I had a one-year-old baby, had just broken up with my husband, and was in a new job as an assistant professor, so I was desperate. I found a Polish caregiver who turned out, God help her, to be pregnant and abandoned. As fate would have it, we became a family of four, with relationships with men on the side. My ex-husband wanted to return to me, but by then I'd gotten involved with someone else, though I didn't want to live with him either. Maria's romantic arrangements were just as crazy. So our kids have grown up as near-siblings. We were two heterosexual women with complicated love lives, but for the children, I was the professor dad and she was the paid stay-at-home mom. It may seem odd but it worked.

Can relations ever become too close for comfort, I wondered—either those between client and caregiver, or between caregiver and cared-for? One man faced that question after hiring a Filipina caregiver named Rosario to look in on his ailing widowed mother a few hours each day. He and his sister, who lived hundreds of miles from their mother, had carefully interviewed Rosario, phoned her weekly, and checked in with her on their twice-a-year visits to their mother. At first, he was pleased to notice a warm bond between Rosario and his mother. While considering it highly unusual, he was not alarmed when the caregiver proudly told him that sometimes, if his mother felt in physical discomfort, she climbed into bed to comfort her. When Rosario called to say his mother was dying, he and his sister rushed to her bedside:

> As my mother's breathing faltered, Rosario was weeping. My sister and I love our mother very much but we aren't big weepers so we just stood there quietly. Then Rosario made the sign of the cross over my mother's entire face and said a Catholic prayer in Spanish. I told her, "No, no!" We're Jewish. My sister and I felt awful about that. We still do.

With limits in place, Joann was happy with her arrangement. So was Nolan and, as far as we know, Joann's father. The relationship was wondrously intricate and probably rare. But as the elderly continue to rise to an estimated one out of six Americans by 2020, as the stay-at-home mother becomes ever more rare, and as global migration continues to supply caregivers to homes and institutions, the well-being of families may hinge on the subtle art of weaving village "just do" into market bonds.[2]

In her bare nursing-home room in another corner of the world, my aunt Elizabeth was still in misery—and now blaming me. "Why are you keeping me here?" she cried when I visited her. "I'm trying to get you out of here," I reminded her. But to no effect. "I'll remember this as *long* as I live," she replied menacingly. She's losing her mental grip, I thought to myself. The one upside was that she seemed to be losing her memory, too, and was likely to forget how betrayed she was now feeling. Finally exhausted by her fury, she fell into a pouting silence. I asked if she wanted me to wheel her outside to see the garden. "I don't care," she sulked. "Why don't we go, then," I proposed. As I wheeled her out of her room and down the corridor, she commented to no one in particular, "Well, they mean well anyway."

In my search for a caregiver, I had looked through newspaper and Internet advertisements, called friends of friends and friends of their friends in the surrounding area. My calls had led me to a cat-loving cheese-maker at a local organic store, a desperate nonstop-talking single mother of three who didn't return phone calls, and a woman with a bad back who lived in a nearby trailer park. I recalled Joann's words about Nolan, "I feel I'm in her hands, and she feels she's in mine."

I could settle for less, but who was out there? How could I find her? Did I need to visit a nail salon?[3]

Chapter 12

Anything You Pay For Is Better

It was evening. We were seated at an ocean-view table at a beachside Miami hotel restaurant, lingering over dessert. Across from me was Gloria Gomez, a svelte twenty-three-year-old Cuban, her black hair drawn into a bun held high on her head with a large gold clip. She had a wide brow, large brown doe eyes, and a sad smile. A rising star in hotel management, she was smartly dressed in a gray, thin-striped tailored suit and white floral scarf. If her family had "lost everything" when they fled Cuba, as she was to tell me, there was no trace of that loss now. Gloria did not aspire to the millionaire life of Norma Brown overseeing a busy traffic of servants tending to her many homes, although that would have been fine. Rather, she was making the case for paid service as a permanent extension of personal life—hers and everyone else's.

> I may be at the extreme, but it seems to me paid services are always better than help you can get from family or friends—given what paid services can do and given what family and friends can't. I couldn't turn to my own family for help, and I

> know many others who couldn't turn to theirs. So we're always going to need to pay for services. The more the better, I say. The only sad thing is that we can't all afford them.

Listening to Gloria, I realized that nearly every person I'd spoken with looked upon paid services as a source of expertise and a way to compensate for lack of time. But no one had made the case for the market as a whole-scale replacement for the village, especially not with Gloria's tone of resolve.

I asked her why she thought families and friends did such a bad job of meeting people's needs:

> Well, take the family I grew up in. It fell apart. It didn't work. Maybe my parents didn't love each other enough. But the closer you inspect any family, the more you see how poorly things work out. Enclosing family members in a small space is terribly bad for the people inside.
>
> I wish my parents had had marriage counseling. Actually they both needed individual therapy, too, my mother for her narcissism and my father for his manic depression. Maybe then they could have handled their divorce better. As it was, their divorce was devastating for all their four daughters. It's why we've never been friends with each other as adults.

Although Gloria was attractively dressed in civilian clothes, I began to imagine her as a war-weary veteran in green and brown army fatigues on a corpse-strewn battlefield. She'd survived a war. She was a determined peace advocate in her new marriage and vowed to be an attentive mother to the children she hoped to have. But this resolve grew out of a dark view of family life. It was with calm conviction that she continued:

> Most families are places of deep injury. You can't really rely on them for the kind of help you need to grow up happy and

> well. If we can afford it, I'd very much like to hire a lifetime counselor to guide my marriage from beginning to end, and I'd like a personal therapist besides.[1]

I asked her what services might interest her, if she had children:

> I'd like to hire an overnight sleep coach, a potty trainer, a birthday planner, someone to drive the kids to soccer and dance class and anything else that needs to be done. That way, I could always be the loving mother they come home to.

All Americans were in the same boat, she felt, drifting helpless and alone, without a tow in sight: "I really think families can't be happy by themselves. They need help from experts, the more the better."

Gloria remembered her mother, a gifted engineer, not as a shining role model balancing love and work but as a self-absorbed career woman for whom family definitely came second:

> My mother was a career girl before it was fashionable. And smart, too. But she was hugely self-centered. She didn't nurture Dad or us; she just disappeared into the office and came home, her briefcase stuffed with engineering reports. The family shattered around her. I only knew that when I grew up I didn't want to be anything like her.

Gloria's father was affectionate with his daughters, but after his small air-conditioning repair business and marriage both failed, he fell into a deep depression from which he never reemerged. It was Gloria's nanny who really loved her, she said: "Anna-May was with me until I was eight and was the only person in the world who gave me unconditional love. Without her I wouldn't be who I am today."

Is a Friend as Good as a Therapist?

What about friends? I wondered. In the absence of family, could a person turn to friends?

> No. The way it is with family, that's how it is with friends. You can't turn to them because they have the same kinds of problems you do. They've gone through the same emotional meat grinder you have. They need all their energy to take care of themselves.

I asked her what she would look for in a friend and she said:

> You need someone to talk to, someone you can be completely honest with, and someone who will ask nothing whatever of you. Friends have problems of their own. And they have their own opinions. You need a blame-free zone so you can really look at yourself. And for that you have to pay.

Besides, if a friend helps you, the help is never free, she thought, adding:

> Friends are very entangling. My friend Carmela is a kind, outreaching person, but she's had a recent breast cancer scare and her insurance company is contesting the medical bills. Meanwhile, her husband's just lost his job, and she needs a lot of support. You have to pay for help one way or another, so you might as well pay for it with money.

So what did she imagine it would feel like to have a true friend? Gloria answered:

> A real, true friend should focus on your needs and be a truly gifted listener. She shouldn't give advice that fits her but not you. A really good friend is a person who doesn't make demands

> on you, and such people are very rare. Frankly, if a friend can't listen in a skilled way or stop herself from loading you down with her issues, the biggest gift she could give you is money to hire a psychotherapist. I may be extreme, but I don't think families and friends can help each other much.

There was also no time in America's golden past when family and friends were any better, Gloria felt sure. In the past, when family and community were all you had to turn to, you had fewer options. So people in the past, she felt, lived more unhappy lives.

Gloria's view was, indeed, extreme. In *Made in America: A Social History of American Culture and Character*, the sociologist Claude Fischer tells us, eighteenth- and nineteenth-century Americans relied heavily on friends not only to "discuss important matters"—a modern measure of friendship—but also to borrow tools, raise a barn, get the hay in before the rain. Scholars disagree on whether the average number of "close friends" has suffered a recent decline from three in 1985 to one in 2006, as one research team claims, or remained the same, as Fischer states or—counting Internet friends—actually expanded.[2]

But by any account, the importance of close friends remains uncontested. The many people I had spoken to who had hired love coaches, wedding planners, and gestational surrogates wove friends in and out of their stories. The lovelorn Grace knew her new Match.com beau, Marcel, was "serious" when he praised her to "all his friends." Grace's twelve-year-old daughter, who claimed three hundred Facebook friends, looked forward to meeting her own future beau through off-line friends. Many busy professionals—the household manager Rose Whitman, for example, had friends as busy as she, but that didn't mean they weren't in touch and on call. It was by talking to a San Jose friend who had a New York friend that Joann Mills found her beloved Nolan.

Have these friendships changed, though, if we no longer turn to them to help us find a mate, put on a wedding, or potty train our babies? In this context, it seems more true to say that while friends haven't disappeared, the market has reshaped friendship as it has so much else. Friends stand beside people like Grace and Laura as they search for the right babysitter, coach, or therapist, and they stand by people like Evan Katz or Rose as they coach and assist. Rather than disappear with the advance of the market, friends now assemble alongside it, as we buy and sell its wares.

Fees and Friendship

It is possible to discover friends in the market. Joann Mills found a good friend in Nolan, for example. But friendships-for-hire are, by definition, different. Liz O'Mally, a forty-two-year-old curly-haired Irish American Boston high school counselor, intentionally set out to acquire new friends. She had recently lost Janet, her "best friend in this life," in a car accident. "She's irreplaceable. But now I have three paid mothers—my therapist, my masseuse, and the trainer at my gym":

> I see my therapist once a week. For pain in my lower back, I see my masseuse every other week. Twice a week, I'm the first to arrive at the gym and always find "my" trainer free. I'll be going to all three until they die or I do. I plunk down the money; I don't think a thing about it.

It was to these helpers that Liz had turned with a very personal problem. Married for fifteen years to a man she described as a "wonderful father" but with "very different interests," Liz had developed a strong crush on an "exciting" older teacher who had guided her step-by-step to the publication of her first article. She e-mailed him three times a week and invited him to lunch several times a year. He was married, however, and kept a proper distance, signing his short e-mail messages "Best Wishes" or "Best," not "With affection" or "Love." Liz was deeply preoccupied with her dangerous wish for a response from him. Were Janet still alive, Liz would have turned to her. Now her paid confidants advised her. The trainer was encouraging her to imagine that when James signed his e-mail messages "Best, James," it meant "he's interested but he can't express it." Her masseuse advised her to "be hopeful but go slow," and her therapist was helping her look more closely at her marriage.

Such intimacy between service provider and client can last a long time and is not unusual. Life coaches hired to help clients meet agreed-upon goals might phone them weekly for three to eight months, help them launch a new career, finish a project, go through a divorce, resolve a dispute, vacate a house, birth a child. In a 1998 survey, Amy Watson, of Houston-based Coach University, found that substantial proportions of clients found their life coaches to be a "sounding board" (85 percent), a "motivator" (78 percent), a "spiritual guide" (30 percent), and over half (56 percent) described them as a "friend." Although most training programs advise coaches to keep a professional distance, half the clients Watson surveyed said they confided in their coach "as much as in their best friend, spouse, or therapist." Twelve percent said they "confided more in their coach than in anyone else."[3] Legacy coaches—therapist, mentor, and taskmaster combined; mentioned in *U.S. News and World Report* as one of the twenty hot job tracks—help clients set priorities and even find purpose in life.[4]

These client-provider bonds feel like real relationships with one important difference. In Liz's case, Janet was her friend before Liz ever called on her for help. Her "three mothers," on the other hand, became friends after she hired them for a specific purpose. She and Janet spent money casually to buy gifts for each other or their children, pay for dinners, or make loans. But Liz's relation to her providers depended first and foremost on money, which put subtle limits on their intimacy. Liz decided not to tell her masseuse about her husband's raise "because I didn't want her to increase her rates." She also said, "My masseuse listens more than she talks, and probably tells me just enough about herself to make me feel okay talking about my marriage." Was the masseuse offering an ear as a part of her paid service? I asked Liz. "Maybe, maybe not." She wasn't sure. But her very uncertainty on this point suggested that, in her mind, money was known to buy certain things friends offer for free.

The same ambiguity dogs friends who become paid workers, raising another delicate issue. I spoke to a fifty-year-old full-time hospital administrator named Louise, who remained devoted, long after their divorce, to her older, wheelchair-bound ex-husband. She secretly hired a longtime mutual friend to help him out.

> I wanted to pay my friend so I could ask things of her I otherwise wouldn't feel comfortable asking. Lenny's bones had become so brittle, he could barely walk. The worst was he didn't admit he needed help, and resented my offering it, and that drove me nuts. So I hired Christine to take him shopping and to the dentist.

Louise and Christine agreed on twenty dollars an hour, but not on what hours to count.

> The first time Christine drove out to see Lenny in his nursing home, she shopped with him for three hours, chatted with him for another two. The commute is an hour each way. I insisted on paying her for seven hours.

Louise and the friend warmly bargained.

"I only want five hours' worth. You don't have to pay me for getting there."

"It's a long drive. Then there's gas."

"Well, okay, but just one way."

Christine strongly resisted the idea that this was "just" a commercial transaction because that would imply Lenny was not or had never been a friend. And that wasn't true. Still, being with Lenny now required great forbearance, time, and, in that sense, work. As Christine recounted:

> Just going with Lenny to buy two pears and one avocado at the supermarket . . . wow! When I'm alone, I zip in and zip out. Lenny examines *all* sides of each pear. He handles a couple of them before deciding which one is best. Avocados, we handle at least ten. One is too soft, another too hard. Then he wants doughnuts, and why aren't there buttermilk doughnuts? I have to find the attendant to find out why they don't have buttermilk doughnuts. It takes a lot of patience and the minute I'm impatient, Lenny senses it—not good.

Louise and Christine danced another minuet around telling Lenny that his ex-wife was paying his good friend to be more patient than she herself could manage and to pretend to mutual enjoyment. Part of being a paid friend to Lenny, Christine felt, was to sustain a small white lie: that Lenny was still the same guy he had been a decade back and that getting together was "just as much fun" for Christine as it was for him.

Louise's daughter strongly disapproved of this white lie. The family was Jewish, and as Louise's daughter put it, "Christine's been a wonderful friend to Dad for thirty years. Why is she accepting money from you? I thought she was doing a mitzvah [a good deed]. You can't get paid to do a mitzvah." Her mother explained, "Your dad isn't who he was. He'll get to the doctor but won't remember a damn thing about what was said. Christine takes notes. She unpacks and packs his wheelchair from the back of the car, gets him to the bathroom, waits. It's a lot to ask." Her daughter remained doubtful. Then Louise put it differently: "Christine needs the money to help her daughter, who's a single mom. We're giving her money she needs." This was fine with the daughter because now Louise was also doing a mitzvah.

Money between friends was fraught with the danger of insult. Christine had, for example, accepted pay to visit the cantankerous elderly mother of another friend. While the elderly mother was delighted with Christine's visits, her help sorting family photos, her companionship on trips to art museums, she became highly upset when she accidently discovered that Christine had not been coming out of pure affection. "Oh then," the mother had declared, "that's dirty liking." The friend later told me, "I didn't have the heart to tell my wonderful friend Christine."

Christine's client-friends felt obliged to back-channel the fact that they paid her to do friendlike things. This was yet another way people protected the intimacy of personal bonds from the depersonalization usually attached to fee-for-service. As Louise said:

> I'm close to Lenny but I don't want to take him to the dentist, which makes me feel guilty. Paying Christine relieves me of guilt. But I'm embarrassed to hire a friend, so I don't talk about it.

Louise's lie protected Christine from the accusation of not loving Lenny enough or of wanting money too much. It protected Lenny from feeling unlovable, and it helped Louise think of herself as—and be—a caring ex-wife. Other people I spoke with also tried to conceal their outsourcing for a variety of reasons. One hostess invited a large gathering of friends to dinner and served them a delicious store-bought roast lamb, which her friends assumed she had made herself. This proved such a big hit that friends asked her for the name of the butcher and cut of the lamb, shopped at the butcher's, and promptly discovered her white lie. Lies have a purpose, of course; hers was intended to preserve the identity of someone who "cares enough" about her friends to devote hours cooking for them while also working full time and raising kids. Guests warmly understood, but it took her a long time to laugh about it.

The Market as Savior

Most people fit services around friendships. But for Gloria, friends you paid were more reliable than the kind that came free. Was that always true? I asked her. Among help-for-hire, weren't there sometimes incompetents or frauds, people who did more harm than good? "Sure," Gloria said. "I once went to a therapist who later lost his license for sleeping with a patient." She also thought therapists could foster a false need for their services by making a patient feel it was "neurotic" not to hire them.

> I was shopping for a good therapist and I was trying out my third. I didn't like her. So I told her I was quitting. She said, "The reason you're quitting is that you can't commit. To deal with your problem, you need to commit to therapy with me." The symptom of the disease was that I refused to be her client. But that wasn't true! I just didn't like her. And her comment was one more reason I didn't like her. The next therapist I tried was too scattered. I would have stuck with her, but she couldn't do the job.

But even bad therapy was better than no therapy, Gloria thought. For all the pitfalls, she deeply believed that experts of all kinds could alleviate the fallout from a toxic family:

> My mother wouldn't let my sister wear her wedding dress because my sister was a few sizes larger than she was. My sister felt terribly hurt. Now they could have gotten past that impasse with a wedding planner, a family therapist, or both.

"Family baggage" could spoil any event, especially holidays, so a Christmas planner, say, could be of benefit, too, Gloria explained:

> Suppose you had an estranged mother dying of cancer and your two ex-husbands and their new wives and children all coming over for Christmas. It can get very complicated. Plus, what will you feed them? If I'd heard of a great party planner, I'd hire her. Planners help families that can't manage on their own.

"Would you mention to your family and friends that the planner had helped out?" I asked.

"I might not." She giggled.

"Would the planner stay for Christmas dinner?"

"Definitely not. She has her own Christmas to go to," Gloria replied.

"But what if the planner has an unwell mother and two ex-husbands coming to dinner?"

"I guess she'd need to hire a planner, too." We both laughed. But Gloria wasn't joking.

More than in the past, business is ready to meet the needs of the Glorias of America. For the last three decades, the consumer market has pursued the strategy of appealing to customers' emotional desires. In his book *Emotional Branding: The New Paradigm for Connecting Brands to People*, Marc Gobé proposes ways of persuading customers to buy things by appealing to their emotions. Customers seek connection, he notes, citing research showing that while one out of four Americans say they do not have "close friends," consumers are seeking a "lasting relationship."[5] A successful brand meets that need, Gobé says, by fostering a bond between customer and purchase. In fact, good brands transform goods and services from "mere" commodities into close—if imaginary—friends.

Some services go further still, actually disparaging a potential customer's real friends. For example, Bob Grant advertises his e-book *How to Make a Man Fall in Love with You and Win His Heart—Even If He's Distant Now*, by saying:

> The main obstacle women face in their effort to understand men is that they . . . seek advice from their friends. . . . By all means, seek the listening ear of a friend if you simply want to *unburden* and if talking to your friend makes you feel better. But always remember that talking to your friends results in deeper and better friendships with your friends—but does little to improve your relationships with men.

At the same time, some new services boldly advertise themselves as a missing piece of family and friendship: "Rent-a-Mom," "Rent-a-Dad," "Rent-a-Grandma," and "Rent-a-Friend." One woman started her "Rent-a-Mom" service to offer customers "everything a mother does"—including waiting for the kids to come home for school and baking cookies with them. "When I was married, my husband never appreciated all the things I did," she explained. "So I figured I might as well get paid for it."

"Rent-a-Friend" offers a partner with whom one can eat dinner, see movies, sort photos, or go on trips. Such workers are not, like Christine, longtime friends slipped a little money to walk the extra mile; they are strangers who straightforwardly propose to act, for cash, like friends. One online entrepreneur, Holly, who advertised friendship for hire, catered directly to the desire for entanglement-free support:

> Ever have a day when you just needed to vent to a good friend and get their feedback to give you another perspective, or to validate your thoughts, or to tell you that you really are fine? What happens if you don't have the energy to do the other side of the friendship, where you support them in their struggles? And suppose you were starting to feel like their solutions fit them but not you? That's when you need me to be your *rent-a-friend*.

Holly continued: "If you are ready to rent my friendly attention for a while, go to the Fee-for-Service." There, Holly spelled out fees that vary according to the severity of a client's problem:

Short & Sweet	$50.00
Average	$75.00
Complex	$100.00

Holly's sample of a "Short & Sweet" problem began, "My husband died of a heroin overdose in April, his second go-round in 5 years with it, but is it normal for me to be so pissed off at him for such stupidity?" Holly's sample answer started, "I'm sorry to hear about your husband's fatal overdose. It seems very acceptable to me to experience anger about that, and anger is an early stage in the grief process. . . ." The "Average" and "Complex" samples described equally disturbing—though more expensive—problems. Shown this ad, Gloria shook her head, "No, charging different amounts for different-sized problems—that was 'too much.'" But renting a friend, that seemed like a good idea. Why not?

Though still new and small, such services seem to be gaining ground. Started by Scott Rosenbaum of Stewartsville, New Jersey, a former marketer for dating Web sites, Rentafriend.com now receives 100,000 unique views a month and has recruited nearly 2,000 members. These members pay $24.95 a month to review profiles and photos of 167,000 possible pals. Once hired, hourly rates range from $10 to $160, none of it for sex work. One friend-for-hire, a thirty-four-year-old married mother with a full-time regular job, told journalist Leanne Italie, "If you need someone to work out or just hang out with, I'm your girl. I'm pretty peppy and bubbly if you just need a smile and I have lived a life of someone twice my age if you need an ear and some advice." She's trying to buy a house and the extra money helps.[6]

A deep hopelessness seemed to underlie Gloria's faith in care she could purchase and distrust of anything she could not. In her charming way, she was a loner—not the self-sufficient Robinson Crusoe, hero to free-market advocates such as Milton Friedman, but the kind of market-dependent loner who might make brand consultants such as Marc Gobé lick their lips.

Were America to move toward Gloria's dark vision—of frosty family, semihelpful friends, and a growing friendship market—these professional services might well become the new standard. After all, Gloria's description of a good friend was "one who made no demands and listened without judgment." Relative to their market competition, one could come to see a sister as a lesser therapist, a friend as a bumbling coach, and a brother as an incompetent party planner.

In response to the prospect of marketized friendship, Carol Quinn and Anny Beck—two friends—developed "3Lunches," a free program offering guidelines and training for how to be a better friend in three lunchtime meetings. Such training, they hope, can counter the "expensive therapist mentality and the even more expensive life-coach trend." Quinn describes the small movement as "generosity-inspired."[7] Told of 3Lunches, Gloria smiled, shook her head, and replied, "Carol and Anny should get trained and paid."

But one paradox of Gloria's position seemed to have escaped her. Relying so completely on paid services would require her to work longer hours and earn more money to buy what she felt she needed. These hours would limit the time she might spend hiking, volunteering, or having coffee with someone who might, despite all her reservations, become a friend. That was a problem, Gloria conceded. In the meantime, she was trying to decide between two therapists. As we parted, she gave an ironic—and was it sad?—smile: "I wonder if I should talk it over with a friend."

Chapter 13

I Would Have Done It If She'd Been My Mother

With her panting dachshund, Itty-Bitty, and me in tow, Barbara Strand was driving a red van toward Pleasant Vista, a tree-shrouded nursing home on the outskirts of Boston. I had asked Barbara if I could join her for a typical day on her rounds as an elder-care manager. I was in for a surprising ride along the edge of the market frontier that was advancing the fastest—care for the elderly. A short, vital woman of forty-three, with curly blond hair and wide-set, alert blue eyes, Barbara had me laughing within minutes. ("Hey, Itty-Bitty, do you think this lady's good for a back scratch?") She had started out as a dental hygienist, become a personal shopper, and then a personal assistant, hunting down rare parts for her boss's antique car, sand for the dance floor of his karaoke restaurant, and tropical flowers for his dining-room table. But it was as a visiting elder-care worker, and later as an elder-care manager, that she finally discovered her true calling.

At the turn of the century, no large nursing homes dotted the landscape of rural or suburban America. Most people died before they grew—in today's sense—"old." The average American born in 1900 could expect to live to forty-nine.[1] Those who did become elderly or infirm were cared for at home by wives and unmarried daughters or in the case of affluent families by private servants. Even as people came to live longer, care of the elderly remained largely a family affair; no one specialized in helping offspring "manage" a father lost in a parking lot or a mother with a broken hip. It was only in the 1970s, when women left the home for paid work that elder care began to move into the hands of professionals.

Today the average American can expect to live to age seventy-eight and stands a 40 percent chance of ending up, at some point, in one of the country's sixteen thousand nursing homes.[2] In another sign of market encroachment, we have gone, in the words of Jim Wilkes, an attorney representing home residents, from "nonprofit and faith-based" rest homes to "large, corporate-owned nursing home chains."[3] These places suffer higher rates of staff turnover, offer patients fewer hours of care, and even show, shockingly, higher rates of resident death, compared to their nonprofit counterparts with clients in comparable states of health.[4]

In the course of a stay in a nursing home, an elderly resident might encounter maids, cafeteria workers nurses, nurse's aides, doctors, interns, hospitalists, physical therapists, social workers, hospice workers, administrators, and privately hired visiting care workers. Care for the elderly has become a hugely diversified field with a bewildering array of services and specialists, which is where a geriatric-care manager comes in—to make sense of it all.

And that's what Barbara did: meet with worried middle-aged clients who hired her for $50 an hour (some managers charge up to $200) to guide them through a maze of choices. "I arrange for a cognitive and physical assessment," Barbara explained. "Then I see what the family wants and can agree on. I review their budget and options. Do they want their mother in home care? Assisted living? In a nursing home? Large, small? Ambulatory only? An Alzheimer's unit? I check prices, waiting lists, terms of contract, and make out the application. I help the family not freak out."

As we drove to her first visit with an elderly patient, I asked Barbara what kind of situations brought clients into her office. She replied:

> A man gets a call in the night; his elderly dad is in Emergency after a heart attack. Or the police call; his mother has been found wandering around in a shopping mall and can't remember her address. He's intimidated by the fast-talking doctor, the make-you-feel-stupid intake clerk, the can't-catch-her-eye nurse. He has no clue what to do next. So he hires me.

Her first task, she said, was to help clients stop feeling guilty for hiring her:

> A client will say, "I visited mom every day. I brought her food in Tupperware and marked the date. I showed her how to use the microwave." I tell them, "You did everything you could." I alleviate their guilt.

Barbara observed that, for their part, parents often needed help but didn't want "to be a burden":

> By the time it comes to moving to a nursing home, maybe the elderly person has fallen once or twice, is afraid of falling again, and doesn't want to trouble her kids. She might say, "I don't want my daughter to stay home and take care of me until I die like I did for my mother," and to some extent she'll mean it.

Others of Barbara's clients were less anxious about an aged parent than about a relationship with their siblings:

> You've got an elderly mother who's broken her hip in Massachusetts. One let-everything-slide sibling is in California. The second is a busy teacher raising her family in Minnesota.

> The third lives in Massachusetts and he's been doing all the goddamned work. California gets on an airplane, visits, and every so often sends a check. Massachusetts is ready to kill someone; he's so pissed at his siblings. The parent says to Massachusetts, "I know you've done a lot. California has let you down and Minnesota is busy. I'll go to a nursing home and it'll be okay."

Often it was Barbara's task to comfort the sibling on whom the burden fell.

> I had a man and three older sisters who put everything on him. They had to move their mother into a nursing home. He would have liked me to persuade his sisters to pitch in, so he could live his life in peace. But I couldn't do that. It was up to him. He'd call me every day: "Oh, God. Where are my mother's bank statements? Where's her social security card? I forgot to go to the bank. I should be able to do this myself. . . ." So I would sit with him and write down on a piece of paper, "Go to bank. Open account. . . ."

Barbara's job shifted with the needs of each client but one task remained constant: checking in on the elderly person whose fate she was helping to manage.

> Sometimes I visit them at nine at night. They usually aren't asleep and no one else is around. The nurses are writing up their reports. The floor is quiet. The woman I currently look in on is lonely and watches *General Hospital*, which makes her feel lonelier. I get there and she talks my head off.

As we pulled into the Pleasant Vista Nursing and Rehabilitation Home, Barbara reached her arm back to scratch her dog's wrinkled ear. "Itty-Bitty's the secret to my success, aren't ya, Itty?

Some nursing homes don't allow dogs," she said, "so I carry her in my yellow canvas bag with a cloth over her head and walk fast. Itty-Bitty's cool, stone silent as we pass the guard." We got off the elevator at the third floor and stepped into a birthday party for Erik, a ninety-year-old divorcé who had taped on the wall by his bed a photo of his family with one face snipped out. "His ex-wife," Barbara later whispered. Surrounded by a circle of half a dozen female residents, he sat in his wheelchair eating small spoonfuls of vanilla ice cream served to him by a rotund aide.

Barbara was not actually paid to look in on Erik, but rather on his neighbor, eighty-nine-year-old Milly. As we made our way over to Milly's room, Barbara addressed one wheelchair-bound resident after another. "Hey, Ted. . . . How's the cake?" "Alice, I didn't see you last week when I dropped by. Were you visiting your daughter?" "Dot, you're looking spiffy in that pink dress." Milly's children were concerned that she felt isolated in the nursing home, so Barbara always made a point of socializing with Milly's neighbors to help forge connections.

We found Milly in her room, a small, quiet woman recovering from a stroke. Barbara sat down next to her and, bending forward, held a slow, soft conversation with the disheartened woman. A while later, Barbara stood up and we left. She had felt Milly's depression. She would convey this to Milly's children and think what else to advise—maybe more family visits.

Then we clambered back in the van and headed out to visit another client's parent in another nursing home. On the way Barbara recounted the story of Victoria Ganio, a marine biologist who had written five books on sea mammals and cofounded one of the nation's most innovative public aquariums. A kindly niece who lived in Charlottesville, North Carolina, had engaged Barbara to visit Victoria twice a week. As Barbara put it, "The niece hired me to love Victoria. And that was easy because Victoria was great." But loving Victoria exposed the contradictions of a bond that, in the end, was neither familial nor, strictly speaking, professional.

Barbara described the photos on the walls around Victoria's nursing-home bed, which showed a radiant young woman enthralled by the natural world around her. In one she held up two large-eyed otter pups by the napes of their necks; in another, she bent down to a penguin as if in conversation; in a third, she stood beaming beside an enormous whiskered walrus. "At one time," Barbara said in awe, "Victoria was magnificent."

By the time Barbara got the call from the niece, Victoria had been devastated by Parkinson's disease:

> She weighed eighty pounds. She couldn't walk or talk much. When I first saw her, it was shocking to imagine she was the gifted, playful woman in the photos I saw taped around her bed. It broke my heart. I was looking at what we all dread.

But Barbara discovered that Victoria was of sound mind and that she could make Victoria feel better simply by sitting beside her:

> I could tell when I locked her in the eye: she was all there. Her mind was fine. It's just that it was hard to move the muscles around her mouth. She would speak very little. But when she did, she was brilliant and sharp. I'd say, "Victoria, d'you mind if I put the dog in bed with you?" Victoria's reply, "Why don't you ask the dog?"

A reserved person who'd lived alone all her life and had no children, Victoria had few visitors. The niece who had engaged Barbara sent cheerful postcards of otters and seals, now also taped to the walls. A young woman who waited tables at the luncheonette where Victoria used to eat regularly brought her issues of *National Geographic*. For a time, a thoughtful cousin had driven down from Maine to visit every year but, discovering that Victoria could barely talk, had given up. Other relatives and friends living busy lives far away lost contact.

Barbara was hired to make up for the absence of people in Victoria's life, but she did far more.

> I started by taking Victoria to the best Parkinson's doctor in Boston for a second opinion and asking him, "Is this the right diagnosis? Is she on the right meds? The right dose?" The answers were "Yes."

Knowing of her love for animals, Barbara usually brought biscuits for Victoria to feed to Itty-Bitty, along with other treats.

> I'd say, "Victoria, would you like a chocolate-chocolate ice-cream soda?" She'd take a sip and her eyes would light up with pleasure. I'd ask, "Do you like it?" She'd say, "Take a guess." She wanted to connect. She'd take my hand.

Barbara also drove Victoria to the local aquarium, to an aviary, to the zoo. When, over time, Victoria lost interest in such trips and special treats, Barbara found Victoria's decline painful to watch:

> I told her, "I'll do anything for you. We'll get in the car. We'll take Itty-Bitty and go to the ocean. Please, what would you like to do?" But she'd say: "I don't want to go anywhere."

This broke Barbara's heart: "I knew I couldn't fix her, but I couldn't bear to see that my visits no longer gave her pleasure."[5] Barbara's job had turned into a calling and her paid visits had come to express friendship. But she was disturbed to also realize that, for her, the friendship depended on being able to give Victoria some measure of joy. "The niece paid me thirty dollars an hour for the visits. It was good money, but I couldn't bear to see Victoria withdraw from me and from life. I had to quit."

"What if you'd been offered sixty dollars an hour?" I probed.

"No, it wouldn't have made a difference."

> It hurt that I couldn't make her smile, laugh, show interest in life. What made this job hard was not Victoria's disability. It was that the family hired me to love her but I couldn't do it if we couldn't connect. People relate to each other through pleasure. When Victoria ceased to feel pleasure, she couldn't connect with me. I even live near the nursing home, but I just couldn't make myself walk in. It wasn't worth the money. I would have done it anyway if it had been my mother but Victoria wasn't my mother.

Barbara didn't completely give up. On Victoria's next birthday, she dropped in to the nursing home:

> Victoria's hair was filthy, not just a week's filthy, a month's. I stalked up to the nurse's station, livid. I pulled a nutty. I said, "Give me the soap! Get me a basin! Give me water—now!" They said "Oh, we'll do it." I said, "I'll do it. Just because her family lives in New Jersey, don't think no one's watching." I reacted like family.

A year later, Barbara stopped by again, this time discovering Victoria sitting in the lounge bent over a watery bowl of oatmeal. Barbara offered her a "chocolate-chocolate ice-cream soda." Victoria drank it but without comment, smile, or upward glance, then slowly returned to her oatmeal. "That was the worst," Barbara said. "She had improved physically, but ceased to enjoy anything."

As Barbara struggled to make sense of her feelings about Victoria, I asked Barbara what she might have done if she had been Victoria.

> Me? I'd find a way to lick a typewriter with my tongue. Or I'd use my nose, like some of these quadriplegics on *60 Minutes* and my sentence would read "U-s-e m-e f-o-r r-e-s-e-a-r-c-h o-n a-n e-x-p-e-r-i-m-e-n-t-a-l d-r-u-g t-o c-o-

> n-q-u-e-r t-h-i-s d-i-s-g-u-s-t-i-n-g d-i-s-e-a-s-e. J-u-s-t d-o-n-'-t h-u-r-t m-e."

A few years later, when Barbara got word that Victoria Ganio had passed away, she paid her own way to travel to New York to attend the funeral.

"It's Unprofessional to Be Upset"

Barbara could stride cheerfully through a series of dreary nursing homes, but she couldn't bear Victoria's retreat from pleasure—and her own inability to halt it. "It's unprofessional to be upset at such a thing. I'd rather hire a person less emotionally involved," one working parent with an ailing mother mused, when I told her of Barbara's decision to quit. But I wondered, wasn't it precisely Barbara's unusual level of care that brought Victoria joy in the first place? And how was it possible to hire one person to love another but expect them to remain uninvolved?

I also kept thinking of Barbara's comment about Victoria not being her mother. For a time, Barbara had given Victoria more loving care than many adult children give their aging parents. Indeed, during the period she had been bringing chocolate sodas to Victoria, meeting clients who were placing disabled elders in facilities, and reviewing medical reports, Barbara had begun to worry about her own mother, a widow, now diabetic, blind, and living alone in Florida.

> I was helping others. But I badly needed help myself. After Dad died, Mom fell into a slump. My brother was furious at our mother and wanted nothing to do with her—which I understood. For seven years, my father had beaten me and my brother, and my mother let it happen. She was a weak person

> and barely a so-so mother. Even with that, I still couldn't stand by and watch Mom sink.

So in stolen moments during her workday, Barbara swung into action:

> I put an ad in the paper for someone to live with Mom in her home. I wanted a person who would watch her meds, wouldn't steal the television or hurt her. I found someone good but she didn't last. I called my mother's friends in Florida. I called her neighbors. I called and called.

Having no other choice, Barbara first placed her mother in a Florida nursing home but after three months moved her to one in Boston:

> In the last six months of her life, I visited my mom two or three times a week. When I was alone with her, I'd bring up the past. "Mom, why didn't you protect me from Dad?" I asked her. She said, "I didn't think he was hurting you much" or "I tried." And I asked, "How did you feel about him hurting me at all?" She said, "Not good but what was I going to do?" I wanted to know why she never said she loved me. She cried and said, "My parents never said it to me." I told her, "Look how miserable you are! Do you want me to be that miserable?" Then my mother'd laugh. So I told her, "Start saying it to me, if you feel like it." When I visited the nursing home, I'd crawl into bed with her and Itty-Bitty would lie between us. The nurse thought we were hilarious. The month before she died, she told me she loved me all the time.

Day after day, Barbara drew out the appreciative mother she'd wished for from the listless mother she had. As with Victoria, it was uphill work, but unlike with Victoria, Barbara did not walk away. Her actions in both cases revealed the delicate boundary between choice and duty. Barbara felt that she could choose to end a commercial relationship, even a loving one, if it caused her pain. But she made no such calculation when it came to family, even with a barely "so-so" mother.

Living in the Now

It was evening when we arrived at Sunrise Senior Home, an enormous white building edged by newly planted shrubs, pines, and maple trees, a landscaper's failed attempt to curtain off a vast parking lot and the nearby juncture of two four-lane freeways. This was Barbara's last stop of the day. As we entered the building, she ducked Itty-Bitty's head down into her canvas shoulder bag again, covered her up, and walked with authority through the front door. We took the elevator to the fourth floor and were buzzed in through two heavy doors to the Alzheimer's ward—a vast room in which we found a stony-faced man pushing a walker along the marbled linoleum floor, a woman clutching a pocketbook and staring at us, and, along the wall, a row of slumped white-haired figures in wheelchairs. "They call this the recreation room," Barbara whispered. She asked a Jamaican nurse's aide to take us to Bill, the father of Barbara's client.

Widowed, Bill had been spending days wandering about subway stations. His devoted daughter had him evaluated, diagnosed, and placed, for the moment, in Sunrise Senior Home. Now she wanted to move him in with her, hoping to help him improve. Barbara was advising her on what to do and in the meantime checking in on Bill.

Bill was seated at what looked like an old-fashioned school desk, hunched over his dinner tray, fork in midair. Barbara wanted to get a better sense of him to help advise his daughter.

"Hi, Bill, my name is Barbara. Remember me?"

He stared at Barbara but said nothing.

"No? I'm a friend of your daughter, Dorothy."

Still no response.

"This is Itty-Bitty. Say hi, Itty-Bitty. Sometimes Itty-Bitty's shy but she does say hi. Do you remember I brought her the last time I came? We fed her potato chips. She loves potato chips."

. . .

"Do you have any potato chips?"

. . .

"No? Okay."

. . .

"I brought you some clean shirts. Dorothy asked me to drop them off. Here they are. Shall I put them in your room?"

Bill nodded.

"Okay, good. I'll put them in your room."

Barbara took Bill's shirts to his room, returned, and eased herself into a chair next to Bill.

"So how do they feed you in this place? Is that lamb chop any good?"

He offered an ambiguous nod.

"Good. And that sweet potato looks pretty good, too. Itty-Bitty doesn't go for sweet potato; otherwise she'd ask you for some. So did Dorothy drop by yesterday? I called her and she said she was going to drop by yesterday."

Bill was staring intently at Barbara now.

"Say, where do you come from, Bill?"

He looked puzzled.

"I mean where were you born? I was born in New York. You can probably tell." She laughed. "Where were you born?"

For the first time, distinctly, he spoke. "Scotch. . . ."

"I didn't ask what you *drank*."

Suddenly Bill's face lit up and he guffawed. Pause. More guffaws.

"So you like your Scotch because you were born in Scotland!"

Scotch and Scotland, Barbara kept the ball in motion. Bill laughed some more, and slowly the "conversation" trailed to an end. He returned his attention to the plate on his tray. After a while, Barbara, Itty-Bitty, and I said our good-byes. An attendant punched in a code. One large steel door, then another, opened. We walked out of the building into the early June evening. Barbara remarked, "Bill has no past or future. He just has now. I'd like to learn to live in the now. Shouldn't we all?"

Barbara offered care to people at moments of great vulnerability, it occurred to me, in a society that separates young from old, beams commercial headlights on fourteen-year-olds, casting the old in shadows, and requires money most don't have to afford the extra services of a Barbara. The need is great and Barbara's gift is rare. But what was in it for her? I wondered. She could earn the same money hunting down rare wines and parts for antique cars. Instead she did what looked like the hardest work in the world. Why?

Barbara lifted the bag with Itty-Bitty off her shoulder, set it down, and looked back across the vast empty parking lot at Sunrise Senior Home.

> So many Victorias and Bills get lost in the shuffle. That doesn't have to be. America needs more people who really like this work. Maybe you need some weird childhood like mine to motivate you. Maybe you don't. But, God knows, we need laughter. I was visiting a severely ill patient one day and four dull-faced doctors trotted into her room, stethoscopes hanging from their necks. And I said, "So what organ are you here for?" Everyone laughed. I wish laughter were on the Medicare wellness checklist—I'd go check-check-check.
>
> But what do *you* get out of it? I asked.
>
> Take that moment when I said to Bill, "I didn't ask you what you drink." He lit up like a Christmas tree! That's why I love my work. I don't need to be thanked. "Thank you" is such an

intimate thing to say, and some people don't say it because it means "I need you." But this isn't thankless work. Some people think visiting elderly people is for the birds. But man, are they wrong. You can make a real difference. If I sit beside an elderly person and slowly rub cream on their hand, or comb their hair, I've made their life better.

Chapter 14

Endings

In March of 1901, when Edith Pratt's mother died and had to be buried, the small plot with tilted granite markers in a nearby cemetery in Turner, Maine, was probably still frozen. So the family might have waited to bury her ashes until after the April thaw. Family and friends, the women in long, dark dresses, tight about the collar, might have gathered on the slope. A grave digger, a neighbor, bowing his head in condolence, might have waited for a folded bill clapped in handshake between two rough hands. A service at the white-steepled wooden church down the road, hymns sung to a wheezing pump organ, words of remembrance, food and drink back at the house; that might have been it.

Many early gravestones in the New England hills tell of people who lived close to farm and village and died at home. Compared to the past, modern death in America most often occurs away from home: three-quarters of American deaths now take place in hospitals or nursing homes. And death is often managed not by the local community and church but by the ministrations of the market.[1]

To be sure, death in America has long been a business, as Jessica

Mitford described so well in her 1963 book, *The American Way of Death*, but the end of life has greatly expanded its market share since then. In what is now a $15-billion-a-year industry, large national chains of funeral homes have crowded out small, local funeral parlors, paralleling the growth of for-profit chains of nursing homes. The largest chain among them, the Houston-based Service Corporation International, now outsources funeral billing to anonymous back-office workers in India, even as it offers a promise of a highly personal experience to mourners at home.[2]

A grieving family today can, for example, express their loved one's individual personality by selecting an urn in the shape of a football helmet with a favorite team logo emblazoned on the side, a teddy bear with pockets for the ashes of the deceased, a NASCAR-themed casket, or a biodegradable one for the environmentally conscious. Bessemer Brown Funeral Home in North Bessemer, Alabama, offers, through its Celestis space memorial service, to launch a payload of memorial ashes into lunar orbit, with a videotape of the launch included in the price of burial. Eternal Reefs places structures containing cremains, as the ashes of the deceased are called, twenty feet below the ocean's surface, creating artificial reefs. The ashes of hunters can be loaded into specially produced "ammunition" and shot out of guns. For four thousand dollars, Maritime Funeral Services in Long Island, New York, offers to pack cremains into fireworks and send them aloft from a barge three miles offshore, timed to go off to music chosen by family and friends watching from a distance. Maritime and others also sell a line of lockets and pendants that hold tiny amounts of loved ones' ashes.[3]

Such modern funerals are not more personal than the 1901 funeral in Turner—but they are more personalized. As in the past, families are expressing love for the deceased and grief at their loss. But they are now expressing these feelings in a context far more oriented to consumerism. Their choices are personal in the sense that they have been individually selected—from a fixed list of options featured by a commercial service in a brochure or online. But in that very list of options we see how far the market has reached into the final moments of intimate life.

Into the Waters

Gus Hald is the founder of Maritime Funeral Services and the captain of the *Determination*, a forty-three-foot yacht docked off the coast of Long Island. An earnest, cherub-faced man, he has scattered at sea the cremated remains of over a thousand people. "It's a business and a service both," he explained. Water burial is, in fact, a growth business, as over one-third of all families choose to cremate the remains of loved ones and 18 percent of those are scattered on some body of water. To honor the solemn spirit of this activity, Gus assures his clients, he will not combine the burial of ashes with other purposes—fishing, weddings, diving, sightseeing—for which his yacht can also be used.

On three-quarters of his burial-at-sea trips, relatives and friends come on board ($675 for six passengers) to accompany the ashes to their final resting place. For a quarter of the trips, however, no one accompanies the ashes, and Gus himself scatters them for a $150 fee. What was the difference, I asked Gus, between the two types of trip? He replied:

> When relatives are on board, before we set out, I carefully pour the ashes from a cardboard box into a beautiful china urn. I drape a brocade cloth on a table and place the urn on it. The relatives can look at the urn on the cloth. When I get three miles out, I turn off the motor. I take the urn from the table, slowly walk it over to the bow of my yacht, and set it down. I pull out my bag of nasturtium blossoms and toss them into the water. Then I pour the ashes onto the waves. If the relatives are there, I enjoy dropping the flowers as part of the ceremony.

"What happens if the relatives don't come with you?" I asked.

> Then I keep the ashes in the cardboard box. I don't pour them into the urn or put the fancy cloth on the table. When I get three miles out, I drop the nasturtium blossoms and then pour the ashes over the side of the boat.

Why did he scatter the blossoms, I wondered, even when the family wasn't in the launch? "I do it with respect," he answered. "But I also need to know which way the flowers are floating. That's how I can tell which way the wind is blowing so the ashes don't stick to the side of the boat."

Besides dealing with death and the disposition of the body, survivors face the task of honoring the memory of the deceased. Concierge services have sprouted up in the niche between traditional funeral parlors and church, mosque, or synagogue. The Los Angeles–based event-planning company Shiva Sisters, which serves Jewish clients, gets involved before death takes place. It then secures the death certificate, organizes the funeral, orders food, and arranges valet parking and video production for the post-funeral reception and seven-day period of mourning. Danna Black, an event planner who started the company in 2009 with her partner, Allison Moldo, a mortgage specialist, described a woman dying of cancer who hired Shiva Sisters to buy her burial plot and plan a service because "she didn't want her husband or son to have to deal with this."[4] Houston-based Everest Funeral Package also helps families write obituaries and gather information on prices of caskets and cemetery services, thereby "removing the family," they claim, "from a sales-focused environment."[5]

Following the funeral, bereaved Catholics may ask for the repose of the soul of a deceased relative through a "Mass Intention," a blessing for the dead to be offered by a priest in church during a mass. The blessing helps the soul win forgiveness, Catholics believe, and ascend to heaven. Decades ago, an American believer could pay a priest in one's local church to say a mass in English for the soul of a departed. Today, however, some American and Canadian Catholic churches outsource the task of offering blessings for the dead to foreign priests for a price. Given the declining numbers entering the American priesthood, and financial hard times in the American Catholic Church, requests for Mass Intentions are now routed through a special department at the Vatican to Catholic churches in southern India. As Bishop Sebastian Adayanthrath, the auxiliary bishop of the Ernakulam-Angamaly diocese in the state of Kerala, told the *New York Times*, his diocese receives an average of 350 Mass Intentions a month from overseas. Priests say the prayers in Malayalam, the local language of Kerala. Prayer requests average five dollars in the United States and 90 cents (40 rupees) in Kerala. Bishop Adayanthrath received fewer requests during the global financial crisis, he said, but predicts the number to rise with an economic recovery.[6]

Care of the gravesite, a practice traditionally expected of family and friends, can also be outsourced. Terry Marotta-Lopriore, a Bronx-born Catholic paralegal and mother of three, earns extra money hiring herself out to visit graves ($25 for Westchester cemeteries and $35 for longer trips to Putnam County). She also offers to do $50 per hour "energy readings," which pass messages, she says, from the dead to the living.[7] Los Angeles–based Headstone Butler offers to clean and polish the gravestones, deliver flowers, light incense, and visit graves for $29.95 a month, "further elevating the spiritual aura of the final resting place." The company also offers "prearranged future care" and notes, in its Internet ad, that "taking care of our departed loved ones is very important for the development of our children's character." One caption under a photo of a small boy, smiling by a gravestone, reads, "Look Grandpa Mike, it's already clean. Well that takes care of that."[8]

From the folded bill pressed in a handshake on a hillside in a New England cemetery long ago, to the fee paid to priests to bless a departed spirit, to the outsourcing of Catholic blessings to Kerala, the market has long been a breath away from life's most sacred moments. But with NASCAR-themed caskets, hunter's ash-ammunition packed in guns, and Celestis space orbits, it seems that we Americans no longer feel confident relying on traditional practices or on ourselves to gather together in gentle dignity to say goodbye to someone we love.

Conclusion

The Wantologist

In the sprawling outskirts of San Jose, California, I found myself at the last stop on my journey, standing at the apartment door of Esther James, wantologist. Could it really be, I wondered, that before doing anything else—hiring a love coach, a wedding planner, a surrogate mother, a nameologist, or an elder-care manager—we should enlist a wantologist to help us sort out what we want? Had I arrived, I wondered, at some final telling moment in my search or at the absurdist edge of the market frontier?

A willowy woman of fifty-five, with inquiring blue eyes and a shy manner, Esther beckoned me in. Did I want to take my shoes off, she asked softly as she took my coat. She pointed to a pair of small slippers tucked by the door should I choose to. On her living-room wall hung a framed PhD degree in psychology from New York University, colorful Indian quilts, and a collage of images clipped from magazines—the back of a child's head, a gnarled tree, a wandering cat—that seemed to invite one to search for a coherent story to connect them. We had met weeks before at a dinner sponsored by the San Francisco chapter of the Professional Coaches and Mentors Association. I'd asked to meet again and she had kindly invited me to lunch. Between bites of a delicious home-cooked curry chicken, I asked Esther how she had found her way to wantology.

"I practiced for twenty years as a Jungian psychologist," she answered with a disarming smile, "but I've studied many thinkers along the way":

> I'm a therapy junky. Ten years ago, I took a nine-day course at the College of Executive Coaching in Pismo Beach, California, and started coaching Silicon Valley executives. I earned two hundred and fifty dollars an hour, but after the economic downturn jobs like that were hard to find. So I got interested in life coaching, and that led me to wantology.

It was originally a method, she explained, invented by Kevin Creitman, an aerospace engineer, designed to help corporate planners double-check their purchasing decisions. ("I help them see that the fantasy they attach to a purchase may not correspond to what it can actually accomplish.")[1] Creitman set up a two-day class to train life coaches in how to apply her (Kevin is a woman) method to individuals and, not long afterward, she certified Esther in the new field. Esther reverently showed me her Wantology Workbook, subtitled: "The first steps to Really Get What You Really Want is to really KNOW what you really want." Printed in large type, the cover featured a solitary man in a white T-shirt facing a large sun illuminating a blue sky. "So how do you practice wantology?" I asked Esther. She explained the first step in thinking about a "want":

> First you ask your client, "Are you floating or navigating toward your goal?" A lot of people float. Then, you ask, "What do you want to *feel like* once you have what you want?" A person can earn four hundred thousand dollars a year, you know, and still not feel secure. We set every kind of trap for ourselves.

She described a client she had recently helped:

> This woman lived in a medium-sized house with a small garden but she wanted a bigger house with a bigger garden. She dreaded telling her husband, who had spent five years renovating their present home. She also feared her son would criticize her for being too materialistic. So she wanted a bigger house and garden but didn't dare ask for it.

Esther took me through her conversation with this woman:

"What do you want?"
"A bigger house."
"How would you feel if you lived in a bigger house?"
"Peaceful."
"What other things make you feel peaceful?"
"Walks by the ocean." (The ocean was an hour's drive away)
"Do you ever take walks nearer where you live that remind you of the ocean?"
"Certain ones, yes."
"What do you like about those walks?"
"I hear the sound of water and feel surrounded by green."

Through such conversations, Esther helped her client redefine her desire. In the end, the woman dedicated a small room in her home to feeling peaceful. She filled it with a wall-high Benjamin fig tree, an Australian tree fern, and lacy maidenhair ferns, some hanging from the ceiling, others perched on upturned pots. The greenery encircled a bubbling slate-and-rock tabletop fountain. Sitting in her new room, the woman found peace in her newly renovated medium-sized house and garden.

I was touched by the woman's story. Perhaps all she needed was someone wise to help her articulate her desire—an Esther offering her wisdom and working for hire had provided this most human of services—albeit one with a wacky name. But the mere existence of a paid "wantologist" indicates just how far the market has penetrated our intimate lives. Can it be that we are no longer confident to identify even our most ordinary desires without a professional to guide us?

Over the last century, the world of services has changed greatly. A hundred—or even forty—years ago, human eggs and sperm were not for sale nor were wombs for rent. Online dating companies, nameologists, life coaches, party animators, and paid graveside visitors did not exist, even as ideas. Nor had a language developed that so seamlessly melded village and market—as in "Rent-a-Mom," "Rent-a-Dad," "Rent-a-Grandma," "Rent-a-Friend"—insinuating itself, half joking, half serious, into our culture.

These services are only likely to proliferate in a world that undermines community, disparages government, marginalizes nonprofits, and believes in the superiority of what's for sale. A cycle effect gets going: The more anxious and isolated we are and the less help we receive from nonmarket sources, the more we feel tempted to fill the void with market offerings. As our California survey shows, greater isolation results in greater demand for market services and professionals—life coaches, party planners, photograph-album assemblers—to fill in for what's missing.[2]

The market is now present in our bedrooms, at our breakfast tables, in our love lives, entangled in our deepest joys and sorrows. And the more the market is the main game in town, the more hooked we get on what it sells, and the more convinced that paid expertise is what we lack and an even larger service mall is the only way to go.

The market is ever too willing to oblige. Take eHarmony, for example. This successful champion of the "M" (marriage) market is rapidly expanding its operations into later stages of adult life, into workplace and college relationships, and into relationships in other societies—Japan, Argentina, Australia, and Eastern European countries, with more to come. So as community-starved people come to crave company-provided counsel, comfort, and support, companies extend services—for those who can pay. The cycle takes another turn.

Ironically, the greater our dependence on the market, the greater its power to subtly undermine our intimate life. As the ex–advertising executive and author of *In the Absence of the Sacred*, Jerry Mander, observed, "With commerce, we always get the good news first and the bad news after a while. First we hear the car goes faster than the horse. Then we hear it clogs freeways and pollutes the air." The bad news in this case is the capacity of the service market, with all its expertise, to sap self-confidence in our own capacities, and those of friends and family. The professional nameologist finds a more auspicious name than we can recall from our family tree. The professional potty trainer does the job better than the bumbling parent or helpful neighbor. Jimmy's Art Supply sells a better Spanish mission replica kit than your child can build from paint, glue, and a Kleenex box. Happiest Day promises a more personally uplifting wedding. Happy Travels promises a more carefree holiday. Our life coach is more upbeat than our friend. Our imperfect, homemade versions of life seem to us all the poorer by comparison. Consider some recent shifts in language. Care of family and friends is increasingly referred to as "lay care." The act of meeting a romantic partner at a flesh-and-blood gathering rather than online is disparaged by some Internet coaches as "dating in the wild." We picture competition as a matter of one business outdoing another. But the fiercest competition may be the quietly ongoing one between the market and private life. As a setter of standards of the ideal experience, it often wins, whether we buy a service or not.

The very ease with which we reach for market services may also prevent us from noticing the remarkable degree to which the market has come to dominate our very ideas about what can or should be for sale or rent, and who should be included in the dramatic cast—buyers, branders, sellers—that we imagine as part of a personal life. Most important of all, it may prevent us from noticing how we devalue what we don't or can't buy.

Even more than *what* we wish, the market alters *how* we wish. Wallet in hand, we focus in the market on the thing we buy. In the realm of services this is an experience—the perfect wedding, the delicious "traditional" meal, the well-raised child, even the well-gestated baby. What escapes us is the *process* of getting there—and the appreciation we attach to the small details of it. A busy executive detaches himself from the need for patience. Norma Brown, the wealthy employer of a household manager, detached herself from the act of making out Christmas-present labels. The Headstone Butler does a more efficient job of beautifying a grave. Riveting our attention on the destination, we detach ourselves from the many small—potentially meaningful—steps in our journey. Confining our sense of achievement to results, to the moment of purchase, so to speak, we unwittingly lose the pleasures of accomplishment, the joy of connecting to others, and even, in the process, our faith in ourselves.

In the face of the market's depersonalization of our bonds with others, we do what we can, consciously or not, to repersonalize them, to make the market feel less like a market. We blow up the birthday balloons ourselves, we befriend the babysitter, we lie about cooking the lamb roast. We don't see these moves as defenses against anything; they feel as natural and unproblematic as opening an umbrella in a storm. Reasonably enough, we adapt our identities to life on the market frontier and try to protect ourselves from its potentially depersonalizing effects.

How do we do it? We demarcate symbolic artifacts or places that represent cherished moments of unoutsourced life; we reclaim a home activity that friends and neighbors might have conceded to the realm of paid services; we engage the market via a secret back channel to avoid embarrassment or hurt feelings; we compensate for outsourcing in one area of life by setting up a market-free realm or restoring a human touch by forging an emotional connection to the service provider. We avoid. We substitute. We compensate. We take back. We encapsulate. We compartmentalize. We reach out. We subordinate. We can use several mechanisms of defense, serially or at the same time, or none at all. These can be so strong as to define our whole character, or they can be almost inconsequential. These defenses apply to consumers and service workers both.

It's so easy to do this, and we do it so automatically, we forget how quickly things that only yesterday seemed bizarre have become the norm today. As a people, Americans are brilliant at adapting to change. In a world that changes so rapidly, it's a useful skill. But there is a hidden danger attached to it. For without quite naming it, we're all busily adapting, trying to "regulate" the market from the inside. And what we're not doing is altering the basic imbalance between market, state, and civic life that caused us to need to draw line after line in the first place.

It's become common to hear that the market can do no wrong and the government—at least its civilian part—can do no right, and to hear scant mention of community at all. Curiously, many who press to expand the free market are the same people who call for stronger families. But do freer markets lead to stronger families? Those who make this claim point to the service mall, and say yes. Far less visible, however, are the harmful effects of free-market policies—deregulation, service cuts, privatization—on families. Unregulated televisions ads for junk food may be good for the market, for example, but bad for children. Cuts in public funding that shorten library hours, close state parks, or speed up staff turnover in nursing homes may be a plus for the free market, but they are a blow to families. Less visible, too, is the way in which market values subtly distort family values. For the more we apply market language, habits of emotional detachment, and focus on "the purchase moment" to our most intimate life, the more fragile it becomes. And while we've become very clever at seeing how market and family mix, we're less clever at seeing how they don't. In

Capitalism and Freedom, the economist Milton Friedman offered the dream of pure capitalism as an antidote to a monstrous overreach of Russian communism. But every system reflects a contradiction between its ideals and its reality. Soviet-style communism had its. Theocracies have theirs. And we have ours.[3]

What's at stake in ignoring this contradiction is not simply family life, but the marginalization of our entire public realm. Public libraries, parks, wilderness preserves, free information—the commons—all exist outside the for-profit sphere.[4] All are available to rich and poor alike. As the class gap widens, it's the one remaining social space within which the poor can enjoy equal respect. We mostly talk about the balance of power within the government between the executive, legislative, and judicial branches, but we badly need to confront the larger and looming imbalance between the market and everything else.

If the wantologist were to put on her couch some of the caregivers in this book and ask them what kind of society they wanted to live in, what would she hear? "If the government had the budget to pay me to help inner-city school dropouts get back on track," one life coach told me, "I'd take it in a heartbeat." As the elder-care manager Barbara mused, "I think America needs a lot of people like me dropping in on poor isolated elderly folks—and that's not going to be a big money maker." "I'd love to play the guitar in children's cancer wards," a guitarist who worked private birthday parties told me, "if I could make a living at it." If jobs corresponded to social needs, they agreed, we'd have plenty of jobs to go around. And more time as well. One Sri Lankan nanny who quit her job in a for-profit nursing home with a low staff-to-patient ratio and high turnover said, "why not bring families into the lives of the old, like we do in Sri Lanka?" And if Maricel, the Filipina nanny, had her way, parents would work shorter hours and send nannies home earlier.

Curiously, it was indirectly, through talk about memories, that I caught a glimpse into the deeper feelings of many people I talked with about the encroachment of the market into their personal lives. The memories they treasured did not center on the professionally planned birthday party, picture-perfect wedding, or hassle-free vacation tour. Instead, they vividly remembered times when things went haywire or otherwise surprised them. One man remembered his dad sitting at a picnic table in the pouring rain, doggedly conversing with a neighbor "as if the sun was shining," as he'd rashly predicted it would on the day when he'd organized a picnic. A single working mother remembered laughing with her girls in disbelief at the floor-to-ceiling kitchen mess after a full day of holiday cooking. Other people remembered moments of spontaneity. Rose Whitman fondly recalled her father rousting his sleepy children from bed to go *schlumpking* to an open field at the edge of town to peer up at the spectacle of the northern lights.

My aunt Elizabeth's story ended with its own welcome blend of village and market. After a long search, I had, at last, found Shawn DePerrio, a caregiver, to live with my aunt—a lively young woman who instantly bonded with her. At last, she was free to live full-time at home, to admire the peanut butter jar holding up her living-room window, sit back in her favorite chair, and look out on the stony hills her ancestors had long ago tilled.

She recovered her capacity to scold, to tease, and to feel glad to be alive. In Shawn's hands, my aunt became the kind, bright, funny, and, for the most part, good-humored person of my childhood memory. Shawn planted red geraniums in front of the house and a vegetable garden to the side of it. "We need it larger," my aunt commented. "Where's the corn going to grow?"

Often Shawn would pack my aunt into her old car and head out for a nearby apple orchard to "harvest apples" out of a rolled-down passenger-side window. "The apples on this tree are too small," my aunt would say. "Can you drive a little farther in?" When they'd collected a bag of apples, they went home to bake a pie. Some evenings the two sang together, Shawn related by phone laughingly, "like Barbra Streisand." In her last years, Elizabeth totally forgot the time she had passionately refused the idea of "a stranger in the house."

By the time my aunt died in peace at home at the age of ninety-eight, just as I was finishing this book, she had forgotten quite a lot. But, to the end, she would tilt her head in laughter at the memory of her last Turner Fourth of July parade. Unable to walk, she was transported to the town's main street by two husky off-duty EMTs in their ambulance and then hoisted onto a stately, white, open-topped buggy pulled by a horse whose tail was braided with red, white, and blue ribbons. The horse stomped and whinnied impatiently, waiting for the parade to begin. The buggy driver, flicking the reins across his steed's mane, was a kindly neighboring farmer. And, seated beside Elizabeth on a plush red velvet seat was Shawn DePerrio, paid and loving.

First came the beating of a drum strapped to a lean, serious-faced boy. Then came the whole Turner High School band, dressed in white shirts and blue shorts—four horns, clarinets, a flute, and two sets of cymbals—followed by the baton twirlers, two by two. The floats from the Turner History Museum, the flower show, and the Veterans of Foreign Wars—old men waving from wooden chairs set on the back of a flatbed truck—were the heart of the parade, along with a 1920s dairy truck, a reaper, a harvester, and a thresher that looked like a giant cricket.

Then came my aunt Elizabeth, waving left and right like a queen, and there was Shawn, beaming at her side. To most observers, my aunt was a white-haired lady in a buggy. To those in the know, she was a lively, strong-willed villager who had needed the help of a range of caretakers, paid and unpaid, in order to sit happily there that day. And to a few townspeople in the crowd, there was the lady who'd taught a parent or grandparent to hold a pencil and sing a song in a one-room schoolhouse long ago.

Notes

Introduction: Villager and Outsourcer

1. In his 1899 *Theory of the Leisure Class*, the Norwegian-born sociologist Thorstein Veblen peevishly observed that servants separate the rich from usefulness. The ideal of the upper class—nobility, priests, captains of industry—was to show that it was not they who husked the corn, but they who cultivated cultural taste. Typically the wife "consumes for" the male head of household, he argued, in "conspicuous leisure." Society had things backward, Veblen felt: the more necessary a person's work, the less honor attached to it. Thorstein Veblen, *The Theory of the Leisure Class* (New York: B. W. Huebsch, 1912 [1899]), p. 63. For their part, my parents soon tired of the high life and occasionally subverted it. One evening my father dressed in a tuxedo and my mother in evening gown arrived at an obligatory cocktail party, for example, apologizing that they had to leave shortly to attend a formal dinner. They made the rounds at the cocktail party, said their good-byes, returned home, and snuck into bed with good books.
2. On the gift exchange, see Lewis Hyde, *The Gift: Imagination and the Erotic Life of Property* (New York: Vintage Books, 1983); Marcel Mauss, *The Gift: The Form and Reason for Exchange in Archaic Societies*, trans. W. D. Halls (New York: W. W. Norton, 2000 [1954]).

3. See Carolyn Dimitri, Anne Effland, and Neilson Conklin, "The 20th Century Transformation of U.S. Agriculture and Farm Policy," *Electronic Information Bulletin* 3(2005), http://www.ers.usda.gov/publications/eib3/eib3.htm; USDA Economic Research Service, "A History of American Agriculture: Farmers & the Land," United States Department of Agriculture, http://www.agclassroom.org/gan/timeline/farmers_land.htm.
4. Between 1992, when the North American Free Trade Agreement (NAFTA) was signed, and 2002, many manufacturing jobs were lost in Maine—including nearly 5,000 in footwear, 6,000 jobs in other leather products, and over 3,000 in other forms of manufacturing. See Congressional Record of the Senate, "Proceedings and Debates of the 107th Congress: Second Session" (Washington, DC: U.S. Government Printing Office, 2002), p. 8802. Many shoe factories relocated abroad. The Maine-based Bass shoe factory, for example, relocated to Puerto Rico and the Dominican Republic, where shoes cost sixteen dollars less to produce than in Maine. See Gerald M. Carbone, "Town Awaits Closing of Bass Shoe Plant with Fear, Sadness," *Providence Journal*, March 1, 1998.
5. In 1910 (the first year the Census Bureau defined metropolitan populations), three in ten (28 percent) of Americans lived in these areas. By 2000, eight in ten (80 percent) did. Through the century, not only did more people come to live in cities, those in cities had more money to spend. See fig. 1–14 in Frank Hobbs and Nicole Stoops, "Demographic Trends in the 20th Century" (Washington, DC: U.S. Government Printing Office, 2002). For the relation of residence to income, see Claude S. Fischer and Michael Hout, *Century of Difference: How America Changed in the Last One Hundred Years* (New York: Russell Sage Foundation, 2006); Hobbs and Stoops, "Demographic Trends in the 20th Century."
6. See Claude Fischer, "Ever-More Rooted Americans," *City and Community* 1:2 (June 2002), 177–98. Relative to most Europeans, Americans have always been more mobile, but they are not more mobile now, Fischer notes, than in the past. Nevertheless, from 1900 on, some evidence suggests, Americans placed less emotional focus on community, nation, and church, and more focus on family. In our study of words used in the *New York Times* from 1900 to 2004, Sarah Garrett and I found that terms such as "sacrifice" and "loyalty" were less and less often coupled with terms denoting the civic sphere (community, nation,

neighbor, church, temple, or synagogue) and more coupled with terms suggesting family (family, children, and kids). See Hochschild and Garrett, "Beyond Tocqueville's Telescope: The Personalized Brand and the Branded Self," *Hedgehog Review* 13, no. 3 (2001): 82–95. See also John Gillis, *A World of Their Own Making: Myth, Ritual, and the Quest for Family Values* (Cambridge, MA: Harvard University Press, 1996).

7. Ashley English, Heidi Hartmann, and Jeff Hayes, "Are Women Now Half the Labor Force? The Truth about Women and Equal Participation in the Labor Force" (Institute for Women's Policy Research, 2010). See also Bureau of Labor Statistics, "11. Employed persons by detailed occupation, sex, race, and Hispanic or Latino ethnicity—2010," Household data, Annual averages, ftp://ftp.bls.gov/pub/special.requests/lf/aat11.txt. On proportion of children in households with working adults, see Joan C. Williams and Heather Boushey, "The Three Faces of Work-Family Conflict," Center for American Progress, January 25, 2010. Today, middle-income families are also working eleven more hours a week than they did in 1979 (Williams and Boushey, p. 1).
8. For data on divorce rates of Americans born in the early 1970s, see Rose M. Kreider and Renee Elli, "Number, Timing, and Duration of Marriages and Divorces: 2009," *Current Population Reports* (2011), http://www.census.gov/prod/2011pubs/p70-125.pdf, p. 16. For lifetime likelihood of divorce, and the notable class and race differences in these rates, see Andrew J. Cherlin, "Demographic Trends in the United States: A Review of Research in the 2000s," *Journal of Marriage and Family* 72, no. 3 (2010): 403–19; Paul R. Amato, "Research on Divorce: Continuing Trends and New Developments," *Journal of Marriage and Family* 72, no. 3 (2010): 650–66; R. Kelly Raley and Larry Bumpass, "The Topography of the Divorce Plateau: Levels and Trends in Union Stability in the United States after 1980," *Demographic Research* 8 (2003); and Andrew J. Cherlin, *The Marriage-Go-Round: The State of Marriage and the Family in America Today* (New York: Alfred A. Knopf, 2009).
9. Robert Kuttner, *Everything for Sale: The Virtues and Limits of Markets* (New York: Alfred A. Knopf, 1997). Compared to today, the companies of the 1950s were more loyal to workers and workers to them. Older workers were paid more than younger ones, not because they contributed more—sometimes they did less—but because companies rewarded loyalty. If a worker worked less efficiently the day he had a cold, he wasn't paid less. All told, life inside the 1950s workplace was more removed from the auction-block model of pure market relations than

its counterpart today. Today, not only workers but entire corporations are treated as commodities. As Kuttner writes: "When the intellectual history of the Reagan era is written, one of the more revealing artifacts will be a chapter in the 1985 Economic Report of the President, titled, 'The Market for Corporate Control.'" The title was drawn from work by Henry Manne who, Kuttner reports, viewed corporations as pure commodities, "like apples" in auction markets (p. 183).

10. Kuttner, ibid., p. 74. Reviewing over a dozen research reports in 2006—before the 2008 recession—economist Francis Green noted a rising rate of involuntary job separation due to permanent layoffs and dismissals. Of dismissed workers, he found that a third find a lower-paying job within six months, a third find a higher-paying one, and a third find no job at all. Even workers who keep their jobs these days often count themselves among the so-called insecurely employed. Francis Green, *Demanding Work: The Paradox of Job Quality in the Affluent Economy* (Princeton, NJ: Princeton University Press, 2006), pp. 148–49.
11. Manpower, Inc., "About Manpower," Manpower, Inc., http://us.manpower.com/us/en/about-manpower/default.jsp.
12. Phoebe Taubman, "Peaceful Revolution: Time to Stop Free-Riding on Families," *Huffington Post*, February 9, 2010, http://www.huffingtonpost.com/phoebe-taubman/ipeaceful-revolutioni-tim_b_455765.html.
13. Edward Zigler and Mary Elizabeth Lang, *Child Care Choices: Balancing the Needs of Children, Families, and Society* (New York: Free Press, 1991), p. 45.
14. To gauge the growth in personal services from 1900 to 2004, Sarah Garrett and I traced the use of words denoting personal services in the pages of the *New York Times*. Using its online historical archive, we tracked the appearance of terms indicating child care and elder care and found them more prevalent in recent decades (child care, day care, babysitter, and related terms in singular and plural form). The mention of the ambiguous terms "servant" and "governess"—older words denoting similar jobs—declined through the century, leaving a mixed picture of change in child- and elder-care services. Over this period the *Times* also shows dramatic growth in mention of newer specialized services—pet care (and related terms such as dog walker, doggy day care), marriage counseling, personal assistants, personal trainers, life coaching, dating services, and wedding planners, for example.

15. From the 1970s onward, conservative thinking that had lain dormant, Kuttner argues, found new audiences among academic economists, government officials, and many Americans. Many were inspired by the Chicago economist Milton Friedman, whose popular book *Capitalism and Freedom* went far beyond classical Adam Smith. Friedman believed in complete freedom for a market that should, he felt, take over the functions of the government, nonprofit organizations, charities, labor unions, and, though this was tacit, the local community and family as well. Friedman called for privatizing public parks, highways, libraries, schools, prisons, the post office, parts of the army. He opposed a minimum wage, progressive taxation, state licencing of doctors, dentists, and air traffic controllers (pp. 150–51 in *Capitalism and Freedom*). He saw no danger in the concentration of power in the market, which he saw as a one-vote, one-purchase democracy (p. 23). Tacitly, Friedman imagined every person and relationship as living on the market auction block. Milton Friedman, *Capitalism and Freedom* (Chicago: University of Chicago Press, 1962); *Take It to the Limits: Milton Friedman on Libertarianism* (Palo Alto, CA: Hoover Institute, Stanford University, 1999), video interview; Milton Friedman and Rose D. Friedman, *Free to Choose: A Personal Statement* (New York: Harcourt Brace Jovanovich, 1980).
16. From Adam Smith, Karl Marx, Jurgen Habermas, Max Weber, Karl Polyani, Erich Fromm, George Simmel, and Christopher Lasch to Viviana Zelizer and Eva Illouz, many thinkers have asked how the market influences our emotional lives and notions of self. Weber focused on fear and anxiety as an engine of capitalism, Erich Fromm, on the market distortion of love, and Karl Marx, in the *Economic and Philosophic Manuscripts*, on our emotional detachment from the work we do or the things we buy. I've been most inspired by the brilliantly innovative corpus of work by the sociologist Viviana Zelizer. To this I've tried to add a "structural roof" and "emotional basement," moves that bring to light, I hope, dilemmas otherwise hard to see or name.

    The first to call this intersection between market and personal life "emotional capitalism" were those interested in the financial uses of it: Kevin Thomson (*Emotional Capital*, 1998), Marc Gobé (*Emotional Branding*, 2001), and Martyn Newman (*Emotional Capitalists*, 2005). In her very illuminating 2007 book *Cold Intimacy*, Eva Illouz zeroes in on the absorption by capitalism of what she calls "the psychoanalytic repertoire." I've also drawn on a line of psychoanalytic thinking from Freud to Erik Erikson and Neil Smelser—on unconscious mechanisms of defense. These are ways of responding to anxiety we sense as violations, large and small, of the principle of the gift exchange, and the generosity we express quite beyond it. Drawing threads from all these works, and adding to them thoughts from my own 1983 book *The Managed Heart,* I focus on small internal moments—which could add up to collective "tipping points" in Gladwell's sense—in which clients feel anxious that they have outsourced "too much" or "too little" of intimate life or thought about personal things in "too marketlike" a way. Please see references in the bibliography.

17. Extending the market metaphor, Jean Slatter, the author of *Hiring the Heavens*, imagines heaven as a great employment agency. Using our "celestial credit card" we can hire a love coach, wedding planner, or personal shopper, although Slatter offers her services as a wantologist back down on earth for $195 an hour. Slatter pictures the outsourcer sitting with God behind her—but on the same level, thereby elevating the believer into "the director's chair" from which one manages "staff meetings" and gives orders to "heavenly hires" (Jean Slatter, *Hiring the Heavens* [Novato, CA: New World Press, 2005], pp. 24, 34, 45, 62).

18. Indeed, as a style, market ways of talking and thinking began to catch on within the nonmarket world of charities, museums, and volunteer groups. As Mark Friedman, seasoned executive director of Civic Ventures, a nonprofit organization that recruits retired professionals into "make a difference" lines of charity work, described this shift: "We used to describe to our funders the number of retired corporate executives we'd placed in inner city 8th grade math classes—who were taking risks and making a real difference—and they'd say, 'It's a miracle. Do it again.' Now a new bus-ed type has come in who says, 'Fine. But double it or we don't fund you.'"

    New feeling rules came in with this shift. If the government or the labor union is the main game in town, and things go wrong, you have a right to get mad and want to "kick the bums out." But if the company goes offshore, you are only justified in feeling sad, since the company—influenced by the modern pure market zeitgeist—was only there for its own profit anyway. The institutions that "owe us something" are weaker, those that owe us nothing are stronger.

19. According to a 2004 national survey conducted by the New American Dream, 88 percent of Americans described the United States as

"too materialistic." See "New American Dream Survey Report" (Charlottesville, VA: New American Dream, 2004).

20. See Harwood Group, "Yearning for Balance: Views of Americans on Consumption, Materialism, and the Environment" (Milton, MA: Merck Family Fund, 1995). The United States had 46,438 shopping malls as of 2003—"20.2 square feet for every man, woman and child in the United States," Lee Drutman and Charlie Cray, "The People's Business: Controlling Corporations and Restoring Democracy," *In These Times* (February 18, 2005), http://www.inthesetimes.org/article/1971/the_peoples_business/.

Chapter 1: You Have Three Seconds

1. Rural New England of 1900 had few paid matchmakers, and they were fading from the great cities of the East Coast. Between 1899 and 1900, there was no mention of matchmakers or dating services in the pages of the *New York Times*. Such services were thriving at the time in Europe and Britain, however, where *The Matrimonial Post and Fashionable Marriage Advertiser* (founded in 1860) and *The Matrimonial Times* (founded in 1904) had a flourishing readership. Earnest S. Turner, *A History of Courting* (New York: E. P. Dutton and Co., 1954). As one matchmaker lamented in an 1893 interview with the *New York Tribune*, "most marriageable men and women [in the Jewish quarter of New York] depended on me to make them happy. Now they believe in love and all that rot. They are making their own marriages." Another matchmaker complained that the *shadkan* (Yiddish for matchmaker) was being replaced by city parks and beaches (Elliott Robert Barkan, Hasia R. Diner, and Alan M. Kraut, eds., *From Arrival to Incorporation: Migrants to the U.S. in a Global Era* [New York: New York University Press, 2007], p. 11).
2. For "sobriety of conduct," see William Cobbett, *Advice to Young Men and (Incidentally) to Young Women in the Middle and Higher Ranks of Life in a Series of Letters Addressed to a Youth, a Bachelor, a Lover, a Husband, a Citizen or a Subject* (New York: John Doyle, 1833). For "chastity of intention," see David Starr Jordon, *The Call of the Twentieth Century: An Address to Young Men* (Boston, MA: American Unitarian Association, 1903), pp. 63–64. For early risers, see E. E. Moise, "New Orleans Marriage Guide Caused Duels: Review of 1858 'How to Get a Rich Wife,'" *New Orleans Item-Tribune*, June 24, 1928. For front and

back hair, see Charles Reynolds Brown, *The Young Man's Affairs* (Oakland, CA: First Congregational Church, 1909).

3. Evan Marc Katz and Linda Holmes, *Why You're Still Single: Things Your Friends Would Tell You If You Promised Not to Get Mad* (New York: Plume, 2006).
4. "Online Daters More Confident Than Offline Daters," *Online Dating Magazine* (2004), http://www.onlinedatingmagazine.com/news2004/onlinedaters.html.
5. Match.com is the largest American dating site, and as the so-called Google of the dating world, it's bought up some of the larger of the other 1,500 dating services in the United States (Abby Ellin, "The Recession, Isn't It Romantic?" *New York Times,* February 12, 2011). Estimates of Match.com's subscribers and users vary widely. IAC/INTERACTIVECORP, Match.com's parent Internet company, wrote on p. 6 of their annual report to the U.S. Securities and Exchange Commission that "As of December 31, 2009, we collectively provided online personals services to approximately 1.3 million subscribers," IAC, "Form 10-K: Annual Report Pursuant to Section 13 or 15(d) of the Securities Exchange Act of 1934 for the Fiscal Year Ended December 31, 2009" (New York: IAC/INTERACTIVECORP, 2010). The *Wall Street Journal* reported in 2009 that the Web site had three million unique users per month, Carl Bialik, "Marriage-Maker Claims Are Tied in Knots (Interactive Graphic)," *Wall Street Journal*, July 29, 2009, http://online.wsj.com/article/SB124879877347487253.html#articleTabs=article. A 2009 Match.com research release reported that it had 2.8 million users; IAC Advertising, "Align Your Brand with the Leading U.S. Online Relationship Site," IAC Advertising and Match.com, http://datingsitesreviews.com/images/other/match/Match-Stats-2009-Q1.pdf. Conversely, some dating review Web sites say that Match.com has as many as 15 million, 20 million, or 29 million members: Dating Sites-Reviews.com, "Match.com Review," DatingSitesReviews.com, http://datingsitesreviews.com/staticpages/index.php?page=2010000100-Match; Consumer-Rankings.com, "Match.com," Consumer-Rankings.com, http://www.consumer-rankings.com/Dating/MatchReview.aspx?li=42.
6. Most cases of violence in the United States are actually committed within families or by neighbors or friends. But a small proportion of

cases occur through Internet dating. Robert Jerin and Beverly Dolinsky, "Cyber-victimization and Online Dating," in *Online Matchmaking*, ed. M. T. Whitty, A. Baker, and J. Inman (New York: Palgrave Macmillan, 2007); Brian H. Spitzberg and William R. Cupach, "Cyber-stalking as (Mis)matchmaking," in *Online Matchmaking*.

7. New firms offer to perform background checks to help online date-seekers to screen potential dates. Two retired police officers, Robert Buchholz and Andrew Scott, founded MyMatchChecker.com, which, for $9.95, offers to perform a basic background check on anyone a person has met on a dating site. MiliMate has created a new mobile phone app—the Instant National Criminal Search—which even offers to send background information on a particular date to the client's friend, just as a precaution. See Stephanie Rosenbloom, "New Online-Date Detectives Can Unmask Mr. or Ms. Wrong," *New York Times*, December 19, 2010.
8. Nick Paumgarten, "Looking for Someone," *New Yorker*, July 4, 2011.
9. For the 2005 Pew study findings, see Mary Madden and Amanda Lenhart, "Online Dating" (Washington, DC: Pew Research Center, 2006). One recent article puts the number of dating Web sites at 1,500, and the number of Americans using dating sites at 20 million—"more than double the number 5 years ago," Rosenbloom, "New Online-Date Detectives Can Unmask Mr. or Ms. Wrong." The article drew on industry research for this, available through Caitlin Moldvay, "Dating Game: With Increasing Internet Penetration, Online Dating Is on the Rise" (IBISWorld, Inc., December 2010). For the 40 million figure, see Anita Dufalla, 'Online Dating Discovers a New Age," *Pittsburgh Post-Gazette*, January 3, 2006. For the quotation about "dating in the wild," thanks to Jennifer Randles, assistant professor of sociology at Austin College.
10. This survey was administered by UC Berkeley's Survey Research Center as part of their Golden Bear Omnibus program. Using random digit telephone sampling and computer-assisted telephone interviewing, investigators surveyed Spanish- and English-speaking adults eighteen years of age or older, residing in households with telephones, within the state of California, between April 30, 2007, and September 2, 2007. 1,186 phone interviews were completed, with an overall response rate of 15.9 percent. Our module about engaging personal services was completed by 978 respondents.

11. This rate is based on data collected in a 2009 Harris Interactive poll, reported here: Dr. Gian Gionzaga, senior director of research and development, eHarmony Blog, "How You Meet Your Spouse Matters," February 10, 2011, http://advice.eharmony.com/blog/2011/02/10/how-you<#213>meet-your-spouse-matters; and eHarmony press release, "Study: 542 People Married Every Day in U.S., on Average, Through eHarmony," August 16, 2010, http://www.eharmony.com/press/release/31.
12. Match.com, "Match.com and Chadwick Martin Bailey 2009–2010 Studies: Recent Trends: Online Dating," http://cp.match.com/cppp/media/CMB_Study.pdf; Gionzaga, "How You Meet Your Spouse Matters."
13. Gionzaga, "How You Meet Your Spouse Matters."
14. For-pay companies are engaged in research battles among themselves and with free online sites as well. The general counsel for Match.com (a for-pay company) accused Plentyoffish (a free service) of publishing "misleading and/or false" claims—for example, that it generates 18 million dates a year. But Plentyoffish founder Markus Frind blogged back that Match.com's claims were "absurd." Another free site, OKCupid, blogged that "you are 12.4 times more likely to get married this year if you *don't* subscribe to Match.com." The company has since removed that posting following its purchase by Match.com. See Chris Morrison, "Match.com Reveals the Dark Side of the Online Dating Business," Plentyoffish.com, April 28, 2010; Letter to Markus Frind, http://www.plentyoffish.com/matchcomletter.pdf; and Adrianne Jeffries, "OK Cupid: We Didn't Censor Our Match.com-Bashing Blog Post," *New York Observer*, http://www.observer.com/2011/tech/okcupid-we-didnt-censor-our-matchcom-bashing-blog-post.

    In response to skepticism from the scientific community about their "happier eHarmony couple" finding, eHarmony psychologists shared via a conference presentation how they compared eHarmony and non-eHarmony couples. (See Steve Carter and Chadwick Snow, "Helping Singles Enter Better Marriages Using Predictive Models of Marital Success," poster presented at the sixteenth annual convention of the American Psychological Society, Chicago, IL, May 24–30, 2004.) This, too, met a critical response (e.g., Houran et al., 2004). eHarmony used conceptually questionable measures, the critics argue, and inadequate study design. For example, the critics claimed, eHarmony compared "apples to oranges"—i.e. highly motivated couples who had paid eHarmony to find them a match with less motivated couples who had paid nothing. Without some independent measure of desire to marry, the critics observed, the eHarmony study may have been comparing eager beavers with non-eager beavers. Their results "might well reflect the result of diversity in the . . . characteristics of the samples, and not necessarily in the effectiveness of the matching system." The eHarmony study argued that it was the program itself, not the different characteristics of those who signed up for it, that led to the "happier" finding. See James Houran, Rense Lange, P. Jason Rentfrow, and Karen H. Brookner, "Do Online Matchmaking Tests Work? An Assessment of Preliminary Evidence for a Publicized Predictive Model of Marital Success," *North American Journal of Psychology* 6, no. 3 (2004): 507–26.

15. Caitlin Moldvay, "Dating Game"; Nick Baumgarten, "Looking for Someone," *New Yorker*, July 4, 2011.
16. For revenue, see IAC Advertising, "Align Your Brand with the Leading U.S. Online Relationship Site." This dipped slightly in 2009: Rob Reuteman, "Technology: How No. 1 Dating Site Match.com Came to Be," *FOXBusiness*, February 12, 2010, http://www.foxsmallbusinesscenter.com/entrepreneurs/2010/02/12/matchcom-eharmony-plentyoffish-love-valentines-day/; for information about the recession "boost," see Sarah Butler, "Recession Boost for Online Dating Sites," *Telegraph*, January 4, 2009, http://www.telegraph.co.uk/finance/newsbysector/mediatechnologyandtelecoms/4109637/Recession-boost-for-online-dating-sites.html.
17. For the international market quote, see Ryan Naraine, "Online Personals: Big Profits, Intense Competition," *Clickz*, June 27, 2003, http://www.click.com/2228891; Lisa Doucette, "Paying for Dates—WhatsYourPrice.com: A Sleazy Proposition or a Personal Investment?" April 19, 2011, http://www.forbes.com/sites/elisadoucette/2011/04/19/paying-for-dates-a-sleazy-proposition-or-personal-investment/. See also WhatsYourPrice.com, "The Media Likens It to Prostitution but Over 60% of the Public Says It's Okay," April 25, 2011, http://www.whatsyourprice.com/img/pressrelease4252011.pdf.

Chapter 2: The Legend of the Lemon Tree

1. One source estimates 15 percent: Bridal Association of America, "The Wedding Report," Bridal Association of America, http://www.bridalassociationofamerica.com/Wedding_Statistics/. David Wood is quoted on p. 37 in Elka Maria Torpey, "Jobs in Weddings and Funerals: Working with the Betrothed and the Bereaved," *Occupational Outlook Quarterly* 50, no. 4 (Winter 2006–7). Interest in professional wedding planning grew through time. The Association of Bridal Consultants appeared in 1955, the Association of Certified Professional Wedding Consultants in 1990, the Bridal Association of America in 1999, and the American Academy of Wedding Professionals in 2004. See Elizabeth Hafkin Pleck, *Celebrating the Family: Ethnicity, Consumer Culture, and Family Rituals* (Cambridge: Harvard University Press, 2000), and Cele Otnes and Elizabeth Hafkin Pleck, *Cinderella Dreams: The Allure of the Lavish Wedding* (Berkeley: University of California Press, 2003).
2. For the $161 billion figure, see Rebecca Mead, *One Perfect Day: The Selling of the American Wedding* (New York: Penguin Press, 2007). For average wedding cost reporting, see PRNewswire, "Brides.com 2009 American Wedding Survey Reveals: Popping the Question Has Popped in Price," PRNewswire, February 23, 2009.
3. Kathryn Edin and Maria Kefalas, *Promises I Can Keep: Why Poor Women Put Motherhood before Marriage* (Berkeley: University of California Press, 2005).
4. As explained by Linda Gordon and Sara McLanahan, information on unwed motherhood is quite limited for the years before 1940. Drawing on historical census data, however, they are able to produce estimates that hint at nonmarital childbearing. They find that in 1900 4.6 percent of children under fourteen lived in households headed by their never-married mothers, Linda Gordon and Sara McLanahan, "Single Parenthood in 1900," *Journal of Family History* 16, no. 2 (1991). Considering these data and evidence of significant measurement and reporting errors, Gordon concludes that much lower figures around the same time period—e.g., a Children's Bureau estimate of 4.6 out of 1,000 births in 1915—may be "distinct understatements"; see pp. 21–22 and footnote 22 (p. 320) in Linda Gordon, *Pitied But Not Entitled* (New York: Free Press, 1994). In 1920, Cutright (1940) calculated that 3 percent of births were to unmarried women, increasing to 4 percent in 1940, Phillips Cutright, "Illegitimacy in the United States: 1920–1968," in *Demo-*

graphic and Social Aspects of Population Growth, ed. C. F. Westoff and R. Parke Jr. (Washington, DC: U.S. Government Printing Office, 1972). For the most recent rates of unwed motherhood—currently about 40 percent—see Children's Defense Fund, "The State of America's Children, 2010" (Washington, DC: Children's Defense Fund, 2010); B. E. Hamilton, J. A. Martin, and S. J. Ventura, "Births: Preliminary Data for 2007" (Hyattsville, MD: National Center for Health Statistics, 2009).

5. Some wedding planners reported encountering mothers-of-the-bride who were highly upset to find themselves "replaced" by them. One warm Harlem-based planner recalled, "We all met together, and every time I opened my mouth about venue, flowers, food, the bride's mother would snap, '*I know all that*.' The bride was hiring me to avoid her mother. After that first meeting, I told my husband, 'I'm backing out of this one.'"
6. Cherlin, *The Marriage-Go-Round*. For divorce rate comparisons, see "Chart SF8.5: The increase in crude divorce rates in all OECD countries from 1970 to 2006/2007" in OECD, "SF 3.1 Marriage and Divorce Rates," OECD Family Database/Directorate for Employment, Labour and Social Affairs, http://www.oecd.org/dataoecd/4/19/40321815.pdf. For the most recent U.S. rates, see B. Tejada-Vera and P. D. Sutton, "Births, Marriages, Divorces, and Deaths: Provisional Data for 2009," *National Vital Statistics Reports* 58, no. 25 (2010). This report reveals that since 2007, both the marriage and divorce rates have modestly declined: per 1,000 individuals, 7.3 to 6.8, and 3.6 to 3.4, respectively.
7. Thorstein Veblen, *The Theory of the Leisure Class* (New York: A. M. Kelley, 1965 [1899]).
8. In fantasy, many link such love with the bygone world of front-porch farmhouse courtships and village weddings.

Chapter 3: For as Long as We Both Shall Live

1. Devon Leonard, "Match.com Is Crunching The Data Of Love," *Business Week*, April 29, 2011. Gottman's "love lab" became a model for eHarmony's "relational lab." Most commercial dating sites rely on extensive questionnaires—and people place faith in the results scientists derive from them. In studying what makes people sign up for eHarmony, company researchers found that a person's "confidence that science and technology could improve the way things work was the most significant predictor of willingness to join an online dating site, and how much they would pay" (Mark Thompson, Philip Zimbardo, Glenn

Hutchinson, "Consumers Are Having Second Thoughts about Online Dating," March 9, 2005, weAttract.com). Gottman, a Seattle-based psychologist, drew, in turn, on a decades-long tradition of university-based research. Academic psychologists such as Lewis Terman, a Stanford psychologist, and Ernest Burgess, a University of Chicago sociologist, devised questionnaires, tests, adjustment and prediction scales, tables, and charts to measure and demonstrate a couple's compatibility, adjustment, and—the same thing, they felt—happiness. By the 1930s, this science and its therapeutic popularizers had begun to wedge itself between newlyweds and their ideas about happiness. This science focused on a couple's similarity—in religion, education, social class, and race. Indeed, under the guise of scientific neutrality, Rebecca Davis observes, couples were steered away from unions that crossed barriers of race and faith. The premise hidden behind measures of compatibility was "stick to your own." Rebecca Davis, *More Perfect Unions: The American Search for Marital Bliss* (Cambridge, MA: Harvard University Press, 2010), pp. 102–4. See also Nick Paumgarten, "Looking for Someone," *New Yorker,* July 4, 2011.

2. In the first decades of the twentieth century, marital problems themselves differed although they were at least equally serious. There were the challenges of mental illness, alcoholism, drug abuse. Suicide rates in the mid-2000s were about what they were in 1900. (National Institute of Mental Health, "NIMH: Questions and Answers on Army STARRS," 2009, http://www.nimh.nih.gov/health/topics/suicide-prevention/suicide-prevention-studies/questions-and-answers-on-army-starrs.shtml, retrieved June 6, 2011.) From the 1860s on—especially between 1890 and 1910, increasing numbers of people were also being identified as insane. But it's hard to know whether that's because more people were crazy or because more psychiatric hospitals were built that defined them as such. In *The Invisible Plague: The Rise of Mental Illness from 1750 to the Present*, E. Fuller Torrey and Judy Miller document the dramatic rise to this day in patients admitted to mental hospitals. Was this rise due to the dislocating strains of industrialization, trauma of war, or the breadlines? To a lower community tolerance for unusual behavior, especially that of the poorer classes? Or was it due to the rise of extrafamilial institutions built to cope with it and to the rising number of psychiatrists, psychologists, psychiatric nurses, and aides who serviced them? Perhaps all were true. As for drinking, Americans averaged an annual 5.80 liters of alcohol per drinking-age person in

1790, 2.39 in 1901–5, and 2.58 in 1985. No twentieth-century Americans matched the big drinkers of the 1790s (considering liquor safer than water, the pilgrims on the Arabella brought over more beer than water). See Mark Edward Lender and James Kirby Martin, *Drinking in America: A History* (New York: Free Press, 1982). Deaths from cirrhosis of the liver declined since 1900; Angela K. Dills and Jeffrey A. Miron, "Alchohol, Prohibition and Cirrhosis," *American Law Economic Review* 6 no. 2 (2004): 283–318. Another study found a rise in young drinkers between the early and mid-twentieth century; less than half the people between ages 20 and 25 drank who were born between 1894 and 1937, whereas three-quarters did for those born between 1968 and 1974. Shanta R. Dube, Vincent Felitti, Maxia Dong, Wayne Giles, and Robert Anda, "The Impact of Adverse Childhood Experiences on Health Problems: Evidence from Four Birth Cohorts Dating Back to 1900," *Preventive Medicine* 37 (2003): 268–77.

3. American Association for Marriage and Family Therapy, "About AAMFT," http://www.aamft.org/iMIS15/AAMFT/About/About_AAMFT/Content/About_AAMFT/About_AAMFT.aspx?hkey=a8d047de-5bf7-40cd-9551-d626e2490a25, retrieved October 2, 2011.
4. Elizabeth Geick, "Should This Marriage Be Saved?" *Time*, February 27, 1995. As historian Rebecca Davis notes, "Seizing a means of staying relevant, mid-twentieth-century religious leaders integrated psychology . . . into marriage-focused ministries." Ministers, priests, and rabbis officiate at over three-quarters of American weddings, and most clergy, Davis notes, require that the couple receive counseling, even if just for a session or two. Davis, *More Perfect Unions*, p. 3.
5. Couples can begin therapy well before they marry or even before they make a commitment. An Internet ad for a $165, four-hour course offered by Rosalind Graham, licensed Marriage and Family Therapy counselor, for example, showed an image of a white couple with the caption "Pre-Marital Therapy," and of a black couple in normal clothing captioned "Pre-Commitment Counseling" (both images featured a man and woman). But in Graham's course, you got something extra if you planned to marry: graduates received a discount on their Shelby County State marriage license. The state of Florida now offers reduced marriage license fees for those who take a premarital course.
6. Jennine Estes, "PreMarital Therapy: The Training Wheels for Marriage," *Relationships in the Raw*, April 20, 2009, http://estestherapy.com/relationshiptips/2009/04/20/the-training-wheels-for-marriage.

7. StayHitched.com, "Marriage Success Training: Build the Foundation for Your Lifetime Together," http//stayhitched.com<#213>prep/htm (accessed June 23, 2011).
8. "In 2007, 44,000 couples met and married through eHarmony," the Director of eHarmony lab, Dr. Gian Gonzaga, told me. "That's a lot of marriages. And we want them to last."
9. Paumgarten, "Looking for Someone," p. 47.
10. Available now is an iPhone application, "personal use Cognitive Behavioral Therapy tool," that helps you "manage your stress and anxieties instantly." On the "Describe" screen, it reads, "I said something negative about my boss to a coworker, now I'm sure I'll get fired. I feel . . ." (you can adjust a dial-like point on the screen) "anxious, angry, dread" or "add emotion." At another click the screen reads "Evaluate": "I always do these stupid things" or "I dread having to deal with this. It is going to make my whole life a mess." It moves on to "Rationalize" and "Review" screens, which include "My rational thoughts" ("I need to ask him to keep it private") and "Now I feel . . ." (the anxious, angry, and dread gauges pointing toward empty). iTunes App Store Web site, http://iTunes.apple.com/US/App/icbt. There are other applications designed for therapists, including one on "Dementia Symptoms" (in case one forgets).
11. Jill Lepore, "Fixed: The Rise of Marriage Therapy, and Other Dreams of Human Betterment," *New Yorker*, March 29, 2010.
12. In this, he also differed from the hay-trusser in Thomas Hardy's 1886 novel, *The Mayor of Casterbridge*. In a rum-soaked moment at a county fair, he auctions off his quiet wife and baby daughter to a sober and kindly bidder. Reflecting a mentality of nineteenth-century England, the bidder didn't pay the wife directly, or separate out services, each with its own rate, nor was the seller in his right mind.
13. A June 2009 report by the AARP Public Policy Institute estimates that "on average, the Medicaid program can provide HCBC [home- and community-based care] to three people for the cost of serving one person in a nursing home," AARP Public Policy Institute, "Providing More Long-Term Support and Services at Home: Why It's Critical for Health Reform" (Washington, DC: AARP Public Policy Institute, 2009). Researching Medicaid expenditures from 1995 to 2005, H. Stephen Kaye, Mitchell P. LaPlante, and Charlene Harrington also show that an increase in home-based care could save states money over the long run (H. Stephen Kaye, Mitchell P.

LaPlante, and Charlene Harrington, "Do Noninstitutional Long-Term Care Services Reduce Medicaid Spending?" *Health Affairs* 28, no. 1 [2009]). See also Joseph Shapiro, "Home Care Might Be Cheaper, But States Still Fear It," *Home or Nursing Home: America's Empty Promise to Give Elderly, Disabled a Choice*, NPR, December 2, 2010, http://www.npr.org/2010/12/10/131755491/home-care-might-be-cheaper-but-states-still-fear-it.

Chapter 4: Our Baby, Her Womb

1. An American seeking a less costly tooth implant could fly to a clinic in Cuernavaca. An Englishman could get a cheaper knee replacement in Delhi. A Canadian might arrange an affordable facelift in São Paulo. Joining this North to South stream of medical tourists are millions of northern retirees who live—and sometimes die—in the global South. According to *International Living*, the top four American retirement havens in 2008 were Mexico, Ecuador, Panama, and Uruguay. Nearly 890,000 U.S. citizens live permanently in Mexico and Panama. The monthly retiree budget that that magazine (targeting American retirees) proposes to "live well"—which includes "housekeeper and gardener three days a week"—is $2,135. Many French retire to Morocco or Tunisia. Some middle-income Japanese and South Koreans move for a season or longer to Thailand, Singapore, or Malaysia. With each move, clients of the North are moving to less expensive service providers in the South. See Chee Heng Leng, "Medical Tourism in Malaysia: International Movement of Healthcare Consumers and the Commodification of Healthcare," Asia Research Institute Working Paper No. 83, National University of Singapore, January 2007. Tim and Lili had joined this larger two-way global flow of client to worker in their poignant search for a baby. See Arlie Hochschild, "The Back Stage of a Global Free Market: Nannies and Surrogates," in *Care und Migration*, ed. Ursula Apitzsch and Marianne Schmidbaur (Opladen, Germany and Farmington Hills, MI: Verlag Barbara Budrich 2010).
2. India's National Commission for Women estimated 3,000 clinics, as reported here: Shilpa Kannan, "Regulators Eye India's Surrogacy Sector," BBC News, India Business Report, March 18, 2009, http://news.bbc.co.uk/2/hi/business/7935768.stm. For the 2012 industry prediction, see Devon M. Herrick, "Medical Tourism: Global Competition

in Health Care" (Dallas, TX: National Center for Policy Analysis, 2007).

3. For information about the Levine study, see: Aaron D. Levine, "Self-Regulation, Compensation, and the Ethical Recruitment of Oocyte Donors," *Hastings Center Report* 40, no. 2 (2010); and David Tuller, "Payment Offers to Egg Donors Prompt Scrutiny," *New York Times*, May 11, 2010.
4. See Xytex Cryo International Sperm Bank, "Patient Section: Information Options," http://www.xytex.com/sperm-donor-bank-patient/index.cfm#infooptions.

Chapter 5: My Womb, Their Baby

1. Some surrogates are more attached to their babies than others. In Elly Teman's study of Israeli surrogates, she discovered many who felt highly detached. Some blamed their detachment on the "alien" hormones they were forced to take, and called their child "fetus" instead of "him" or "her." One remarked, "My brain doesn't even know that I am pregnant." Elly Teman, "Technological Fragmentation and Women's Empowerment: Surrogate Motherhood in Israel," *Women's Studies Quarterly* 31, no. 3/4 (2001).
2. Amrita Pande, "'It May Be Her Eggs but It's My Blood': Surrogates and Everyday Forms of Kinship in India," *Qualitative Sociology* 32, no. 4 (2009a): 379–405; Pande, "Not an 'Angel,' not a 'Whore,'" *Indian Journal of Gender Studies* 16, no. 2 (2009b): 141–73. Some information in this chapter comes from personal communication with Amrita Pande. See Arlie Hochschild, "Childbirth at the Global Crossroads," *American Prospect,* October 2009, pp. 25–28.
3. Pande, "'It May Be Her Eggs but It's My Blood,'" p. 386.
4. A shockingly widespread crime in India, the Indian National Crime Records Bureau reported 8,172 so-called dowry deaths in 2008—an increase of 14 percent over 1998, "Crime in India 2008: Figures at a Glance," National Crime Records Bureau, Indian Ministry of Home Affairs, http://ncrb.nic.in/cii2008/cii-2008/figure%20at%20a%20glance.pdf. The men who perpetrate such murders often evade prosecution for a variety of reasons, including bribing officials, Shally Prasad, "Medicolegal Response to Violence Against Women in India," *Violence Against Women* 5, no. 5 (1999); Prachi Sanghavi, Kavi Bhalla,

and Veena Das, "Fire-Related Deaths in India in 2001: A Retrospective Analysis of Data," *Lancet* 373, no. 9671 (2009).

5. On routine cesarean sections, see Scott Carney, "Inside India's Rent-A-Womb Business," *Mother Jones* (March/April, 2010), http://motherjones.com/politics/2010/02/surrogacy-tourism-india-nayna-patel.
6. The Indian gynecologists I spoke with were divided among themselves on whether or not to accept gay clients for surrogacy. Dr. B. N. Chakravarty, the Chair of the National Drafting Committee (to regulate surrogacy) told me, "In India we don't have this problem" (referring to homosexuality). On the other hand, Dr. Allahbadia of Mumbai's Rotunda Clinic proudly arranges surrogacy for gay men. Clients also had their attitudes: some rejected potential surrogates "because she looked too dark" even though the woman bore no genetic relation to the child to which she would give birth.
7. Thanks to N. B. Sarojini and Vrinda Marwah of Sama Resource Group for Women and Health, B 45, 2nd Floor, Shivalik Main Road, Malviya Nagar, New Delhi, 110017, India. www.samawomenshealth.org. See N. B. Sarojini and Vrinda Marwah, *Shake Her, She Is Like the Tree that Grows Money!* (New Delhi, India: Sama Resource Group for Women and Health, forthcoming).
8. Pande, "'It May Be Her Eggs but It's My Blood,'" p. 384.
9. It seems as though there are "hard rules" set by law and the courts, and "soft rules" set by custom. Since 2002, the hard rules governing Indian commercial surrogacy have changed; it's legal and unregulated. But the soft rules are various, confusing, and up for grabs. Should the genetic parents try to bond with the surrogate, and accept the baby as a personal gift, as in the gift exchange? Or should they treat this service as a strictly impersonal transaction?
10. Carney, "Inside India's Rent-A-Womb Business."
11. See Harry Braverman, *Labor and Monopoly Capital: The Degradation of Work in the Twentieth Century* (New York: Monthly Review Press, 1998).
12. Not only are surrogates privately poor but the Indian public sector provisions of health and education are also abysmal. The United Nations recently rated Indian reproductive medical care the seventh worst in the world. Just 17 percent of Indian women have had any contact whatever with a health worker. Ironically, while India, one of the poorest nations in the world, has accomplished little to help women

control fertility, "Mother India" has become a huge commercial enterprise, Amit Gengupta, "Medical Tourism: Reverse Subsidy for the Elite," *Signs: Journal of Women in Culture and Society* 36, no. 2 (2011): 312–18. See also Amrita Pande, "Commercial Surrogacy in India: Manufacturing a Perfect 'Mother-Worker,'" *Signs: Journal of Women in Culture and Society* 35, no. 4 (2010): 969–92.

13. Namita Kohli, "Moms on the Market," *Hindustan Times*, March 13, 2011.
14. While Dr. Patel focused exclusively on their "carrier" wombs, much else of their person—their ankles, backs, breasts, their appetite, their sleep, their dreams—was affected.
15. William Greider, *One World, Ready or Not: The Manic Logic of Global Capitalism* (New York: Simon and Schuster, 1997).
16. Sama Resource Group for Women and Health, "Constructing Conceptions: The Mapping of Assisted Reproductive Technologies in India," New Delhi, Sama Resource Group for Women and Health, 2010, p. 155.
17. Ibid., p. 161.
18. Ibid., p. 165.
19. Ibid., p. 171. While fertility clinics compete for business with such boasts as "First Laser Hatching Baby of Allahabad" or "Over 455 Pregnancies in Last Six Years by IVF," little mention is made of research on the risks. A study comparing 301 infants conceived with ICSI (intracytoplasmic sperm injection) or IVF (in vitro fertilization) with a matched sample of naturally conceived infants, found the ICSI and IVF infants to have twice as many major birth defects, M. Hansen, J. J. Kurinczuk, C. Bower, and S. Webb, "The Risk of Major Birth Defects after Intracytoplasmic Sperm Injection and In Vitro Fertilization," *New England Journal of Medicine* 346, no. 10 (2002): 725–30.
20. For Saudi Arabia's law, see p. 2 of Rachel Cook, Shelley Day Sclater, and Felicity Kaganas, *Surrogate Motherhood: International Perspectives* (Portland, OR: Hart Publishing, 2003). The most recent international report on policies regarding assisted reproductive technologies was unable to get "reliable full information" from Saudi Arabia, Howard W. Jones et al., eds., *IFFS Surveillance 07, Fertility and Sterility* 87, Supplement 1 (American Society for Reproductive Medicine, 2007). For Israel, see Elly Teman, "Embodying Surrogate Motherhood: Pregnancy as a Dyadic Body Project," *Body & Society* 15, no. 3 (2009); D. Kelly Weisberg, *The Birth of Surrogacy in Israel* (Gainesville:

University Press of Florida, 2005); Elly Teman, "The Last Outpost of the Nuclear Family: A Cultural Critique of Israeli Surrogacy Policy," in *Kin, Gene, Community: Reproductive Technology among Jewish Israelis*, ed. Daphna Birenbaum-Carmeli and Yoram Carmeli (Oxford: Berghahn Books, 2010). For countries allowing noncommercial surrogacy, see Sylvia Dermout et al., "Non-commercial Surrogacy: An Account of Patient Management in the First Dutch Centre for IVF Surrogacy, from 1997 to 2004," *Human Reproduction* 25, no. 2 (2010); and Jones et al., eds., *IFFS Surveillance 07*. In the United Kingdom, for example, surrogacy is allowed "provided it is consensual and involves the payment of no more than reasonable expenses," see Natalie Gamble, "Crossing the Line: The Legal and Ethical Problems of Foreign Surrogacy," *Reproductive Biomedicine Online* 19, no. 2 (2009).

21. For reviews of surrogacy and assisted reproduction laws in the United States, see Jessica Arons, "Future Choices: Assisted Reproductive Technologies and the Law" (Washington, DC: Center for American Progress, 2007); Carla Spivack, "The Law of Surrogate Motherhood in the United States," *American Journal of Comparative Law* 58, Supplement 1 (2010). A recent article published in a French journal (Jennifer Merchant, "Assisted Reproductive Technology (ART) in the United States: Towards a National Regulatory Framework?" *Journal International de Bioéthique* 20, no. 4 [2009]) describes the contemporary U.S. situation this way: "Four states do not recognize the validity of a surrogacy contract, four states recognize the validity of a surrogacy contract but do not authorize payment for the gestational mother, four states fully recognize the validity of a surrogate contract and authorize payment for the gestational mother, and seven states formally prohibit surrogacy arrangements and have erected severe sanctions" (pp. 68–69). Florida, New Hampshire, and Virginia "recognize the validity of a surrogacy contract but only allow payment to cover medical costs, clothing, food, and salary loss of the gestational mother. These states also signify to the gestational mother that she can change her mind and keep the child without any threat of sanction. . . . The remaining states have no legislation regarding surrogacy and leave it up to the courts to handle conflicts of any kind" (p. 69). Spivack reports that in 27 states—Alaska, California, Colorado, Connecticut, Delaware, Georgia, Hawaii, Idaho, Kansas, Maine, Maryland, Massachusetts, Minnesota, Mississippi, Missouri, Montana, New Jersey, Ohio,

Oklahoma, Oregon, Pennsylvania, Rhode Island, South Carolina, South Dakota, Vermont, Wisconsin, Wyoming—couples entering surrogacy contracts run the risk that a court will later determine that the agreement was unenforceable or illegal. In 1989, two attempts were made to introduce national legislation regulating surrogacy. Both failed.

Some market enthusiasts have extended the logic of commercial surrogacy to older children. In "The Economics of the Baby Shortage," Elizabeth Landes and Richard Posner, for example, complain that American adoption agencies are "restricted" from operating as "efficient profit-maximizing firms." Comparing the "thousands of children in foster care" to "unsold inventory stored in a warehouse," the authors argue for paying parents to relinquish their children to high-bidding adoptive parents. While not a mainstream idea, we can hardly dismiss its authors as marginal crackpots: one author, the Right Honorable Judge Posner, is a judge on the U.S. Court of Appeals, the second-highest court in the land, and is identified by the *Journal of Legal Studies* as the most cited legal scholar of all time. "The Economics of the Baby Shortage," in Martha M. Ertman and Joan C. Williams, eds., *Rethinking Commodification* (New York: New York University Press, 2005), pp. 46–57.

22. "Surrogacy: Wombs for Rent," *NOW ON PBS,* September 18, 2009, http://www.pbs.org/now/shows/538/index.html. See also *Bloodlines: Technology Hits Home*, an award-winning 2003 PBS documentary produced and directed by Noel Schwerin. In another case, a Michigan surrogate decided to claim legal parenthood of twins she had carried for clients when she discovered, at a guardianship hearing, that the intended mother—who had bought an egg, sperm, and engaged a surrogate—suffered from schizophrenia. Stephanie Saul, "Building a Baby, With Few Ground Rules," *New York Times*, December 13, 2009.

Chapter 6: It Takes a Service Mall

1. According to the historian Janet Golden, breast-feeding at that time was seen by many upper-class women as "immodest, wearisome and déclassé." In 1906, Dr. Thompson S. Wescott, associate professor at the University of Pennsylvania medical school, noted the passing of wet nurses, Golden writes, "with regret." She continues, "Like servants, whose loyalty and hard work increased in memory as their numbers

diminished, wet nurses benefited from misguided nostalgia" (p. 178). In turn-of-the-century Boston, one-third of private-duty wet nurses came from Ireland, one-third from coastal towns of Canada, and most of the rest were native born, primarily, Golden speculates, of Irish descent (p. 109, Table 4.11). Working in the houses of the wealthy, many impoverished wet nurses were tragically forced to leave their own babies in orphanages such as the Massachusetts Infant Asylum, where many languished or died. For quotations in this paragraph of the text, see pages 45, 46, and 57 of Janet Golden, *A Social History of Wet Nursing in America: From Breast to Bottle* (New York: Cambridge University Press, 1996). To my knowledge, the only wet nursing services available today are through Certified Household Staffing in Beverly Hills, California. See Florence Williams, "Human Milk For Sale," *New York Times Magazine*, December 19, 2010; and Carol Lloyd, "Modern-Day Wet Nursing," *Broadsheet*, Salon.com, April 26, 2007.

2. The Baby Naming Experience: http://thebabynamingexperience.com/products/consultations.html. Korwitts even offers a "Free Baby Name Report Card," saying on her Web site: "Might as well see how a name is graded regarding things like health, finances, job success, relationship compatibility, and communication ability before you put that name on your baby's birth certificate." (The lower the grade, the more in need of her service, of course.) She also asks the potential client if the spelling of one's child's name is "balanced for success." If not, for seventy-five dollars, one can get a child's name "attuned." As reported in Alexandra Alter, "The Baby-Name Business," *Wall Street Journal*, June 22, 2007, http://online.wsj.com/article/SB118247444843664288.html, one woman who hired a nameologist remarked, "She was an objective person for me to obsess about it with rather than driving my husband crazy," and Bruce Lansky, author of *100,000+ Baby Names*, said, "We live in a marketing-oriented society. People who understand branding know that when you pick the right name, you're giving your child a head start."
3. Jessica Yadegaran, "Baby Planners Pave Way for Little Ones," *Oakland Tribune* (posted January 25, 2010). An International Academy of Baby Planner Professionals was launched in 2007.
4. See the following Web sites for examples of these services: http://thepottytrainer.com; http://www.3daypottytraining.com.
5. http://thepottytrainer.com, 2010.
6. Elissa Gootman, "The Job Description: Life of the Party: The Proper

Motivator Ensures That the Bar Mitzvah Celebration Boogies," *New York Times*, May 30, 2003, B6.

7. Rima D. Apple, *Perfect Motherhood: Science and Childrearing in America* (New Brunswick, NJ: Rutgers University Press, 2006), p. 14. See also chapter 6 in Barbara Ehrenreich and Deirdre English, *For Her Own Good: Two Centuries of the Experts' Advice to Women* (New York: Anchor Books, 1978).
8. Kathryn E. Walker and Margaret E. Woods, *Time Use: A Measure of Household Production of Goods and Services* (Washington, DC: American Home Economics Association, 1976).
9. In a study of working parents for my 1997 book, *The Time Bind*, I was already discovering busy couples doing similar things not just for their kids but for themselves—buying camper trucks no one had time to drive, workshop tools that would never be used, and guitars that no one got around to learning to play. Such items became totems in the fantasy life of the family, in the bolstering of hypothetical selves—selves that couples would have been, or so they imagined, if only they had the time.

Chapter 7: Making Five-Year-Olds Laugh Is Harder Than You Think

1. Nannies and housekeepers remain a small part of the total U.S. workforce—in 2007 about 0.4 percent. See Table 2.5 in Mignon Duffy, *Making Care Count: A Century of Gender, Race, and Paid Care Work* (New Brunswick, NJ: Rutgers University Press, 2011).

Chapter 8: A High Score in Family Memory Creation

1. Paul Tough, "The Year in Ideas: Dad's Performance Review," *New York Times Magazine*, December 15, 2002.
2. See Perry M. Christensen and Benson L. Porter, *Family 360* (New York: McGraw Hill, 2004), p. 83.
3. Ibid., p. 40. For the best practices, see pages 139 (dinner plates), 140 (classical music), 141 (writing letters), 142 (auditing conversation), 146 (discussing articles), and 153 (impatience).
4. Ibid. See p. 41 for "communication opportunities" and similar examples. For change management, see the affiliated Web site: http://www.family360.net/howitworks.html.

5. See Ann Hulbert, *Raising America: Experts, Parents, and a Century of Advice About Children* (New York: Alfred A. Knopf, 2003), and Peter N. Stearns, *Anxious Parents: A History of Modern Childrearing in America* (New York: New York University Press, 2003).
6. According to Steven Mintz, "Mothers and Fathers in America: Looking Backward, Looking Forward," Digital History, http://www.digitalhistory.uh.edu/historyonline/mothersfathers.cfm: "Influenced by the evolutionary theories of Charles Darwin, a 'child study movement' in England and the United States conducted detailed observations of children's weight, height, and activities, delineated stages of child development, and called on mothers to respond appropriately to each developmental stage." See also Steven Mintz and Susan Kellogg, *Domestic Revolutions: A Social History of American Family Life* (New York: Free Press, 1989).

Chapter 9: Importing Family Values

1. Maricel's voyage would have seemed both familiar and new to the Irish immigrant community of J. Porter and Edith's early twentieth-century New England. The young, single Irish women boarding boats for the docks of Boston shed tears for parents and siblings left behind. But children, if they had them, were likely to be born on American shores. Carried along in that wave of migration was a twenty-two-year-old named Mary Burn, who arrived in Boston at the turn of the last century, by steerage, with her brother, a wheelwright. Within the year, she was hired by the Russell family—my grandparents—to become a Maricel to my aunt Elizabeth.

   At the turn of the century, over half of twenty-five- to thirty-four-year-old Irish women were unmarried and impoverished. Only oldest brothers inherited the family farm in largely rural Ireland, so many younger men migrated, too. See Pauline Jackson, "Women in 19th Century Irish Emigration," *International Migration Review* 18, no. 4 (1984): 1004–20; and also Donald Harman Akenson, *The Irish Diaspora: A Primer* (Belfast, Northern Ireland: Queen's University of Belfast, 1993). British administrators of Ireland touted better job and marriage prospects in America, too, but, like many of her countrywomen in America, Mary remained single and childless for the rest of her life. Like Maricel, Mary had been a "little mother" to eight young siblings and had left them in Ireland, with their mother, in order to care for my aunt, then a baby, in America. In this way she became part of an earlier, and different, Europe-to-United States care chain.

2. After Maricel migrated to America she wired money back to her mother, but not to Nanay, and when she tried to bring relatives to the United States, Nanay was not among them. Nanay was Maricel's mother of sentiment; her birth mother was a mother of responsibility. Despite the shame in a middle-class Filipino home to work as a nanny, Maricel became the envy of her siblings and a heroine in her neighborhood. She outearned her older sister, Yoli, a trained accountant, now selling women's clothes in a Manila department store. She outearned a younger sister, trained to teach high school math, now filing back-office papers in an insurance company; a brother with a BA in engineering, now hired as a laborer in a chemical factory; and another brother trained as an accountant, now working as a bank guard. Maricel, the unschooled black sheep, now earned nearly as much as her whole family—including her father—combined. See Hochschild and Barbara Ehrenreich, eds., *Global Woman: Nannies, Maids, and Sex Workers in the New Economy* (New York: Metropolitan Books, 2003).
3. Suspecting infidelity at one point, Janek beat Maricel, saying, "I'll give you a green face." Although Maricel's son, a gentle, lanky young man who worked the night shift in a convalescent home, moved out of his mother's house, he visited her twice a week in order, he said quietly, "to make sure she's okay."
4. See Table 13, "Niños y niñas que vivan sin padre y madre" in Rodolfo García Zamora, "Un pasivo: Mujeres y niños en comunidades de alta migración internacional en Michoacán, Jalisco, y Zacatecas, México": Jalisco, 35%, Michoacán, 30%, Zacatecas, 33%. This working paper reports data from a 2006 survey and is part of a larger unpublished UNESCO field report, "Las remesas de los migrantes Mexicanos en Estados Unidos y su impacto sobre las condiciones de vida de los infantes en México."
5. For the 40–50 percent estimate see the extensive interview study by Pierrette Hondagneu-Sotelo, "Families on the Frontier: From Braceros in the Fields to Braceras in the Home," in Marcelo M. Suarez-Orozco and Mariela M. Paez, eds., *Latinos: Remaking America* (Berkeley: University of California Press, 2003), p. 267. A growing number of scholars have investigated the effects of such migration on women and children. In 2002, Carola Suarez-Orozco and colleagues studied school-age children—from 51 schools in Boston and San Francisco

whose parents had recently immigrated from China, Mexico, and a variety of Central American countries—regarding their experiences of separation from their parents. Seventy-nine percent of the children had been separated by immigration from their fathers and 55 percent from their mothers. The rate of separation from mothers was highest (80 percent) for children from Central America, and lowest (23 percent) for children from China, Carola Suarez-Orozco, Irina L. G. Todorova, and Josephine Louie, "Making Up for Lost Time: The Experience of Separation and Reunification among Immigrant Families," *Family Process* 41, no. 4 (2002). For more background on these issues, see also Rosalia Cortés, "Children and Women Left Behind in Labour Sending Countries: An Appraisal of Social Risks" (Brighton, UK: Child Migration Research Network, 2007); and Woodrow Wilson International Center for Scholars and the Migration Policy Institute, "Women Immigrants in the United States: Proceedings of a Conference at the Center" (paper presented at the Women Immigrants in the United States conference, Washington, DC, September 9, 2002).

6. Melanie M. Reyes, "Migration and Filipino Children Left-Behind: A Literature Review" (Quezon City, Philippines: Miriam College/UNICEF, 2008).
7. Rhacel Salazar Parreñas, *Children of Global Migration: Transnational Families and Gendered Woes* (Stanford, CA: Stanford University Press, 2005).
8. According to the 1987 Filipino Family Code, children should be cared for by their own mothers until age seven. See Rhacel Parreñas, *Children of Global Migration.* In Sri Lanka, a struggle is on between the Middle East Employees Federation (representing overseas workers) who resist restrictions on migrant mothers, but advocate welfare programs for children left behind, and the cabinet that has approved a law preventing mothers of children five and under from leaving the country for work. Such a law is unlikely to halt such migration since the Foreign Employment Bureau has "no mechanism to identify women who have small children when they apply for overseas jobs." Anjana Samarasinghe, "Welfare System for Migrant Women Workers, Young Children Favoured," *Daily News* (Sri Lanka), March 15, 2007.
9. See Mignon Duffy, *Making Care Count*, pp. 100, 114.
10. One recent study (Montgomery et al. 2005) found that about 90

percent of long-term care workers in the United States were middle-aged females. More than half were nonwhite and about 20 percent were foreign-born. U.S. Census data show that of all hospital aides in the United States in 2000, 17 percent were foreign-born or noncitizens, as were 13 percent of nursing-home aides and 23 percent of home care aides. Rhonda J. V. Montgomery et al., "A Profile of Home Care Workers from the 2000 Census: How It Changes What We Know," *Gerontologist* 45, no. 5 (2005).

Chapter 10: I Was Invisible to Myself

1. Stay-at-home mothers are just as likely to say they "feel pressured" as working mothers. Kim Parker, "The Harried Life of the Working Mother," *Pew Research Center Social & Demographic Trends* (2009), http://pewsocialtrends.org/2009/10/01/the-harried-life-of-the-working-mother/.

Chapter 11: Nolan Enjoys My Father for Me

1. Cameron Lynne Macdonald, *Shadow Mothers: Nannies, Au Pairs, and the Micropolitics of Mothering* (Berkeley: University of California Press, 2011).
2. For population estimates, see U.S. Census Bureau Population Division, 2009, "Table 3-C. Percent Distribution of the Projected Population by Selected Age Groups and Sex for the United States: 2010 to 2050," in *Summary Tables: Constant Net International Migration Series*, Washington, DC: U.S. Census Bureau, http://www.census.gov/population/www/projections/2009cnmsSumTabs.html.
3. Joann Mills was able to afford private care for her father. But what about average Americans? Surprisingly, home care for an elderly person costs less, on average, than nursing-home care, experts estimate, Joseph Shapiro, "Home Care Might Be Cheaper, But States Still Fear It" in *Home or Nursing Home: America's Empty Promise to Give Elderly, Disabled a Choice*, National Public Radio, December 2, 2010. In 1999, the U.S. Supreme Court case of *Olmstead v. L. C.*, also ruled that under the Americans with Disabilities Act, Medicaid patients who live in institutions (such as state hospitals and nursing homes) and who are able to live at home, have the civil right to receive their paid care there. States have been slow to create

the programs necessary to realize this promise, although the 2010 overhaul of Medicare calls for states to spend more money on such programs.

Chapter 12: Anything You Pay For Is Better

1. In *The Transcendent Child* (New York: Basic Books, 1996), the social psychologist Lillian Rubin interviewed people in just such situations. One was an orphan adopted by a mentally ill woman who clutched the child by her hair and dunked her head in the toilet. Another was beaten as a child by a brutal father. A third was abandoned by her parents. Yet all these victims of terrible family abuse survived as adults in the highly important sense that they could love and work—and often in the field of healing. All of Rubin's survivors stopped looking for nurture within their families, and searched for it—effectively and with success—outside them. One discovered a kindly neighbor. Another found an outreaching teacher. Yet another found a schoolmate's mother. In spirit if not in law, they got adopted. They learned from their new relationships and gradually overcame the torment of life at home. Perhaps Gloria was reaching beyond her troubled family, too—only instead of seeking rescue in a neighbor, a teacher, or a schoolmate's mother, she reached to the market.
2. Scholars differ on the question of whether the typical American in the 2000s had fewer friends than the typical American in 1985. Citing findings from the well-regarded General Social Survey, McPherson, Smith-Lovin, and Brashears (2006, 2008) argue that social networks shrank "precipitously" from an average of three "close friends in 1985 to an average of one in 2006." Nearly one in ten Americans—a much higher share than in 1985—say their spouse is the only person they confide in. But, citing other relevant data as well as problems with these G.S.S. data, sociologist Claude Fischer (2009) challenges this finding. Moreover, in a study of Americans ages twenty-five to seventy-four drawn from the World Internet Project, Hua Wang and Barry Wellman (2010) report expanding social networks among Americans—both online and off—between 2002 and 2007. The mean number of "friends" Americans say they contact at least once a week face-to-face or via phone, they claim, increased from 9.4 to 11.3. Note that respondents were "somewhat more likely to be women, older, and better educated" than average within the U.S. population (p. 1153). But is a Facebook friend a real friend? In "Facebook and the Sense of

Loneliness: How Social Are the New Social Media?" (in progress), Chanqiz Mohiyeddini, S. Bauer, and F. Mohiyeddini report that the more "friends" a Facebook user reports, the more lonely and depressed he or she reports being.

For references see: Claude S. Fischer, *Still Connected: Family and Friends in America since 1970* (New York: Russell Sage Foundation, 2011); Claude S. Fischer, "The 2004 G.S.S. Finding of Shrunken Social Networks: An Artifact?" *American Sociological Review* 74, no. 4 (2009): 657–69; Miller McPherson, Lynn Smith-Lovin, and Matthew Brashears, "Social Isolation in America: Changes in Core Discussion Networks over Two Decades," *American Sociological Review* 71, no. 3 (2006): 353–75; McPherson, Smith-Lovins, and Brashears, "ERRATA: Social Isolation in America: Changes in Core Discussion Networks over Two Decades," *American Sociological Review* 73, no. 6 (2008): 1022; Hua Wang and Barry Wellman, "Social Connectivity in America: Changes in Adult Friendship Network Size from 2002 to 2007," *American Behavioral Scientist* 53, no. 8 (2010): 1148–69. See also the work of Barry Wellman and Jeffrey Boase of the University of Toronto, and coauthors, who claim that the average American feels very close to fifteen other people, Jeffrey Boase, John B. Horrigan, Barry Wellman, and Lee Rainie, "The Strength of Internet Ties," Washington, DC: Pew Internet & American Life Project, 2006.

Note that "friend," for each side of the Fischer/McPherson et al. debate, refers to a person with whom one can "discuss important matters." The ability to trust another to listen, to be concerned about, and to understand an "important matter" surely opens the door to reflection about oneself and the world, and guards against isolation. As such, discussing "important matters" is probably the key to modern friendship. But it differs from a "village" state of being "on call" to haul a generator into a freezing house or answer other practical needs.

3. The 1998 study conducted by Amy Watson with Profusion Public Relations was the first study of clients of American coaches. Another study conducted in 2004 by Richard Zackon and Tony Grant is for sale from the International Coaching Federation.
4. Katherine T. Beddingfield, Dana Hawkins, Timothy Ito, Tracy Lenzy, and Margaret Loftus, "20 Hot Job Tracks when Baby Boomers Retire," *U.S. News and World Report*, October 20, 1996. See also Jan Johnson, *Living a Purpose-full Life* (New York: Doubleday Religious Publishing Group, 1999), p. 4.

5. Marc Gobé, *Emotional Branding: The New Paradigm for Connecting Brands to People* (New York: Allworth Press, 2011), p. xiv, and see especially p. 112.
6. Leanne Italie, "Feeling Lonely? Rent a Friend: Such Websites, Popular in Asia, Gaining Ground in U.S.," Associated Press, 2010, http://www.msnbc.msn.com/id/37760576.
7. Culture Fish, "A New Recipe for Personal Coaching: 3Lunches Is a Book and a Movement Inspiring Friend-to-Friend Coaching and Connection," in *Culture Fish Social Media Release*, 2009. Carol Quinn and Anny Beck, "3Lunches: About," 3Lunches.com, 2010, http://www.pitchengine.com/culturefish/a-new-recipe-for-personal-coaching-127978.

Chapter 13: I Would Have Done It If She'd Been My Mother

1. For life expectancy in 1900, see "Table 11. Life expectancy by age, race, and sex: Death-registration states, 1900–1902 to 1919–1921, and United States, 1929–1931 to 2006," in Elizabeth Arias, "United States Life Tables, 2006," *National Vital Statistics Reports* 58, no. 21 (2010).
2. For 2008 chances of living in a nursing home, see Medicare.gov, "Long-Term Care," Department of Health and Human Services, http://www.medicare.gov/longtermcare/static/home.asp. However, at any one point in time, very few of the over sixty-five live in a nursing home: in 2004, less than 4 percent—1,317,200—lived in nursing homes. See Table 5 in A. L. Jones et al., "The National Nursing Home Survey: 2004 Overview," *Vital Health Statistics* 13, no. 167 (2009). For the number of employees in nursing facilities, see Reimbursement and Research Department of the American Health Care Association, "The State Long-Term Health Care Sector 2005: Characteristics, Utilization, and Government Funding" (Washington, DC: American Health Care Association, 2006). For life expectancy, see Kenneth D. Kochanek, Jiaquan Xu, Sherry L. Murphy, Arialdi M. Minino, and Hsiang-Ching Kung, "Deaths: Preliminary Data for 2009," *National Vital Statistics Reports* 59, no. 4 (2011).
3. Jim Wilkes, "For-Profit Nursing Facilities in Trouble: A Wider Array of Choices and Greater Accountability Are Called For," *South Florida Sun-Sentinel*, July 31, 2000. See Will Mitchell, Aparna Venkatraman, Jane Banaszak-Holl, Joel Baum, and Whiney Berta, "The Commercialization of Nursing Home Care: Does For-Profit Cost-Control Mean Lower Quality or Do Corporations Provide the Best of Both

Worlds?" working paper at the Center for Advancement of Social Entrepreneurship (CASE), Duke University, 2004, http://www.caseatduke.org/documents/FPvNP_NursingHomes_mitchell.pdf.

4. On various types of long-term care of the elderly, see Gooloo S. Wunderlich and Peter O. Kohler, *Improving the Quality of Long-Term Care* (Washington, DC: The National Academies Press, 2001). For characteristics of care providers and clients, see Agency for Healthcare Research and Quality, "Long-Term Care Users Range in Age and Most Do Not Live in Nursing Homes: Research Alert" (Rockville, MD: Agency for Healthcare Research and Quality, 2000), "The Characteristics of Long-Term Care Users" (Rockville, MD: Agency for Healthcare Research and Quality, 2001); and Nora Super, "Who Will Be There to Care? The Growing Gap between Caregiver Supply and Demand" (Washington, DC: National Health Policy Forum/George Washington University, 2002). In fact, Comondore et al. calculate that if all care were nonprofit, the elderly would receive "500,000 more hours of nursing care a day." This exhaustive review of forty studies compared for-profit and not-for-profit care and showed that nonprofit homes deliver far better care, Vikram R. Comondore et al., "Quality of Care in For-Profit and Not-for-Profit Nursing Homes: Systematic Review and Meta-analysis," *British Medical Journal* 339 (2009).

   Turnover rates in care work are high generally, but especially high in for-profit nursing homes. See Nicholas G. Castle and John Engberg, "Turnover and Quality in Nursing Homes," *Medical Care* 43 (2005); William E. Aaronson, Jacqueline S. Zinn, and Michael D. Rosko, "Do For-Profit and Not-for-Profit Nursing Homes Behave Differently?" *The Gerontologist* 34, no. 6 (1994); Michael P. Hillmer et al., "Nursing Home Profit Status and Quality of Care: Is There Any Evidence of an Association?" *Medical Care Research and Review* 62, no. 2 (2005); Jane Banaszak-Holl and Marilyn A. Hines, "Factors Associated with Nursing Home Staff Turnover," *The Gerontologist* 36, no. 4 (1996); and Nicholas G. Castle and John Engberg, "Organizational Characteristics Associated with Staff Turnover in Nursing Homes," *Gerontologist* 46, no. 1 (2006). Staff turnover rates are related to quality of patient care. Castle and Engberg (2005) found, for example, that in institutions where turnover increased, care quality decreased, as measured by higher "rates of physical restraint use, catheter use, contractures, pressure ulcers, psychoactive drug use, and certification survey quality of care deficiencies" (p. 616).

Another recent report on the nation's nursing homes (for-profit and nonprofit combined) found that 44 percent failed to "ensure a safe environment," a third violated rules regarding the clean handling of food, a fifth gave residents unnecessary drugs, and a fifth were found to have "poor infection control." See Charlene Harrington, Helen Carrillo, and Brandee Woleslagle Blank, "Latest Data: Nursing Facilities, Staffing, Residents and Facility Deficiencies 2003 through 2008" (San Francisco: University of California, San Francisco, 2009).

5. One symptom of Parkinson's disease is a loss of emotional reaction, and perhaps this caused Victoria to lose interest in Barbara's offers, though Barbara didn't speak of this as a possible cause.

Chapter 14: Endings

1. In 2001, nearly half of Americans died in hospitals, and nearly a quarter in nursing homes; Center for Gerontology and Health Care Research, "Brown University Atlas of Dying," http://www.chcr.brown.edu/dying/usastatistics.htm. In addition, the for-profit hospice industry grew by 128 percent between 2001 and 2008, while nonprofits expanded 1 percent and government-sponsored hospice rose 25 percent. For-profit hospices select long-term (noncancer) patients and pay lower salaries, Joshua E. Perry and Robert C. Stone, "In the Business of Dying: Questioning the Commercialization of Hospice," *Journal of Law, Medicine and Ethics*, Summer 2011. See also S. Woolhandler and D. V. Himmelstein, "When Money Is the Mission—The High Costs of Investor-Owned Care," *New England Journal of Medicine* 341, no. 6 (1999).
2. Jessica Mitford, *The American Way of Death* (New York: Simon and Schuster, 1963). For industry revenues, see U.S. Census Bureau, "N.A.I.C.S. Industry Data—Other Services: Service Annual Survey" (Washington, DC: U.S. Census Bureau, 2006). For funeral cost information, see National Funeral Directors' Association, 2010, "Statistics: Funeral Costs," http://www.nfda.org/media-center/statisticsreports.html. In 1960 an average American funeral cost $708 to $5,233 in 2010 dollars. In 2009 it averaged $6,560. This cost includes the price of a metal casket, handling, preparation and transportation of remains, use of funeral home facilities, printed funeral materials, and excludes the cost of an outer burial container, cemetery plot, monument or marker costs, flowers or obituary. For information about Service

Corporation International outsourcing, see Russ Banham, "At Peace with Outsourcing," *FAO Today* 3, no. 3 (2006).

3. These examples are drawn from Sanders (2009) and other Internet sites. George Sanders, "'Late' Capital: Amusement and Contradiction in the Contemporary Funeral Industry," *Critical Sociology* 35, no. 4 (2009): 447–70.
4. Tamar Snyder, "Dawn of the Mourning Business," *Jewish Week*, April 18, 2011, p. 4. Mitchell Landsberg, "Shiva Sisters Offer Kind Words, Practical Help for Jewish Families at Times of Loss," *Los Angeles Times*, March 20, 2011, http://articles.latimes.com/2011/mar/20/local/la-me-shiva-sisters-20110321.
5. Everest Funeral Package, "Everest Services," http://www.everestfuneral.com/Services.aspx, accessed August 5, 2011.
6. For information about Bishop Adayanthrath, see Saritha Rai, "Short on Priests, U.S. Catholics Outsource Prayers to Indian Clergy," *New York Times*, June 13, 2004. Since the early days of the Catholic Church, indulgences—"remissions of temporal penalty for sin granted by the Episcopal authority of the Catholic Church" (Shaffern, p. 643)—have been (directly or indirectly) traded for alms, prayers, or good deeds. In the Middle Ages, abuses in selling indulgences became more common, and this was one reason that Martin Luther broke away from the Church. Robert W. Shaffern, "Indulgences and Saintly Devotionalisms in the Middle Ages," *Catholic Historical Review* 84, no. 4 (1998): 643–61. See also Kevin Knight and Inc., "The Catholic Encyclopedia," New Advent, http://www.newadvent.org/cathen/; and F. L. Cross, ed., *The Oxford Dictionary of the Christian Church* (New York: Oxford University Press, 2005).
7. Vincent M. Mallozzi, "For Hire: A Visitor to the Grave of Your Dearly Departed," *New York Times*, July 8, 2011, http://www.nytimes.com/2011/07/10/nyregion/womans-job-is-to-visit-graves-for-loved-ones-who-cannot.html.
8. "Concierge Services," Headstone Butler LLC, http://www.headstonebutler.com/conciergeservices.html, accessed October 10, 2011.

Conclusion: The Wantologist

1. A former trucker and musician, Kevin Creitman also taught career planning to engineering students at San Jose State. She consulted with local governments on supportive housing for the mentally ill, con-

sulted on Total Quality Management in the aerospace industry, and helped Oracle satisfy customers who had purchased expensive IT systems. Now she runs wantology training groups for life coaches and individuals, and estimates she's trained and treated "a few hundred" people. "Part of what I do," she explained in an interview, "is help people question the fantasies they attach to the things they buy. They read the ads. They believe them. Often they believe things have magical properties, and then add to those beliefs their own wishes. So a new computer will write the book. A remodeled living room will open a social world. So I ask them what they imagine a thing or service will make them feel. Often it bears no relation to what the thing or service actually does."

2. Through the UC Berkeley Survey Research Center, I surveyed nearly a thousand Californians from top to bottom of the class ladder in order to learn what, in the world of services, people might want. Consider the idea, I began by asking, "If I had all the money I wanted, I would hire someone to cook all my meals." About a third answered "yes." "Cook some of my meals?" I asked. Forty-five percent said yes. "Assemble a personal photo album and label particular photos?" To this, 30 percent agreed. "Select and purchase gifts and cards for friends and family?" Twenty-two percent. "Plan and supervise a birthday party for my children?" Twenty-six percent. "Pay daily or weekly visits to my elderly parent?" Twenty-four percent. Eighteen percent were ready to hire a life coach. A majority of Californians weren't tempted by such services. Still, a full third wanted to outsource all home cooking. A quarter wanted to hire someone to visit their elderly parents, and a fifth wished to hire a life coach.

   The poor wanted all these services more than the rich did. More than twice as many high school dropouts (46 percent) said "yes" to the birthday party planner as did those with a postgraduate education (21 percent). Over twice as many high school dropouts said "yes" to the photo-album assembler, too (39 vs. 19 percent). As for hiring a professional visitor to call on an elderly relative daily or weekly, 44 percent of the less educated would do so but just 21 percent of the more highly educated. Since the more highly educated generally earned higher salaries, a painful irony unfolded; those less interested in such services had the thicker wallets to afford them, and those most interested did not. Wallets and wants did not line up.

   The poorest of Americans in this survey, as in others, were the most socially isolated. They were also the most likely to agree "strongly" with the bleak statement: "You can't always count on family and friends, but you can always count on money." If current social trends continue, we will see more poor in America. And if isolation and poverty drive an understandable desire for personal services, more people will turn—at least in fantasy—to the market in search of all that is missing at home.

3. For this and for general encouragement, I'm grateful for a conversation with Erv Polster, 2010.
4. Activists have been working to spread a spirit of "the commons." In the wake of the 2004 market crash, a Boston-based organizer named Chuck Collins set up a series of "Resilience Circles" (sometimes called Common Security Clubs) through which people gather monthly in one another's homes to lend one another a helping hand. They set up skill banks (one repairs people's computers, another babysits, still another cooks casseroles, another organizes closets—each earning time credits they can cash in for the needed service of another, all without exchanging money). They share baby strollers, battery chargers, and other things. They buy food in bulk. Weekends, some groups have winterized homes, halving heating bills, conserving energy, and later enjoyed potluck dinners. One retired social worker who had become isolated caring for her ill husband, enthused, "I'd been listening to CNN financial news all day alone and getting terrified. Joining this gave me new friends, got me a part-time job, and made me feel a lot safer. Actually, it's the best thing I ever did." As of November 2011, there were 125 circles nationwide, and Interfaith Worker Justice and the NAACP were piloting circles for their networks. See www.localcircles.org and Hochschild, "Common Security Clubs Offer the Jobless a Lifeline," *Los Angeles Times*, May 23, 2010.

Bibliography

Aaronson, William E., Jacqueline S. Zinn, and Michael D. Rosko. "Do For-Profit and Not-for-Profit Nursing Homes Behave Differently?" *Gerontologist* 34, no. 6 (December 1, 1994): 775–86.

AARP Public Policy Institute. "Providing More Long-Term Support and Services at Home: Why It's Critical for Health Reform." Washington, DC: AARP Public Policy Institute, 2009.

Agency for Healthcare Research and Quality. "The Characteristics of Long-Term Care Users." Rockville, MD: Agency for Healthcare Research and Quality, 2001.

Agency for Healthcare Research and Quality. "Long-Term Care Users Range in Age and Most Do Not Live in Nursing Homes: Research Alert." Rockville, MD: Agency for Healthcare Research and Quality, 2000.

Ahluwalia, Indu B., Brian Morrow, Jason Hsia, and Laurence M. Grummer-Strawn. "Who Is Breast-Feeding? Recent Trends from the Pregnancy Risk Assessment and Monitoring System." *Journal of Pediatrics* 142, no. 5 (2003): 486–91.

Akenson, Donald Harman. *The Irish Diaspora. A Primer.* Belfast, Northern Ireland: Queen's University of Belfast, 1993.

Alter, Alexandra. "The Baby-Name Business." *Wall Street Journal,* June 22, 2007, 1, Section W.

Amato, Paul R. "Research on Divorce: Continuing Trends and New Developments." *Journal of Marriage and Family* 72, no. 3 (2010): 650–66.

American Academy of Wedding Professionals. "About American Academy of Wedding Professionals." http://www.aa-wp.com/about/aawp.asp.

American Association for Marriage and Family Therapy. "About AAMFT." http://www.aamft.org/iMIS15/AAMFT/About/About_AAMFT/Content/About_AAMFT-About AAMFT.aspx?hkey=a8d047de-5bf7-40cd-9551-d626e2490a25, accessed October 2, 2011.

Appadurai, Arjun, ed. *The Social Life of Things: Commodities in Cultural Perspective.* Cambridge, UK: Cambridge University Press, 1986.

Apple, Rima D. *Perfect Motherhood: Science and Childrearing in America.* New Brunswick, NJ: Rutgers University Press, 2006.

Arias, Elizabeth. "United States Life Tables, 2006." *National Vital Statistics Reports* 58, no. 21 (June 28, 2010).

Arons, Jessica. "Future Choices: Assisted Reproductive Technologies and the Law." Washington, DC: Center for American Progress, 2007.

Association of Bridal Consultants. "President's Welcome." Association of Bridal Consultants. http://www.bridalassn.com/Welcome.aspx.

Association of Certified Professional Wedding Consultants. "About the ACPWC." Association of Certified Professional Wedding Consultants. http://acpwc.com/content/index.php/about-the-acpwc.

Banaszak-Holl, Jane, and Marilyn A. Hines. "Factors Associated with Nursing Home Staff Turnover." *The Gerontologist* 36, no. 4 (1996): 512–17.

Banham, Russ. "At Peace with Outsourcing." *FAO Today* 3, no. 3 (2006).

Barkan, Elliott Robert, Hasia R. Diner, and Alan M. Kraut. *From Arrival to Incorporation: Migrants to the U.S. in a Global Era.* New York: New York University Press, 2008.

Basinger, Julianne. "Private Sources Play More of a Role in Paying Public-University Chiefs." *Chronicle of Higher Education* (November 30, 2001). http://chronicle.com/article/Private-Sources-Play-More-of-a/19322/.

Bates, Eric. "Private Prisons." *Nation* (January 5, 1998): 1.

Beddingfield, Katherine T., Dana Hawkins, Timothy Ito, Tracy Lenzy, and Margaret Loftus. "20 Hot Job Tracks When Baby Boomers Retire." *U.S. News and World Report*, October 20, 1996. http://www.usnews.com/usnews/biztech/articles/961028/archive_034854.htm.

Bernstein, Beth. *Temporarily Yours.* Chicago: University of Chicago Press, 2007.

Bialik, Carl. "Marriage-Maker Claims Are Tied in Knots (Interactive Graphic)." *Wall Street Journal*, July 29, 2009. http://online.wsj.com/article/SB124879877347487253.html#articleTabs=article

Bianchi, Suzanne M., John P. Robinson, and Melissa A. Milkie. *Changing Rhythms of American Family Life*. New York: Russell Sage Foundation, 2006.

Boase, Jeffrey, John B. Horrigan, Barry Wellman, and Lee Rainie. "The Strength of Internet Ties." Washington, DC: Pew Internet & American Life Project, 2006.

Bramlett, M., and W. Mosher. "Cohabitation, Marriage, Divorce, and Remarriage in the United States." *Vital Health Statistics* 23, no. 22 (2002).

Braverman, Harry. *Labor and Monopoly Capital: The Degradation of Work in the Twentieth Century*. New York: Monthly Review Press, 1975.

Bridal Association of America. "Our Mission." Bridal Association of America. http://www.bridalassociationofamerica.com/ourmission/.

———. "The Wedding Report." Bridal Association of America. http://www.bridalassociationofamerica.com/Wedding_Statistics/.

Brown, Charles Reynolds. *The Young Man's Affairs*. Oakland, CA: First Congregational Church, 1909.

Brown, Wendy. "Wounded Attachments." *Political Theory* 21, no. 3 (1993): 390–410.

Butler, Sarah. "Recession Boost for Online Dating Sites." *Telegraph*, January 4, 2009. http://www.telegraph.co.uk/finance/newsbysector/mediatechnologyandtelecoms/4109637/Recession-boost-for-online-dating-sites.html.

Camarota, Steven A. "Immigrants at Mid-decade: A Snapshot of America's Foreign-Born Population in 2005." Washington, DC: Center for Immigration Studies, 2005.

Carbone, Gerald M. "Town Awaits Closing of Bass Shoe Plant with Fear, Sadness." *Providence Journal* (March 1, 1998).

Carnesale, Albert. "The Private-Public Gap in Higher Education." *Chronicle of Higher Education* (January 6, 2006). http://chronicle.com/article/The-Private-Public-Gap-in/9033/.

Carney, Scott. "Inside India's Rent-A-Womb Business." *Mother Jones* (March/April 2010). http://motherjones.com/politics/2010/02/surrogacy-tourism-india-nayna-patel.

Carter, Steve, and Chadwick Snow. "Helping Singles Enter Better Marriages Using Predictive Models of Marital Success." Poster presented at the 16th annual convention of the American Psychological Society, Chicago, IL, May 24–30, 2004.

Castle, Nicholas G., and John Engberg. "Organizational Characteristics Associated with Staff Turnover in Nursing Homes." *Gerontologist* 46, no. 1 (February 1, 2006): 62–73.

———. "Turnover and Quality in Nursing Homes." *Medical Care* 43 (2005): 616–26.

Center for Gerontology and Health Care Research. "Brown University Atlas of Dying." http://www.chcr.brown.edu/dying/2001DATA.HTM.

Centers for Disease Control and Prevention. "FastStats: Unmarried Childbearing." CDC/National Center for Health Statistics. http://www.cdc.gov/nchs/fastats/unmarry.htm.

Cherlin, Andrew J. "Demographic Trends in the United States: A Review of Research in the 2000s." *Journal of Marriage and Family* 72, no. 3 (2010): 403–19.

———. *The Marriage-Go-Round: The State of Marriage and the Family in America Today.* New York: Alfred A. Knopf, 2009.

Children's Defense Fund. "The State of America's Children, 2010." Washington, DC: Children's Defense Fund, 2010.

Christensen, Perry M., and Benson L. Porter. *Family 360: A Proven Approach to Getting Your Family to Talk, Solve Problems, and Improve Relationships.* New York: McGraw-Hill, 2004.

Cobbett, William. *Advice to Young Men and (Incidentally) to Young Women in the Middle and Higher Ranks of Life in a Series of Letters Addressed to a Youth, a Bachelor, a Lover, a Husband, a Citizen or a Subject.* New York: John Doyle (Individual), 1833.

Collier, Jane Fishburne. *From Duty to Desire: Remaking Families in a Spanish Village.* Princeton, NJ: Princeton University Press, 1997.

Comondore, Vikram R., P. J. Devereaux, Qi Zhou, Samuel B. Stone, Jason W. Busse, Nikila C. Ravindran, Karen E. Burns, et al. "Quality of Care in For-Profit and Not-for-Profit Nursing Homes: Systematic Review and Meta-Analysis." *British Medical Journal* 339 (2009): 374–90.

Congressional Record of the Senate. "Proceedings and Debates of the 107th Congress: Second Session." Washington, DC: U.S. Government Printing Office, 2002.

Consumer-Rankings.com. "Match.Com." Consumer-Rankings.com. http://www.consumer-rankings.com/Dating/MatchReview.aspx?li=42.

Cook, Rachel, Shelley Day Sclater, and Felicity Kaganas. *Surrogate Motherhood: International Perspectives*. Portland, OR: Hart Publishing, 2003.

Coontz, Stephanie. "How to Make It Work This Time." *New York Times*, May 13, 2011.

Cortés, Rosalia. "Children and Women Left Behind in Labour Sending Countries: An Appraisal of Social Risks." Brighton, UK: Child Migration Research Network, 2007.

Council of Europe. *European Social Charter: Committee of Independent Experts: Conclusions xiv-2*. Council of Europe, 1999.

Cross, F. L., ed. *The Oxford Dictionary of the Christian Church*. New York: Oxford University Press, 2005.

Cross, Gary S. *An All-Consuming Century: Why Commercialism Won in Modern America*. New York: Columbia University Press, 2000.

Cross, Gary S., and Peter. R. Shergold. "The Family Economy and the Market: Wages and Residence of Pennsylvania Women in the 1980s." *Journal of Family History* 11 (1986): 245–65

Culture Fish. "A New Recipe for Personal Coaching: 3Lunches Is a Book and a Movement Inspiring Friend-to-Friend Coaching and Connection." *Culture Fish Social Media Release*, 2009. http://www.pitchengine.com/culturefish/a-new-recipe-for-personal-coaching-/27978/.

Cutright, Phillips. "Illegitimacy in the United States: 1920–1968." In *Demographic and Social Aspects of Population Growth*, edited by C. F. Westoff and R. Parke Jr. Washington, DC: U.S. Government Printing Office, 1972, 377–438.

DatingSitesReviews.com. "Match.Com Review." DatingSitesReviews.com. http://datingsitesreviews.com/staticpages/index.php?page=2010000100-Match.

Davis, Rebecca L. *More Perfect Unions: The American Search for Marital Bliss*. Cambridge, MA: Harvard University Press, 2010.

Dermout, Sylvia, Harry van de Wiel, Peter Heintz, Kees Jansen, and Willem Ankum. "Non-Commercial Surrogacy: An Account of Patient Management in the First Dutch Centre for IVF Surrogacy, from 1997 to 2004." *Human Reproduction* 25, no. 2 (February 1, 2010): 443–49.

Dills, Angela K., and Jeffrey A. Miron. "Alcohol Prohibition and Cirrhosis." *American Law and Economics Review* 6, no. 2 (August 1, 2004): 285–318.

Dimitri, Carolyn, Anne Effland, and Neilson Conklin. "The 20th

Century Transformation of U.S. Agriculture and Farm Policy." *Electronic Information Bulletin* 3 (2005). http://www.ers.usda.gov/publications/eib3/eib3.htm.

Dizard, Jan E., and Howard Gadlin. *The Minimal Family.* Amherst: University of Massachusetts Press, 1990.

Doucette, Lisa. "Paying for Dates—Whatsyourprice.com: A Sleazy Proposition or a Personal Investment?" *Forbes*, April 19, 2011. http://www.forbes.com/sites/elisadoucette/2011/04/19/paying-for-dates-a-sleazy-proposition-or-personal-investment/.

Drutman, Lee, and Charlie Cray. "The People's Business: Controlling Corporations and Restoring Democracy." *In These Times,* February 18, 2005. http://www.inthesetimes.org/article/1971/the_peoples_business/.

Dube, Shanta R., Vincent Felitti, Maxia Dong, Wayne Giles, and Robert Anda. "The Impact of Adverse Childhood Experiences on Health Problems: Evidence from Four Birth Cohorts Dating Back to 1900." *Preventive Medicine* 37 (2003): 268–77.

Dufalla, Anita. "Online Dating Discovers a New Age." *Pittsburgh Post-Gazette*, January 3, 2006.

Duffy, Mignon. *Making Care Count: A Century of Gender, Race, and Paid Care Work.* New Brunswick, NJ: Rutgers University Press, 2011.

Edin, Kathryn, and Maria Kefalas. *Promises I Can Keep: Why Poor Women Put Motherhood before Marriage.* Berkeley: University of California Press, 2005.

eHarmony. "The #1 Most Trusted Name in Online Relationship Services." http://www.eharmony.com/advertising/singles.

———. "Study: 542 People Married Every Day in U.S., on Average, Through eHarmony." eHarmony press release, August 16, 2010. http://www.eharmony.com/press/release/31.

Ehrenreich, Barbara, and Deirdre English. *For Her Own Good: Two Centuries of the Experts' Advice to Women.* New York: Anchor Books, 1978.

Ellin, Abby. "The Recession, Isn't It Romantic?" *New York Times*, February 12, 2011.

England, Paula. "The Gender Revolution: Uneven and Stalled." *Gender and Society* 24 no. 2 (2010): 114–66.

English, Ashley, Heidi Hartmann, and Jeff Hayes. "Are Women Now Half the Labor Force? The Truth about Women and Equal Participation in the Labor Force." Institute for Women's Policy Research, 2010.

Erikson, Erik. *Childhood and Society.* New York: W. W. Norton, 1993 (1964).

Estes, Jennine. "Pre-Marital Therapy: The Training Wheels for Marriage." *Relationships in the Raw,* April 20, 2009. http://estestherapy.com/relationshiptips/2009/04/20/the-training-wheels-for-marriage/.

Everest Funeral Services. "Everest Services." http://www.everestfuneral.com/Services.aspx, accessed August 5, 2011.

Fevre, Ralph. *The New Sociology of Economic Behaviour.* Thousand Oaks, CA: Sage Publications, 2003.

Fischer, Claude S. *Made in America: A Social History of American Culture and Character.* Chicago: University of Chicago Press, 2010.

———. *Still Connected: Family and Friends in America since 1970.* New York: Russell Sage Foundation, 2011.

———. "The 2004 G.S.S. Finding of Shrunken Social Networks: An Artifact?" *American Sociological Review* 74, no. 4 (August 1, 2009): 657–69.

Fischer, Claude S., and Michael Hout. *Century of Difference: How America Changed in the Last One Hundred Years.* New York: Russell Sage Foundation, 2006.

Folbre, Nancy. *The Invisible Heart: Economics and Family Values.* New York: New Press, 2001.

Friedman, Milton. *Capitalism and Freedom.* Chicago: University of Chicago Press, 1962.

———. *Take It to the Limits: Milton Friedman on Libertarianism.* Palo Alto, CA: Hoover Institute, Stanford University, 1999. Video interview.

Friedman, Milton, and Rose D. Friedman. *Free to Choose: A Personal Statement.* New York: Harcourt Brace Jovanovich, 1980.

Fromm, Erich. *The Art of Loving.* New York: Perennial Classics, 2000 (1956).

Gamble, Natalie. "Crossing the Line: The Legal and Ethical Problems of Foreign Surrogacy." *Reproductive BioMedicine Online* 19, no. 2 (2009): 151–52.

García Zamora, Rodolfo. "Un pasivo: Mujeres y niños en comunidades de alta migración internacional en Michoacán, Jalisco, y Zacatecas, México." In "Las remesas de los migrantes Mexicanos en Estados Unidos y su impacto sobre las condiciones de vida de los infantes en México." UNESCO. Unpublished.

Garey, Anita, and Karen Hansen, eds. *At the Heart of Work and Family: Engaging the Ideas of Arlie Hochschild.* New Brunswick: Rutgers University Press, 2011.

Geick, Elizabeth. "Should This Marriage Be Saved?" *Time,* February 27, 1995.

Gengupta, Amit. "Medical Tourism: Reverse Subsidy for the Elite." *Signs: Journal of Women in Culture and Society* 36, no. 2 (2011): 312–18.

Gillis, John R. *A World of Their Own Making: Myth, Ritual, and the Quest for Family Values.* Cambridge, MA: Harvard University Press, 1996.

Gionzaga, Gian. "How You Meet Your Spouse Matters." *eHarmony Blog*, February 10, 2011. http://advice.eharmony.com/blog/2011/02/10/how-you-meet-your-spouse-matters.

Gladwell, Malcolm. *The Tipping Point: How Little Things Can Make a Big Difference.* Boston: Little, Brown and Company, 2000.

Gobé, Marc. *Emotional Branding: The New Paradigm for Connecting Brands to People.* New York: Allworth Press, 2001.

Golden, Janet. *A Social History of Wet Nursing in America: From Breast to Bottle.* New York: Cambridge University Press, 1996.

Gootman, Elissa. "Job Description: Life of the Party." *New York Times*, May 30, 2003, B1.

Gordon, Linda. *Pitied but Not Entitled.* New York: Free Press, 1994.

Gordon, Linda, and Sara McLanahan. "Single Parenthood in 1900." *Journal of Family History* 16, no. 2 (1991): 97–116.

Gottman, John Mordechai, and Nan Silver. *The Seven Principles for Making Marriage Work.* New York: Crown Publishers, 1999.

Grant, A., and R. Zackon. "Executive, Workplace and Life Coaching: Findings from a Large-Scale Survey of International Coach Federation Members." *International Journal of Evidence Based Coaching and Mentoring* 2, no. 2 (2004): 1–15.

Grayson, Katharine. "Need Some Air? Startup Selling Oxygen." *Minneapolis/St. Paul Business Journal*, August 12, 2007.

Green, Francis. *Demanding Work: The Paradox of Job Quality in the Affluent Economy.* Princeton, NJ: Princeton University Press, 2006.

Greider, William. *One World, Ready or Not: The Manic Logic of Global Capitalism.* New York: Simon and Schuster, 1997.

Gross, Neil. "The Detraditionalization of Intimacy Reconsidered." *Sociological Theory* 23, no. 3 (2005): 286–311.

Grummer-Strawn, Laurence M., and Katherine R. Shealy. "Progress in Protecting, Promoting, and Supporting Breastfeeding: 1984–2009." *Breastfeeding Medicine* 4, no. 1 (2009): S31–S39.

Gruneir, Andrea, Vincent Mor, Sherry Weitzen, Rachael Truchil, Joan Teno, and Jason Roy. "Where People Die: A Multilevel Approach to Understanding Influences on Site of Death in America." *Medical Care Research and Review* 64, no. 4 (August 2007): 351–78.

Habermas, Jürgen. *The Theory of Communicative Action*, vol. 2, *Lifeworld and System: A Critique of Functionalist Reason*. Boston: Beacon Press, 1987.

Hamilton, B. E., J. A. Martin, and S. J. Ventura. "Births: Preliminary Data for 2007." Hyattsville, MD: National Center for Health Statistics, 2009.

Hansen, Michael, Jennifer J. Kurinczuk, Carol Bower, and Sandra Webb. "The Risk of Major Birth Defects after Intracytoplasmic Sperm Injection and In Vitro Fertilization." *New England Journal of Medicine* 346, no. 10 (2002): 725–30.

Hardy, Thomas. *The Mayor of Casterbridge*. Ed. James K. Robinson. New York: W. W. Norton, 1977 (1886).

Harrington, Charlene, Helen Carrillo, and Brandee Woleslagle Blank. "Latest Data: Nursing Facilities, Staffing, Residents and Facility Deficiencies 2003 through 2008." San Francisco: University of California, San Francisco, 2009.

Harwood Group. "Yearning for Balance: Views of Americans on Consumption, Materialism, and the Environment." Milton, MA: Merck Family Fund, 1995.

Herrick, Devon M. "Medical Tourism: Global Competition in Health Care." Dallas, TX: National Center for Policy Analysis, 2007.

Hillmer, Michael P., Walter P. Wodchis, Sudeep S. Gill, Geoffrey M. Anderson, and Paula A. Rochon. "Nursing Home Profit Status and Quality of Care: Is There Any Evidence of an Association?" *Medical Care Research and Review* 62, no. 2 (2005): 139–66.

Hirsch, Barry T., and David A. Macpherson. "Union Membership and Coverage Database from the Current Population Survey: Note." *Industrial and Labor Relations Review* 56, no. 2 (2003): 349–54.

———. "U.S. Historical Tables: Union Membership, Coverage, Density, and Employment among All Wage and Salary Workers, 1973–2010." Union Membership and Coverage Database from the Current Population Survey. http://unionstats.gsu.edu/All%20Wage%20and%20Salary%20Workers.htm.

———. "U.S. Historical Tables: Union Membership, Coverage, Density, and Employment among Private Sector Workers, 1973–2010." Union Membership and Coverage Database from the Current Population Survey. http://unionstats.gsu.edu/Private%20Sector%20workers.htm.

Hobbs, Frank, and Nicole Stoops. "Demographic Trends in the 20th Century." Washington, DC: U.S. Government Printing Office, 2002.

Hochschild, Arlie R. "The Back Stage of a Global Free Market: Nannies and Surrogates." In *Care und Migration*, edited by Ursula Apitzsch and

Marianne Schmidbaur. Opladen, Germany, and Farmington Hills, MI: Verlag Barbara Budrich, 2010.

———. "Childbirth at the Global Crossroads." *American Prospect*, October 2009, 25–28.

———. *The Commercialization of Intimate Life: Notes from Home and Work*. Berkeley: University of California Press, 2003.

———. "Common Security Clubs Offer the Jobless a Lifeline." *Los Angeles Times*, May 23, 2010. http://articles.latimes.com/2010/may23/opinion/la-oe-hochschild-unemployed-20100523.

———. *The Managed Heart: Commercialization of Human Feeling*. Berkeley: University of California Press, 2012 (1983).

———. *The Second Shift: Working Families and the Revolution at Home*. New York: Penguin Group, 2012 (1989).

———. *The Time Bind: When Work Becomes Home and Home Becomes Work*. New York: Macmillan, 2001.

Hochschild, Arlie R., and Barbara Ehrenreich, eds. *Global Woman: Nannies, Maids, and Sex Workers in the New Economy*. New York: Metropolitan Books, 2003.

Hochschild, Arlie R., and Sarah B. Garrett. "Beyond Tocqueville's Telescope: The Personalized Brand and the Branded Self." *Hedgehog Review* 13, no. 3 (2011): 82–95.

Holson, Laura. "Wall Street Woos Film Producers, Skirting Studios." *New York Times*, October 14, 2006.

"Homework: Relax, Put Your Feet Up—and Let Someone Else Take Care of the Household Chores." *Economist* 348, no. 8087 (September 26, 1998): 68.

Hondagneu-Sotelo, Pierrette. "Families on the Frontier: From Braceros in the Fields to Braceras in the Home." In *Latinos: Remaking America*, edited by Marcelo M. Suárez-Orozco and Mariela M. Páez. Berkeley: University of California Press, 2002, 259–73.

Houran, James, Rense Lange, P. Jason Rentfrow, and Karen H. Brookner. "Do Online Matchmaking Tests Work? An Assessment of Preliminary Evidence for a Publicized Predictive Model of Marital Success." *North American Journal of Psychology* 6, no. 3 (2004): 507–26.

Hua, Vanessa. "One for the Books: Tutoring Gets Outsourced." *San Francisco Chronicle*, October 22, 2006. http://articles.sfgate.com/2006-10-22/news/17317236_1_tutoring-online-market-face-to-face-instruction.

Hulbert, Ann. *Raising America: Experts, Parents, and a Century of Advice About Children*. New York: Alfred A. Knopf, 2003.

Hyde, Lewis. *The Gift: Imagination and the Erotic Life of Property*. New York: Vintage Books, 1983.

IAC. "Form 10-K: Annual Report Pursuant to Section 13 or 15(d) of the Securities Exchange Act of 1934 for the Fiscal Year Ended December 31, 2009." New York: IAC/INTERACTIVECORP, 2010.

IAC Advertising. "Align Your Brand with the Leading U.S. Online Relationship Site." IAC Advertising and Match.com. http://dating sitesreviews.com/images/other/match/Match-Stats-2009-Q1.pdf.

Illouz, Eva. *Cold Intimacies: The Making of Emotional Capitalism*. Malden, MA: Polity Press, 2007.

International Living. "Mexico—Still the World's Best Retirement Haven." International Living. http://internationalliving.com/2008/08/retire -index-08/, accessed April 13, 2009.

Italie, Leanne. "Feeling Lonely? Rent a Friend: Such Websites, Popular in Asia, Gaining Ground in U.S." Associated Press. http://www .msnbc.msn.com/id/37760576/.

Jackson, Pauline. "Women in 19th Century Irish Emigration." *International Migration Review* 18, no. 4 (1984): 1004–20.

Jeffries, Adrianne. "OKCupid: We Didn't Censor Our Match.com -Bashing Blog Post." *New York Observer* February 2, 2011. http:// www.observer.com/2011/tech/okcupid-we-didnt-censor-our -matchcom-bashing-blog-post.

Jerin, Robert, and Beverly Dolinsky. "Cyber-victimization and Online Dating." In *Online Matchmaking*, edited by M. T. Whitty, A. Baker, and J. Inman. New York: Palgrave Macmillan, 2007, 147–58.

Johnson, Jan. *Living a Purpose-Full Life: What Happens When You Say Yes to God*. New York: Doubleday Religious Publishing Group, 1999.

Jones, A. L., L. L. Dwyer, A. R. Bercovitz, and G. W. Strahan. "The National Nursing Home Survey: 2004 Overview." *Vital Health Statistics* 13, no. 167 (June 2009).

Jones, Howard W., Jean Cohen, Ian Cooke, and Roger Kempers, eds. *IFFS Surveillance 07, Fertility and Sterility* 87, Supplement 1. American Society for Reproductive Medicine, 2007.

Jordon, David Starr. *The Call of the Twentieth Century: An Address to Young Men*. Boston, MA: American Unitarian Association, 1903.

Kannan, Shilpa. "Regulators Eye India's Surrogacy Sector." BBC News, India Business Report, March 18, 2009. http://news.bbc.co.uk/2/hi/ business/7935768.stm.

Katz, Evan Marc, and Linda Holmes. *Why You're Still Single: Things Your Friends Would Tell You If You Promised Not to Get Mad*. New York: Plume, 2006.

Kaufman, Sharon R. *And a Time to Die: How American Hospitals Shape the End of Life*. New York: Simon and Schuster, 2005.

Kaye, H. Stephen, Mitchell P. LaPlante, and Charlene Harrington. "Do Noninstitutional Long-Term Care Services Reduce Medicaid Spending?" *Health Affairs* 28, no. 1 (2009): 262–72.

Kleinberg, S. J. *Women in the United States, 1830–1945*. New Brunswick, NJ: Rutgers University Press, 1999.

Knight, Kevin, and New Advent, Inc. *The Catholic Encyclopedia*. New Advent. http://www.newadvent.org/cathen/.

Kochanek, Kenneth D., Jiaquan Xu, Sherry L. Murphy, Arialdi M. Minino, and Hsiang-Ching Kung. "Deaths: Preliminary Data for 2009." *National Vital Statistics Reports* 59, no. 4 (March 16, 2011).

Kohli, Namita. "Moms on the Market." *Hindustan Times*, March 13, 2011.

Kreider, Rose M., and Renee Ellis. "Number, Timing, and Duration of Marriages and Divorces: 2009." *Current Population Reports* P70-125 (2011). http://www.census.gov/prod/2011pubs/p70-125.pdf.

Kuttner, Robert. *Everything for Sale: The Virtues and Limits of Markets*. New York: Alfred A. Knopf, 1997.

Landes, Elisabeth M., and Richard A. Posner. "The Economics of the Baby Shortage." In *Rethinking Commodification: Cases and Readings in Law and Culture*, edited by Martha M. Ertman and Joan C. Williams. New York: New York University Press, 2005.

Lane, Robert E. *The Loss of Happiness in Market Democracies*. New Haven: Yale University Press, 2001.

Lepore, Jill. "Fixed: The Rise of Marriage Therapy, and Other Dreams of Human Betterment." *New Yorker*, March 29, 2010.

Lender, Mark Edward, and James Kirby Martin. *Drinking in America: A History*. New York: Free Press, 1982.

Leng, Chee Heng. "Medical Tourism in Malaysia: International Movement of Healthcare Consumers and the Commodification of Healthcare." Singapore: Asia Research Institute, National University of Singapore, 2007.

Levine, Aaron D. "Self-Regulation, Compensation, and the Ethical Recruitment of Oocyte Donors." *Hastings Center Report* 40, no. 2 (2010): 25–36.

Liggett, Brit. "Hong Kong Activist Group Selling 'Fresh Air' for 25 Cents a Bottle." Inhabitat.com. http://inhabitat.com/hong-kong-activist-group-selling-fresh-air-for-25-cents-a-bottle/.

Lindheim, Roslyn. "Birthing Centers and Hospices: Reclaiming Birth and Death." *Annual Review of Public Health* 2 (1981): 1–29.

Lloyd, Carol. "Modern-Day Wet Nursing." *Broadsheet*, Salon.com, April 26, 2007. http://life.salon.com/2007/04/26/nursing_6/.

Macdonald, Cameron Lynne. *Shadow Mothers: Nannies, Au Pairs, and the Micropolitics of Mothering*. Berkeley: University of California Press, 2011.

MacDorman, Marian F., Fay Menacker, and Eugene Declercq. "Trends and Characteristics of Home and Other Out-of-Hospital Births in the United States, 1990–2006." *National Vital Statistics Reports* 58, no. 11 (March 3, 2010).

Madden, Mary, and Amand Lenhart. "Online Dating." Washington, DC: Pew Research Center, 2006.

Mallozzi, Vincent M. "For Hire: A Visitor to the Grave of Your Dearly Departed." *New York Times*, July 8, 2011. http://www.nytimes.com/2011/07/10/nyregion/womans-job-is-to-visit-graves-for-loved-ones-who-cannot.html.

Mander, Jerry. *In the Absence of the Sacred: The Failure of Technology and the Survival of the Indian Nations*. San Francisco: Sierra Club Books, 1991.

Manpower, Inc. "About Manpower." Manpower, Inc. http://us.manpower.com/us/en/about-manpower/default.jsp.

Marx, Karl. *Economic and Philosophic Manuscripts of 1844*. Mineola, NY: Dover Publications, 2007.

Match.com, and Chadwick Martin Bailey. "Match.Com and Chadwick Martin Bailey 2009–2010 Studies—Recent Trends: Online Dating." Chadwick Martin Bailey Online (2010). http://cp.match.com/cppp/media/CMB_Study.pdf.

Mauss, Marcel. *The Gift: The Form and Reason for Exchange in Archaic Societies*. Translated by W. D. Halls. New York: W. W. Norton, 2000 (1954).

McDonald, D., E. Fournier, M. Russell-Einhorn, and S. Crawford. "Private Prisons in the United States: An Assessment of Current Practice." Cambridge, MA: Abt Associates, 1998.

McLanahan, Sara S., and Gary Sandefur. *Growing Up with a Single Parent: What Hurts, What Helps?* Cambridge, MA: Harvard University Press, 1994.

McPherson, Miller, Lynn Smith-Lovin, and Matthew Brashears. "Errata: Social Isolation in America: Changes in Core Discussion Networks over Two Decades." *American Sociological Review* 73, no. 6 (2008): 1022.

———. "Social Isolation in America: Changes in Core Discussion Networks over Two Decades." *American Sociological Review* 71, no. 3 (2006): 353–75.

Mead, Rebecca. *One Perfect Day: The Selling of the American Wedding.* New York: Penguin Press, 2007.

Medicare.gov. "Long-Term Care." Department of Health and Human Services. http://www.medicare.gov/longtermcare/static/home.asp.

Mercer. "Worldwide Benefit & Employment Guidelines." Geneva, Switzerland: Mercer, 2010.

Merchant, Jennifer. "Assisted Reproductive Technology (ART) in the United States: Towards a National Regulatory Framework?" *Journal International de Bioéthique* 20, no. 4 (2009): 55–71.

Mintz, Steven. "Mothers and Fathers in America: Looking Backward, Looking Forward." Digital History. http://www.digitalhistory.uh.edu/historyonline/mothersfathers.cfm.

Mintz, Steven, and Susan Kellogg. *Domestic Revolutions: A Social History of American Family Life.* New York: Free Press, 1989.

Mitchell, Will, Aparna Venkatraman, Jane Banaszak-Holl, Joel Baum, and Whitney Berta. "The Commercialization of Nursing Home Care: Does For-Profit Cost-Control Mean Lower Quality or Do Corporations Provide the Best of Both Worlds?" Working paper at the Center for Advancement of Social Entrepreneurship (CASE), Duke University, 2004. http://www.caseatduke.org/documents/FPvNP_NursingHomes_mitchell.pdf.

Mitford, Jessica. *The American Way of Death.* New York: Simon and Schuster, 1963.

Moise, E. E. "New Orleans Marriage Guide Caused Duels: Review of 1858 'How to Get a Rich Wife.'" *New Orleans Item-Tribune*, June 24, 1928, 2.

Moldvay, Caitlin. "Dating Game: With Increasing Internet Penetration, Online Dating Is on the Rise." IBISWorld, Inc., December 2010.

Montgomery, Rhonda J. V., Lyn Holley, Jerome Deichert, and Karl Kosloski. "A Profile of Home Care Workers from the 2000 Census: How It Changes What We Know." *The Gerontologist* 45, no. 5 (October 1, 2005): 593–600.

Morgan, Edmund S. *The Puritan Family: Religion and Domestic Relations in Seventeenth-Century New England.* New York: Harper & Row, 1966 (1944).

Morrison, Chris. "Match.com Reveals the Dark Side of the Online Dating Business." *BNET,* April 28, 2010. http://www.bnet.com/blog/technology/matchcom-reveals-the-dark-side-of-the-online-dating-business/7391.

Nakano Glenn, Evelyn. *Forced to Care.* Cambridge: Harvard University Press, 2010.

Naraine, Ryan. "Online Personals: Big Profits, Intense Competition." *ClickZ* (June 27, 2003). http://www.clickz.com/2228891.

National Crime Records Bureau. "Crime in India 2008: Figures at a Glance." National Crime Records Bureau, Indian Ministry of Home Affairs. http://ncrb.nic.in/cii2008/cii-2008/figure%20at%20a%20glance.pdf.

National Funeral Directors' Association. "Statistics: Funeral Costs" (2010). http://www.nfda.org/media-center/statisticsreports.html.

National Institute of Mental Health. "NIMH Questions and Answers on Army STARRS." http://www.nimh.nih.gov/health/topics/suicide-prevention/suicide-prevention-studies/questions-and-answers-on-army-starrs.shtml, accessed June 6, 2011.

New American Dream. "New American Dream Survey Report." Charlottesville, VA: New American Dream, 2004.

Newman, Martyn. *Emotional Capitalists: The New Leaders.* Melbourne, Australia: RocheMartin Institute, 2005.

OECD. "Sf 3.1 Marriage and Divorce Rates." OECD Family Database/Directorate for Employment, Labour and Social Affairs. http://www.oecd.org/dataoecd/4/19/40321815.pdf.

Online Dating Magazine. "Online Daters More Confident Than Offline Daters." *Online Dating Magazine* (2004). http://www.onlinedatingmagazine.com/news2004/onlinedaters.html.

Otnes, Cele, and Elizabeth H. Pleck. *Cinderella Dreams: The Allure of the Lavish Wedding.* Berkeley: University of California Press, 2003

Pande, Amrita. "Commercial Surrogacy in India: Manufacturing a Perfect 'Mother-Worker.'" *Signs: Journal of Women in Culture and Society* 35, no. 4 (2010): 969–92.

———. "'It May Be Her Eggs but It's My Blood': Surrogates and Everyday Forms of Kinship in India." *Qualitative Sociology* 32, no. 4 (2009): 379–97.

———. "Not an 'Angel', Not a 'Whore.'" *Indian Journal of Gender Studies* 16, no. 2 (June 1, 2009): 141–73.

Parker, Kim. "The Harried Life of the Working Mother." *Pew Research Center Social & Demographic Trends* (2009). http://pewsocialtrends.org/2009/10/01/the-harried-life-of-the-working-mother/.

Parreñas, Rhacel Salazar. *Children of Global Migration: Transnational Families and Gendered Woes.* Stanford, CA: Stanford University Press, 2005.

Passel, Jeffrey S., and D'Vera Cohn. "Unauthorized Immigrant Population: National and State Trends, 2010." Washington, DC: Pew Hispanic Center/Pew Research Center, 2011.

Paumgarten, Nick. "Looking for Someone." *New Yorker,* July 4, 2011.

Perry, Joshua E., and Robert C. Stone. "In the Business of Dying: Questioning the Commercialization of Hospice." *Journal of Law, Medicine and Ethics,* Summer 2011.

Pleck, Elizabeth H. *Celebrating the Family: Ethnicity, Consumer Culture, and Family Rituals.* Cambridge, MA: Harvard University Press, 2000.

Plentyoffish.com. "Letter to Markus Frind," April 23, 2010. http://www.plentyoffish.com/matchcomletter.pdf.

Polanyi, Karl. *The Great Transformation: The Political and Economic Origins of Our Times.* New York: Farrar and Rinehart, Inc., 1944.

Population Projections Program. "N.P.-D1-A: Projections of the Population by Age, Sex, Race, and Hispanic Origin for the United States: 1999 to 2100 (Middle Series)." Washington, DC: Population Division, U.S. Census Bureau, 2000.

Prasad, Shally. "Medicolegal Response to Violence against Women in India." *Violence Against Women* 5, no. 5 (May 1, 1999): 478–506.

PRNewswire. "Brides.com 2009 American Wedding Survey Reveals: Popping the Question Has Popped in Price." PRNewswire (February 23, 2009).

Pulley, John L. "Public Universities' Ambitious Campaigns Vex Many Small Private Institutions: Largest Campaigns by Public Universities." *Chronicle of Higher Education* (1999). http://chronicle.com/article/Public-Universities-Ambitious/12057/.

Putnam, Robert D. *Bowling Alone: The Collapse and Revival of American Community.* New York: Simon and Schuster, 2000.

Quinn, Carol, and Anny Beck. "3Lunches: About." 3Lunches. http://3lunches.com/about/.

Radin, Margaret Jane. *Contested Commodities.* Cambridge, MA: Harvard University Press, 1996.

Rai, Saritha. "Short on Priests, U.S. Catholics Outsource Prayers to Indian Clergy." *New York Times*, June 13, 2004.

Raley, R. Kelly, and Larry Bumpass. "The Topography of the Divorce Plateau: Levels and Trends in Union Stability in the United States after 1980." *Demographic Research* 8 (2003): 245–60.

Rampell, Catherine. "Corporate Profits Were the Third Highest on Record Last Quarter." *New York Times*, November 23, 2010.

Reimbursement and Research Department of the American Health Care Association. "The State Long-Term Health Care Sector 2005: Characteristics, Utilization, and Government Funding." Washington, DC: American Health Care Association, 2006.

Reuteman, Rob. "Technology: How No. 1 Dating Site Match.com Came to Be." *FOXBusiness* (February 12, 2010). http://www.foxsmallbusinesscenter.com/entrepreneurs/2010/02/12/matchcom-eharmony-plentyoffish-love-valentines-day/.

Reyes, Melanie M. "Migration and Filipino Children Left-Behind: A Literature Review." Quezon City, Philippines: Miriam College/UNICEF, 2008.

Richins, Marsha L. "Measuring Emotions in the Consumption Experience." *Journal of Consumer Research* 24, no. 2 (1997): 127–46.

Risman, Barbara, ed. *Families as They Really Are*. New York: W. W. Norton, 2010.

Roschelle, Anne R. *No More Kin: Exploring Race, Class, and Gender in Family Networks*. Understanding Families, vol. 8. Thousand Oaks, CA: Sage Publications, 1997.

Rosenbloom, Stephanie. "New Online-Date Detectives Can Unmask Mr. or Ms. Wrong." *New York Times*, December 19, 2010.

Rowe, Jonathan. "The Promise of the Commons." *Earth Island Institute* 17, no. 3 (2002): 28–30.

Rubin, Lillian B. *The Transcendent Child: Tales of Triumph over the Past*. New York: Basic Books, 1996.

Ruskin, Gary, and Juliet Schor. "Every Nook and Cranny: The Dangerous Spread of Commercialized Culture." *Multinational Monitor* 26, no. 1/2 (2005). http:///www.commercialalert.org/news/featured-in/2005/01.

Sabol, William J., Heather Couture, and Paige Harrison. "Prisoners in 2006." Washington, DC: U.S. Department of Justice, 2007.

Salamon, Lester. "The Marketization of Welfare: Changing Nonprofit and For-Profit Roles in the American Welfare State." *Social Service Review* 67, no. 1 (March 1993): 16–39.

Salamon, Lester, S. Wojciech Sokolowski, and Associates. *The Global Civil Society: Dimensions of the Nonprofit Sector.* Baltimore, MD: Johns Hopkins Center for Civil Society Studies, 1999.

Sama Resource Group for Women and Health. "Constructing Conceptions: The Mapping of Assisted Reproductive Technologies in India." New Delhi: Sama Resource Group for Women and Health, 2010.

Samarasinghe, Anjana. "Welfare System for Migrant Women Workers, Young Children Favoured." *Daily News* (Sri Lanka), March 15, 2007.

Sanders, George. " 'Late' Capital: Amusement and Contradiction in the Contemporary Funeral Industry." *Critical Sociology* 35, no. 4 (2009): 447–70.

Sanghavi, Prachi, Kavi Bhalla, and Veena Das. "Fire-Related Deaths in India in 2001: A Retrospective Analysis of Data." *Lancet* 373, no. 9671 (April 17, 2009): 1282–88.

Sarojini, N. B., and Vrinda Marwah. *Shake Her, She Is Like the Tree That Grows Money!* New Delhi, India: Sama Resource Group for Women and Health, forthcoming.

Saul, Stephanie. "Building a Baby, with Few Ground Rules." *New York Times*, December 13, 2009.

Schor, Juliet. *Born to Buy: The Commercialized Child and the New Consumer Culture.* New York: Scribner, 2004.

Schwerin, Noel. *Bloodlines: Technology Hits Home.* Public Broadcasting Service, 2003.

Shaffern, Robert W. "Indulgences and Saintly Devotionalisms in the Middle Ages." *Catholic Historical Review* 84, no. 4 (1998): 643–61.

Shapiro, Joseph. "Home Care Might Be Cheaper, But States Still Fear It." *Home or Nursing Home: America's Empty Promise to Give Elderly, Disabled a Choice.* NPR, December 2, 2010. http://www.npr.org/2010/12/10/131755491/home-care-might-be-cheaper-but-states-still-fear-it.

Simmel, Georg. *The Philosophy of Money.* London, UK: Routledge & Kegan Paul, 1978.

Smelser, Neil. *The Social Edges of Psychoanalysis.* Berkeley: University of California Press, 1998.

Smith, Adam. *An Inquiry into the Nature and Causes of the Wealth of Nations.* New York: The Modern Library, 1937.

———. *The Theory of Moral Sentiments.* New York: Oxford University Press, 1976.

Spitzberg, Brian H., and William R. Cupach. "Cyber-Stalking as (Mis)-matchmaking." In *Online Matchmaking*, edited by M. T. Whitty, A. Baker, and J. Inman. New York: Palgrave Macmillan, 2007, 127–46.

Spivack, Carla. "The Law of Surrogate Motherhood in the United States." *American Journal of Comparative Law* 58, Supplement 1 (2010): 97–114.

StayHitched.com. "Marriage Success Training: Build the Foundation for Your Lifetime Together." http://www.stayhitched.com/prep.htm.

Stearns, Peter N. *Anxious Parents: A History of Modern Childrearing in America*. New York: New York University Press, 2003.

Streitfeld, David. "Anger as a Private Company Takes Over Libraries." *New York Times*, September 26, 2010, A1.

Suarez-Orozco, Carola, Irina L. G. Todorova, and Josephine Louie. "Making Up for Lost Time: The Experience of Separation and Reunification among Immigrant Families." *Family Process* 41, no. 4 (2002): 625–43.

Super, Nora. "Who Will Be There to Care? The Growing Gap between Caregiver Supply and Demand." Washington, DC: National Health Policy Forum/George Washington University, 2002.

Swidler, Ann. "Culture in Action: Symbols and Strategies." *American Sociological Review* 51 (April 1986): 273–86.

Taubman, Phoebe. "Peaceful Revolution: Time to Stop Free-Riding on Families." *Huffington Post*, February 9, 2010. http://www.huffingtonpost.com/phoebe-taubman/ipeaceful-revolutioni-tim_b_455765.html.

Tejada-Vera, B., and P. D. Sutton. "Births, Marriages, Divorces, and Deaths: Provisional Data for 2009." *National Vital Statistics Reports* 58, no. 25 (August 27, 2010): 2–6.

Teman, Elly. "Embodying Surrogate Motherhood: Pregnancy as a Dyadic Body Project." *Body & Society* 15, no. 3 (2009): 47–57.

———. "The Last Outpost of the Nuclear Family: A Cultural Critique of Israeli Surrogacy Policy." In *Kin, Gene, Community: Reproductive Technology among Jewish Israelis*, edited by Daphna Birenbaum-Carmeli and Yoram Carmeli. Oxford: Berghahn Books, 2010.

———. "Technological Fragmentation and Women's Empowerment: Surrogate Motherhood in Israel." *Women's Studies Quarterly* 31, no. 3/4 (2001): 11–34.

Thompson, Mark, Philip Zimbardo, and Glenn Hutchinson. "Consumers Are Having Second Thoughts about Online Dating." WeAttract.com, April 29, 2005, Version 1.4.

Thomson, Kevin. *Emotional Capital: Maximizing the Intangible Assets at the Heart of Brand and Business Success.* Oxford, UK: Capstone Publishing, 1998.

Timmermans, Stefan. *Sudden Death and the Myth of CPR.* Philadelphia: Temple University Press, 1999.

Torpey, Elka Maria. "Jobs in Weddings and Funerals: Working with the Betrothed and the Bereaved." *Occupational Outlook Quarterly* 50, no. 4 (Winter 2006–7): 30–45.

Torrey, E. Fuller, and Judy Miller. *The Invisible Plague: The Rise of Mental Illness from 1750 to the Present.* New Brunswick, NJ: Rutgers University Press, 2001.

Tough, Paul. "The Year in Ideas: Dad's Performance Review." *New York Times Magazine*, December 15, 2002, 65.

Tronto, Joan C. *Moral Boundaries: A Political Argument for an Ethic of Care.* New York: Routledge, 1994.

Tuller, David. "Payment Offers to Egg Donors Prompt Scrutiny." *New York Times*, May 11, 2010, D5.

Turner, Earnest S. *A History of Courting.* New York: E. P. Dutton and Co., 1954.

Twain, Mark. "At the Appetite-Cure." In *How to Tell a Story, and Other Essays*, edited by Mark Twain. New York: Harper & Brothers Publishers, 1909, pp. 293–310.

Uma Devi, S., and Indian Economic Association, eds. *Economics and Ethics.* Delhi: Deep & Deep Publications, 2003.

Ungerson, Claire. "The Language of Care: Crossing the Boundaries," in C. Ungerson, ed., *Gender and Caring: Work and Welfare in Britain and Scandinavia.* Hemel Hempstead, UK: Harvester-Wheatsheaf, 1990.

UNICEF. "Child Poverty in Perspective: An Overview of Child Well-Being in Rich Countries." In *Innocenti Report Card* 7. Florence: Innocenti Research Centre, 2007.

U.S. Bureau of Labor Statistics. "Foreign-Born Workers: Labor Force Characteristics—2010." Washington, DC: Bureau of Labor Statistics, U.S. Department of Labor, 2011.

U.S. Census Bureau. "N.A.I.C.S. Industry Data—Other Services: Service Annual Survey." Washington, DC: U.S. Census Bureau, 2006.

U.S. Census Bureau. "Quickfacts: USA." U.S. Census Bureau. http://quickfacts.census.gov/qfd/states/00000.html.

U.S. Census Bureau. "Table 1. Intercensal Estimates of the Resident

Population by Sex and Age for the United States: April 1, 2000 to July 1, 2010." *National Intercensal Estimates (2000–2010)*, September 2011. http://www.census.gov/popest/intercensal/national/nat2010.html.

U.S. Census Bureau. "Table 2. Intercensal Estimates of the Resident Population by Sex and Age for California: April 1, 2000 to July 1, 2010." *State Intercensal Estimates (2000–2010)*, September 2011. http://www.census.gov/popest/intercensal/national/nat2010.html.

U.S. Census Bureau Population Division. "Summary Tables: Constant Net International Migration Series." Washington, DC: U.S. Census Bureau, 2009.

U.S. Department of Agriculture. "Food C.P.I. and Expenditures: Table 1." Economic Research Service, U.S. Department of Agriculture. http://www.ers.usda.gov/Briefing/CPIFoodAndExpenditures/Data/Expenditures_tables/table1.htm.

USDA Economic Research Service. "A History of American Agriculture: Farmers & the Land." United States Department of Agriculture. http://www.agclassroom.org/gan/timeline/farmers_land.htm.

Veblen, Thorstein. *The Theory of the Leisure Class*. New York: A. M. Kelley, 1965 (1899).

Wagman, Barnet, and Nancy Folbre. "Household Services and Economic Growth in the United States, 1870–1930." *Feminist Economics* 2, no. 1 (1996): 43–66.

Walker, Kathryn E., and Margaret E. Woods. *Time Use: A Measure of Household Production of Family Goods and Services*. Washington, DC: Center for the Family of the American Home Economics Association, 1976.

Wallulis, Jerald. *The New Insecurity: The End of the Standard Job and Family*. Albany: State University of New York Press, 1998.

Wang, Hua, and Barry Wellman. "Social Connectivity in America: Changes in Adult Friendship Network Size from 2002 to 2007." *American Behavioral Scientist* 53, no. 8 (2010): 1148–69.

Wassener, Bettina. "Fresh Air for Sale, in Hong Kong." *New York Times, Green Blog*. http://green.blogs.nytimes.com/2010/09/01fresh-air-for-sale-in-hong-kong/

Watson, Amy, and International Coach Federation. "Client Survey Results and Press Release: Analysis of 1998 Survey of Coaching Clients." International Coach Federation. http://www.coachfederation.org/includes/redirects/articlecount.cfm?articleID=57&filename=008ICFClientSurveyResults1998.doc.

Weisberg, D. Kelly. *The Birth of Surrogacy in Israel*. Gainesville: University Press of Florida, 2005.

Weitzen, Sherry, Joan M. Teno, Mary Fennell, and Vincent Mor. "Factors Associated with Site of Death: A National Study of Where People Die." *Medical Care* 41, no. 2 (February 2003): 323–35.

WhatsYourPrice.com. "The Media Likens It to Prostitution, but over 60% of the Public Says It's Okay." WhatsYourPrice.com press release, April 25, 2011. http://www.whatsyourprice.com/img/pressrelease4252011.pdf.

White, Tracie. "Outsourcing: Or How to Celebrate a Bat Mitzvah When You're Mormon." *San Francisco Chronicle Magazine*, April 18, 2006, 20.

Williams, Florence. "Human Milk for Sale." *New York Times Magazine*, December 19, 2010, 41.

Woodrow Wilson International Center for Scholars and the Migration Policy Institute. "Women Immigrants in the United States: Proceedings of a Conference at the Center." Paper presented at the Women Immigrants in the United States conference, Washington, DC, September 9, 2002.

Woolhander, S. and D. V. Himmelstein, "When Money Is the Mission—The High Costs of Investor-Owned Care." *New England Journal of Medicine* 241, no. 6 (1999).

Wunderlich, Gooloo S., and Peter O. Kohler. *Improving the Quality of Long-Term Care*. Washington, DC: The National Academies Press, 2001.

Xytex Cryo International Sperm Bank. "Patient Section: Information Options." http://www.xytex.com/sperm-donor-bank-patient/index.cfm#infooptions.

Yadegaran, Jessica. "Baby Planners Pave Way for Little Ones." *Oakland Tribune*, January 25, 2010.

Zelizer, Viviana A. *Economic Lives: How Culture Shapes the Economy*. Princeton, NJ: Princeton University Press, 2011.

———. *The Purchase of Intimacy*. Princeton, NJ: Princeton University Press, 2005.

———. *The Social Meaning of Money: Pin Money, Paychecks, Poor Relief, and Other Currencies*. New York: Basic Books, 1994.

Zerubavel, Eviatar. *The Fine Line: Making Distinctions in Everyday Life*. Chicago: University of Chicago Press, 1993 (1991).

Zigler, Edward, and Mary Elizabeth Lang. *Child Care Choices: Balancing the Needs of Children, Families, and Society*. New York: Free Press, 1991.

Acknowledgments

Many thanks to those who kindly allowed me into their lives. I have disguised their identities but they will know who they are. I want to especially thank "Anastasia Haber" (chapter 7), whose acute perceptions, shared over many hours, truly opened my eyes.

I am blessed with generous, creative, and knowledgeable friends and colleagues. A special thanks to Joan Cole and Deirdre English. Joan held my hand throughout the writing of this book, often beginning a phone talk with a warm "So how's the writing?" Deirdre tried out my ideas in a way that gave them back bigger and better, and it was she who suggested I begin with my own life. Ellie Langer, Barrie Thorne, and Lillian Rubin gave me very helpful detailed responses to an early draft and unfailing encouragement. Ann Swidler helped me get my facts straight and, as often, held a mirror to my mind. Thanks to Harriet Barlow for reflections on the spiritual dimension of this topic, and to Troy Duster and Harry Dwyer for its link to politics. Thanks to Julie Schor for a helpful reminder of centuries of market cultures in India, China, and Europe. Thanks also to Russ Ellis, Cynthia Li, Metta Spencer, and to my German colleagues, Kai Maiwald,

Martin Dorne, and Ursula Apitzsch. I especially want to thank Martin Dorne, whose perceptive ten-page commentary fundamentally reshaped this book. I also thank the Andrew W. Mellon Foundation for generous financial support for this research.

I'm grateful to my two comrades in arms, my gifted and tireless research assistant Sarah Garrett, with whom I carried some research for this book into another essay ("Beyond Tocqueville's Telescope: The Personalized Brand and the Branded Self"), and Bonnie Kwan, who unearthed Internet ads, typed interview transcripts, and who gave me loving support for longer than either of us imagined she'd have to.

While writing and editing *TomDispatch*—a thrice-weekly, illuminating, "beneath-the-news" analysis of breaking events, Tom Engelhardt managed time to wrangle an early bucking bronco idea into the corral of a book. My first draft went off in every direction—the rise of commercial names for sports stadiums, the rising reference to self-interest in church sermons, the European enclosure movement. "Your interviews," he advised, "the surprises are there." When I became bogged down with market theory, he advised me to "write the book without a footnote," whereupon my own voice at last emerged. In editorial skill, no one compares to Tom Engelhardt.

Except for Sara Bershtel. Metropolitan's publisher, Sara, "got" the book instantly. Then she inhaled it and, with architectural brilliance, helped me lay bare the deeper logical story underlying the personal ones. She also urged me to trust my reader to catch understatement, to embrace complexity. For all this, I am more grateful than I can say. I am grateful, too, to Metropolitan's Riva Hocherman, whose intuitions and interventions improved this book in every way. Thanks as well to Rachel Bolten who bravely managed the flow of production with skill and good will.

And a very deep thanks to Adam, my husband and lifelong light of my life. While crafting his own extraordinary book on World War I, Adam shared many thoughts and helped me liberate my personal voice from a more guarded, "academic" one. During one stylistic backslide, he taped a page to the wall behind my desk. At the top left side he drew a smiling face and below it a picture of Snoopy, aspiring dog novelist from Charles Schulz's cartoon *Peanuts*, typewriter atop doghouse, beginning, "It was a dark and stormy night . . ." Below this he mischeviously taped a page of my writing he liked. On the right-hand top side, he drew a scowling face and beneath it, a page of my most deadly prose. If he ever needed another job, he could well hire out as a laughter therapist. In the meantime, the feel of that twinkly, warm, knowing, love underlies every word in this book.

As my long-term mentor and PhD thesis adviser at UC Berkeley, Neil Smelser early gave me the extraordinary gift of his faith in me. During a recent lunch with him, thinking back to my first, unhappy, year of graduate school, I told him, "You lifted me up when I was falling." He replied laughingly, "Don't say more; you'll make me cry." But the truth is he really did. And with so many thanks, I dedicate this book to him.

Index